Reforming
Public Schools
Through
Community Education

Jack D. Minzey • Clyde E. LeTarte

KENDALL/HUNT PUBLISHING

4050 Westmark Drive   P.O. Box 1840   Dubuque, Iowa 52004-1840

DEDICATION

As people grow older and their careers mature, it becomes more evident to them that their remaining years are somewhat limited. It is in this vein that we make the following acknowledgments.

We dedicate this book to our families whose memories of us will give us some degree of personal immortality.

To our wives:

Esther Minzey   Kathleen LeTarte

To our children: *To our grand-children:*

David and Debra Minzey   Christina Minzey
Daniel and Barbara Minzey   Michael Minzey
Debra and Rob Papineau   Stephanie Minzey
John and Anna Minzey   Dorothy Papineau
Richard and Kriss LeTarte   Megan Minzey
Rhonda LeTarte   Robbie Papineau
                                 John Papineau
                                 Samantha Minzey
                                 Caitlin Minzey
                                 Jeffrey Minzey
                                 Karissa LeTarte
                                 Nicole Minzey

We also dedicate this book to our colleagues in education whose activities, successes, and commitments to community education will determine the duration of our professional immortality.

TABLE OF CONTENTS

FOREWORD

In the summer of 1936, a young teen-ager drowned while swimming in the Flint River. Frank Manley, a teacher in the Flint, Michigan, school system asked a very perplexing question, "Why? Why, when we have school playgrounds, swimming pools, school gymnasiums, and classrooms that could be used all year long?"

He spoke his concerns to Flint service clubs. Mr. Charles Stewart Mott, a wealthy businessman, heard him. He offered the Flint Board of Education $6,000 to experiment with Mr. Manley's innovative ideas for using school facilities.

Thus, the modern concept of community education was launched though it was mostly bat and ball programs to start. Over the next 30 years it became a vehicle of change that expanded nationally and internationally into all aspects of education and community life.

As the concepts and philosophies developed from the traditional kindergarten through twelfth grade (K-12) curriculum to the open schoolhouse, to lifelong learning, to community councils, and to business-education partnerships, community education was often misunderstood, misconstrued, and opposed by various elements of education and local service organizations fearful of take-overs. The ubiquitous forces of apathy, status quo, life style, don't-rock-the-boat, and keep-off-my-turf emerged to endanger and delay its adoption and acceptance.

In 1971, Clyde LeTarte and Jack Minzey, professors of education at Eastern Michigan University, recognized the growing concerns and misconceptions confronting community education. They published a book, *Community Education, From Program to Process*. It defined community education, explaining what it was and what it was not. It delineated the amorphous parameters so misunderstood by the K-12 traditionalists, while defining more clearly the coordinating roles of the community educators.

During this period of explorative research, the authors coined the word *process* to explain the creative activities used to identify and attack any destructive community blight. The book was so accepted and adopted by educators that it became "the bible" for all community education protagonists.

New expansionist ideas, creative thinking, changing situations, and ambivalent reform strategies necessitated a review and reworking of the ideas that had successfully withstood the challenges of eight years. Thus, LeTarte and Minzey, in 1979, published a sequel, *Community Education, From Program to Process to Practice.* This was a compilation of the best from their 1971 book plus the accumulation of the community education processes and practices that had developed from 1971 to 1979. This book also became the textbook and "bible" for the succeeding decade.

The universal acceptance of these two books solidified their basis as the definitive publications on community education. In the last two decades, Jack Minzey has so often been requested as a speaker at education, business, and civic meetings that he has become known as the "voice for community education."

The present day demand for change necessitates yet another look at how community education fits into today's compelling need for citizen participation and education responsibilities. Education must certainly be involved. The problems of poverty, family deterioration, teen-age pregnancies, teen dropouts, gangs, drugs, and crime all have one thing in common—lack of education.

The last fifty years of status-quo education has proved lacking and will not suffice in the mountainous tasks facing modern society. The financial crunch alone will mean that education must make every dollar do double duty, increasing the demand and necessity for "year-round" schooling. The teaching profession must be used 52 weeks a year, not nine months. This will enable teachers to obtain better salaries, and it will encourage more applicants and eliminate the need for new expensive facilities.

Partnerships must be developed between education and business, industry, churches, courts, prisons, police, social services, and citizens. An all-out effort to coordinate all the assets of a modern community is absolutely essential to combat the forces making our society a wasteland of despair and wanton destruction. Education must be the leader simply because most, if not all, of our most dangerous problems spring from lack of education.

In their new book, LeTarte and Minzey retain the basic and most relevant parts of books one and two. In the new chapters, they present and explain how community education can and should be an essential participant in the changes facing America and why community education is a social imperative. They describe how learning communities are created and why they are so desirable. They emphasize the importance of maximum use of local school facilities and equipment and how they can be best used. They explore expanded opportunities for children and adults.

Democracy necessitates citizen participation. Community education demands citizen involvement. The two philosophies are complementary and beneficial to the American society according to LeTarte and Minzey. Community education is a vehicle for change. All it needs are the spark plugs to start the engines in every community. Education, because of its inherent cause of America's maladies, must assume the lead in its remedial therapy—from teaching to teacher preparation. The vehicle is ready and in place!

The question is, can the education institutions, from pre-school to post graduate, shake off the shackles of traditional, bureaucratic, status quo empowerment? Can they enthusiastically and totally accept the challenge to provide the leadership in every community? The future of America depends upon it.

Richard C. Pendell

PREFACE

When we first ventured into the writing of a textbook in community education, we were convinced that the concept of community education was about to have widespread expansion into the field of education and that there would be a need for a textbook on this subject for use in teaching the topic in the various colleges and universities throughout the United States. Our first publication, *Community Education, From Program to Process*, lived up to our expectations in that it filled the void we anticipated in the training of community educators. In addition, we had introduced the concept of *process* into community educators' thinking and were credited with moving the philosophy of community education to a new level.

Our first book was published in 1972, and by 1976 we were asked by the Pendell Publishing Company to consider a revision of that publication. We began such a publication, but soon discovered that there was so much new in the field that we would actually end up revising over half of the book. As a result, instead of a revision, we published a new book, released in 1979, *Community Education, From Program to Process to Practice*. This book not only updated our previous work, it also introduced to the field the idea that community education should be viewed as a new role for schools in our educational society.

This new book was well received by our colleagues and others in the field of education, and we believed that this was our last textbook on community education. In 1992, however, we were again approached, this time by the National Community Education Association, to consider updating our previous work. We were convinced that there was a need for such an effort and were thus motivated to produce this book.

As we began our task of rewriting this text, we consciously made a decision about what should be changed and what should remain the same. Perhaps our decision was based on knowing that this will be our last definitive work on this topic, at least in textbook form. Perhaps we were affected by the fact that we are older, if not wiser, and are driven by a different perception of what change is and should be. In any event, we were influenced by our belief that change for change's sake is not necessarily a good direction to go. Having read many of our predecessors' works, those of Maurice Seay, John Dewey, Walter Beggs, Clyde Campbell, Fred Totten, Edward Olsen, Frank Manley, and Ernest Melby, we realized that much of what has been said about community education had been written many years ago. Most new ideas are old thoughts with new titles or the ideas of others who were not given appropriate credit.

The above rationale guided us in revising our text. We are very much aware that many of the quotes and references are old. We have purposely kept them because we feel that:

- ◆ They provide evidence that our current problems have been in existence for a long time, and they make the reader aware that their concerns are not new.

- ◆ They give credit to people who may have perceived the idea originally rather than to someone who more recently has restated the idea.

- ◆ They contradict the implication that change is the prerogative or the invention only of the current generation.

- ◆ They promote interest by younger people to seek solutions to their problems from the thinking of older scholars as well as more recent writers.

- ◆ They affirm the fact that a recent publication date does not assure more wisdom, creativity, or credibility.

- ◆ They remind us that the essence of history is that by knowing our past, we can better build our future. A part of the arrogance of youth is the assumption that only new ideas are worth considering, and as a result, we are constantly "reinventing the wheel." We have failed to use our past history and experiences as a resource for growth.

Thus, in preparing this text, we felt that there is much to be updated and changed, and we have made significant changes in the content. We also felt that much of what we had previously written was accurate and predictive, and the points made in our previous book still needed to be reinforced and reiterated. These ideas include the following:

- There is still a great need for a major change in education, not just in rearranging the current program but in restructuring the very nature of schools and actually redefining and altering the current paradigm we call public education.

- The concepts of community education offer an excellent option for restructuring the schools in a way that will be needed in the twenty-first century.

- Much of what the futurists are suggesting for changing the public schools is based on community education principles developed fifty years ago.

- Many of the programs begun by community educators are now integrated into the regular school program—latch key, pre-school, community use of buildings, involvement of the community in school programs, adult education programs, community councils, parenting programs, home-school counselors, extended school time (days, hours, weeks) and use of the schools by social agencies.

While the number of schools claiming to be community schools has greatly expanded in the last forty years, the major problem in community education is still one of conceptualization—of not realizing the expanded definition or full value of community education and its potential. Thus, we feel that there is still a need for a book like ours. We recognize that we are not the utmost authorities in the "how-to" of community education, but we do feel that we still have much to offer in community education's conceptualization.

CHAPTER I

THE STATUS OF EDUCATION IN THE UNITED STATES

For the past ten years, there has been a major focus on public education in the United States. There were at least 30 major reports, including *The National Science Board's Report on Education, High School—A Report on Secondary Education in America,* and other reports by the Education Commission of the States, The College Board, the Twentieth Century Fund, and the *Report On High School* by John Goodlad. These reports triggered approximately 157 responses by every state department of education as well as separate reports by each state governor.

The most notorious and recognized of these reports was *Excellence In Education—A Nation At Risk,* carried out by the National Commission on Excellence and given national status by being described as a presidential report. This report has had a tremendous impact on schools throughout the United States and is still used as the guideline and major impetus for school reform in the country.

Although there has always been major interest in improving schools, and indeed in constantly criticizing public schools, this new interest has been more compelling and far reaching than other efforts over the past 100 years. Professional educators have learned to expect criticism of their efforts and products and have accepted such criticism in the spirit of the late Will Rogers who purportedly said, "Schools aren't as good as they used to be, but then, they never were."

The new and more sophisticated reports on education, however, have generated an intensity and impact far greater than might have been expected. This intensity and impact might best be explained by asking what the motivation was that caused such a profound interest in the quality of our public schools. The answer can be found in the explanations given in *A Nation At Risk.* In this publication, the following reasons were given to substantiate such a study.

1. The quality of a nation's schools determines its prosperity, security, and civility.

2. Knowledge, learning, information, and skilled intelligence are the new raw materials of international commerce.

3. Individuals in our society who do not possess the levels of skill, literacy, and training essential to this new era will be effectively disenfranchised, not simply from the material rewards that accompany competent performance, but also from the chance to participate fully in our national life.

4. We have engaged in unthinking, unilateral educational disarmament.

5. Our schools have not been responsive to the requests for change by our businesses, civic organizations, or communities.

This report then went on to list the indicators of risk, documenting the indicators with the following allegations:

1. Compared with other industrialized countries, on 19 academic tests, American students were never first or second and were last seven times.

2. Twenty-three million American adults are functionally illiterate.

3. Thirteen percent of all 17-year-olds in the U.S. are functionally illiterate, and for minority youth the number is 40 percent.

4. The average achievement of high school youth on standardized tests is lower than it was 26 years ago.

5. Over half of the gifted do not match their ability with comparable achievement.

6. Standardized Achievement Test scores declined steadily from 1969 to 1980.

7. For the first time in the history of our country, the education skills of the current generation will not surpass, will not equal, will not even approach that of their parents.

8. Secondary school curricula have been homogenized, diluted, and diffused to the point where they no longer have a central purpose.

9. The amount of home work for high school students has decreased while students' grades have risen even though their achievement has declined.

10. In many schools, students are receiving only 17 hours of instruction per week and are in school a maximum of 180 six-hour days per year as compared with eight hours a day of instruction and 220 days per year in other industrialized nations.[1]

The essence of this report was to point out the need for changes in our education system, and efforts were begun throughout the country to attempt to bring about meaningful change. These efforts have resulted in recommendations that, in general, have called for more rigorous standards, more resources, more local, state, and national support, better teachers, better leadership, and more time for education.

For education, the results of these studies have been both good and bad. On the positive side, education has become a major focus throughout the country. Politicians, media, civic groups, and businesses have given a high priority to education, and this has resulted in continued financial support, even in some difficult economic times. The bad news is that while there is common agreement that we all want excellence in education, no one, including educators themselves, has been able to agree on how excellence should be interpreted. To the question, "Excellence for what?" responses are as diverse as the people making them—science, math, English, vocational training, fine arts, humanities, moral education, participatory democracy, technology, back to basics. When the question is, "Excellence for whom?" some say, an elitist group of students; some say, all children; and some say, for everyone in the community.

A part of the problem in deciding what the role of a school should be lies in the different perceptions of the various clients within the community. Another part of the problem is the vast divergence between what schools say they should do and what they actually do. This can best be

---

[1] *A Nation At Risk*, National Commission on Excellence in Education, United States Department of Education, Washington, DC, April, 1983.

presented by looking at the stated goals of public education and identifying which of these goals are partially or totally neglected. The following sets of goals are those which have resulted from extensive study and those to which most professional educators would subscribe.

1. The Seven Cardinal Principles of Education
    a. fundamental processes (reading, writing, math)
    b. vocational education
    c. worthy use of leisure time
    d. worthy home membership
    e. health
    f. citizenship
    g. ethical character

2. National Education Association Goals of Education
    a. vocational training
    b. self development
    c. citizenship
    d. human relations

3. John Goodlad's Goals of Education
    a. vocational education
    b. general education
    c. citizenship
    d. personal development

4. Life Needs
    a. securing food and shelter
    b. protecting life and health
    c. communicating ideas and feelings
    d. adjusting to other people
    e. satisfying sexual desires
    f. enriching family living
    g. rearing children
    h. securing education
    i. sharing citizenship
    j. controlling the environment

k. using leisure time
l. enjoying beauty
m. appreciating the past
n. meeting religious needs
o. finding personal identity
p. adjusting to change
q. growing old and facing death[2]

A perusal of these goals reveals that schools accomplish only a few of these, usually in a limited fashion. It should be said, in defense of the public schools, that a major reason why they are not more successful in achieving these goals is because schools are being given more and more of the tasks that probably should be handled by the family or some other community agency. Further, the atmosphere of the schools has become so contaminated with disruption, discipline problems, and other social issues that conditions within the school are not conducive to learning.

There is, however, a more basic circumstance related to change that is having a major impact on the ability of schools to move forward. Change in public schools in the past has been educational tinkering. The changes sought and accomplished have been incremental. They deal with rearranging the furniture without thought to the shape of the room. They continue to be based on a set of principles that have served us well for many years but may be out of date as guidelines for the twenty-first century. These principles were developed in the late 1800s and formed the basis for the institution we call the public school system. The basic beliefs of this system are:

1. School is the core of society.

2. School is synonymous with education.

3. School provides for two functions—survival of society and knowledge needed for the survival of the individual in that society.

4. School should be compulsory.

---

[2] Kussrow, Paul, Director, Center for Community Education, Appalachia State University, from a speech delivered at Eastern Michigan University, Ypsilanti, Michigan, November, 1983.

5. School is for children only.

6. There is a specific content that all must learn in a graded fashion.

7. The method of learning and the ordering of learning is determined by professional educators.

8. Individuals need not go on to education beyond grade 12 to survive in society.

9. Without school, the individual is absolutely disadvantaged in society.[3]

Various challenges have been made to these premises, but, basically, these ideas have guided our school system for the past 100 years. While many of those making the challenge were viewed as radicals, even some of our more concerned and conservative leaders began to raise questions about the purposes of the public schools. One of these, the late Walter Reuther, said it this way:

> The real measurement of the quality of a society is how does that society order its priorities? We have been more concerned about the quality of our goods than we have about the quality of our goals. We will make more technological progress in the next 25 years than we have made in the last 2,500 years. But the question is to what purpose will we commit that technological progress? The problem is not science or technology, the problem is man, for science and technology are neutral in the affairs of man. The basic dilemma of the human community, as I see it, is that science and technology have expanded man's wealth but not his wisdom. Science and technology have multiplied man's power but have not increased his understanding nor his compassion, nor his sense of human solidarity, nor his sense of community when these are the essential ingredients around which we must build man's future and his very survival.[4]

---

[3] Minzey, Jack D., and Townsend, Anthony C., *Core Plus Education, A Model for Schools of the Future*, Center for Community Education, Eastern Michigan University, Ypsilanti, Michigan, Fall, 1982.

[4] Reuther, Walter, President, United Auto Workers, from a keynote speech delivered at the National Community Education Conference, Detroit, Michigan, December, 1969.

Incremental change in public schools was appropriate for many of the corrections and adjustments education needed in the past, but it is now time to talk of substantive change, for it will take nothing less to accomplish the task public education will face in the future. We need a change in not just the content of schools but in the very paradigm we call public education.

This will not be the first time the paradigm of public education has been changed in the United States. The original school system in our country was the Latin Grammar School. Its purpose was to teach our citizens how to vote and read the Holy Bible. Since only the sons of people who owned land could vote, the school was designed to serve only a certain portion of our society. This school system lasted for 150 years and was changed because society changed. As the country moved from an agricultural society to one composed of a new middle class, there was a need to develop a school system more appropriate to that new society. In the mid 1700s, the American Academy was developed. It was designed to serve all girls and boys whose parents could afford to send them to school. In the 1800s, there was again a need to make a substantive change in education. The need for a more educated population led to the creation of the American Free School. Now all children could go to school through grade eight at public expense. In 1894, a landmark case, the Kalamazoo Case, ruled that all children would be entitled to a free public education through grade 12. Each of these changes was accompanied by great resistance by community members and public educators, primarily based on the uneasy feelings that occur whenever a paradigm is changed. The point is that schools have changed at least three times in a major way, and they have changed to become more relevant to society.

It should also be pointed out that changing the paradigm does not imply that the public schools have been doing a poor job. Our public schools have much to be proud of.

1. We have a higher rate of literacy than any nation in the world.

2. Ninety-four percent of our youth between the ages of 14 and 17 are in school. That number was only seven percent in 1890.

3. Seventy-five percent of high school-age youth are graduating.

4. About 20 percent of our population has graduated from college.

5. Thirty-two percent of our industrial growth is due to education.

6. An individual gets about 25 percent return on his or her investment in education.

7. Eight percent of our gross national product is a result of education.

8. Students learn much more in school at a younger age than ever before.

9. Seventy-one percent of the community has a positive attitude about its schools.[5]

Henry Steel Commanger said that no people have demanded so much from their public schools, and no people have been so well served. Author James Michener claimed that the public schools were a major reason for his success in life. He said that the schools spent $11,000 on his education and that he, in turn, generated $68 million. Most people can tell similar stories about how they owe a great deal of their success in life to the public schools, and, in fact, the public schools probably served our population very well up through the 1960s. Yet in the last 30 years, there have been major changes in our society, and the schools have not responded in an appropriate way. We have shifted from an industrial to an information society with an impact on our society that will probably be greater than the nineteenth century shift from agriculture to industry. In 1950, 65 percent of the U.S. workers were in the industrial sector. Today, that number is 30 percent. In 1950, 17 percent of U.S. workers were in the service sector. Today, that number is 50 percent. While the strategic resource in the industrial society was capital, in the post industrial society it is knowledge.[6]

While all of this is happening, our schools continue to operate with a 1960 orientation. The curriculum that was developed as a response to

[5] Cetron, Marvin, *Schools of the Future*, American Association of School Administrators, Arlington, Virginia, 1986.
[6] Toffler, Alvin, *The Third Wave* (1st. Edition), Morrow, New York, 1980.

A Nation At Risk requires all students to take four years of English, three years of social studies, two years of science, two years of math, and a computer class. This is primarily the same curriculum offered in most high schools in 1960, and one might question its relevance to our current society. As Mario Fantini stated, when you put a new carburetor on a 1960 Chevy, you still have a 1960 Chevy even though it may run a little better. Fantini also stated that when scientists decided to go to the moon, no one suggested a DC 10 with two extra engines. They knew that a new era and task require a new vehicle.[7]

The public schools have not kept pace. Their continuing use of the old curricula has resulted in many hypocrisies.

- ◆ We know that the first few years of life are very important in terms of attitudes and learning, yet generally we provide no education programs for children under age five.

- ◆ We know that a child is a product of his or her total environment, yet we continue to perform as though his or her total education is the result of experiences in school.

- ◆ We have convinced our public of the relationship between education and social and economic success, and yet we deny the opportunity for education to large segments of our society.

- ◆ We put large numbers of dollars into physical facilities, yet we use them only a small part of their potential operational time.

- ◆ We stress local control of schools and then deny input into the operation from many in our communities.

- ◆ We deplore duplication and waste, yet we do little to maximize the efficient coordination of our services with others or help to bring together effectively problems and resources.

- ◆ We preach participatory democracy, yet we do little to encourage the development of local advocacy or problem solving.

---

[7] Fantini, Mario, Dean, College of Education, University of Massachusetts, from a speech delivered at an Eastern Michigan University community education conference, Albion, Michigan, Fall, 1980.

- We believe that education is a lifetime process, yet we operate as though education needs terminate at age 18.

- We have described education as a preparation for life, yet our schools have lost a great deal of their relevance.

With all this in mind, let us look at a basic axiom that should always guide us as we develop goals for our public schools, both now and in the future. Simply presented, this axiom states that the purpose of any institution is to serve the society for which it was created. This implies that the only reason for an institution is to provide something the individual or the family cannot do for itself. Most institutions know this, but in the process of their development and growth, they lose sight of their relationship to the community. New institutions develop professionals who, in turn, tend to be guided by their own standards and perceptions and, as a result, end up losing track of this basic concept.

To apply this concept to the public schools, we must recognize that we are closer to the year 2000 than we are to 1960. We must know what our communities look like now and also what things are likely to happen in the future. We all are probably too painfully aware of what is happening in our communities, but we need to remind ourselves of the nature of our society and attempt to adjust our schools so that they might respond to these conditions. We need to ask ourselves what we are doing in light of the following statistics.

- Five percent of the families in the U.S. are the traditional father working, mother as housewife, and two children. In 1955, that group represented 60 percent of the U.S. families.

- Fifty-nine percent of all children will live with a single parent before they reach age 18.

- Forty percent of parents say they never read to their children.

- Twenty-seven percent of parents say they never help their children with homework.

- Seventy-eight percent of single mothers are on welfare.

- Every day, 40 teen-agers in the U.S. give birth to their third child.

- Of 24,000 students entering ninth grade in our major cities, only 20 percent will graduate four years later.

- The median age of Americans has moved from 16 to 30.

- There was a 24 percent increase in those over the age of 25 between 1970 and 1980.

- The average life expectancy is 79 years of age.

- One half of the women ages 20–24 are single.

- One of two marriages ends in divorce.

- In 1990, there were more people in the U.S. over age 55 than there were between the ages of five and 19.

- Not since 1969 have the majority of people in the U.S. had children in the public schools.[8]

A survey was done in Michigan to ask community members to indicate what they would like their schools to do. The responses follow.

- Seventy-five percent of those polled wanted to be used as volunteers to help educate children, but they did not want to be used for those mundane jobs teachers did not want. They wanted to be used for jobs commensurate with their skills, training, and interests.

- Sixty-six percent wanted adults to be able to take classes at the same time that the traditional students do.

- Sixty-six percent favored letting senior citizens use school space during the school day.

---

[8] Hubbell, Ned, Consultant, Michigan Department of Education, from a speech delivered at an Eastern Michigan University community education conference, East Lansing, Michigan, March, 1982.

- Fifty-six percent favored letting government and social agencies use school facilities during the school day.

- Sixty-two percent opposed the schools providing day care services.[9]

In most school districts, professionals would find it difficult philosophically to support such ideas. Yet, if it is a basic belief that schools should serve the society for which they are created, it would seem that serious consideration should be given to such suggestions. Perhaps the difference between community expectations and school response to these issues partially explains the decrease in public support to the schools. It seems likely that community members are asking, "What's in it for me?" and the schools are not hearing that message.

In looking at the school's role based on the future, the problem of identifying community needs becomes somewhat more difficult. In this case, we must look to our best guesses and information provided through planning and data related to predictions of the future. This might not be as difficult as we expect, since we have developed a discipline of futurism and have available to us recommendations suggested by recognized educators.

One of these futurists is Daniel Yankelovich, a recognized expert on future changes in society. He identifies eight major transformations taking place in our society that will have an impact on education in our country.

1. The aging of America and maturing of the baby boomers
2. The internationalization of the world economy and the related loss of U.S. markets and world economic superiority
3. The technical revolution and its impact on society
4. The loss of U.S. nuclear superiority and resulting vulnerability
5. New living arrangements in society

---

[9] op. cit., number 7.

6. Shifting population and demographics
7. The new expressivism in society—as an individual I no longer suppress my own needs but do the things that are "for me"
8. The growth of fundamentalism and localism[10]

An even more famous futurist is John Naisbitt. His predictions contain what he calls the ten most emerging trends. He presents these trends in terms of what we are changing "from" to what we are moving "toward." Again, these trends should give educators direction on what our education programs will have to reflect in the curricula of the future.

Moving From	Moving To
industrial society	information society
centralization	decentralization
party politics	issue politics
machines	human technology
focus on racism/sexism	focus on ageism
top down management	bottom up management
equal access to capital	equal access to education
bigness	appropriate size
company board of directors	independent board of directors
representative democracy	participatory democracy[11]

In addition to what might be called general futurists, there are a group of professionals who might be called education futurists. Their predictions are specifically aimed at the discipline of education. One of these is Marvin Cetron. In his book, *Schools of the Future*, Cetron makes several points regarding what schools will have to do in the years to come. He feels we will need to train students for a changing job market. Students will need vocational retraining every five to ten years. Since more adults will need to be educated, schools will have to be open all hours

---

[10] Yankelovich, Daniel, "Changes in Society for the 1990's," *NSPRA Scanner*, National School Public Relations Newsletter, Washington, DC, October, 1985.

[11] Naisbitt, John, *Megatrends 2000, Ten New Directions for the 1990's*, Avon, New York, 1991.

and year-round to accommodate this new need. Businesses will rely more on schools to retrain their workers. Greater emphasis will be needed in basic skills since these are the skills needed to adapt to daily work. And finally, he believes that teachers will become managers of education rather than only the dispensers of knowledge.[12]

Nolan Estes, a professor at the University of Texas and the former superintendent of Dallas, Texas, states his futuristic ideas:

- Public schools will become educational freeways with multiple entrances and exits.
- If education is really a life time process, then there is really less reason to stay in the traditional school.
- We should move in education from a choice of futures to a future of choices.
- Schools should become one stop shopping centers for community services.
- Schools must become more ecumenical.
- In the future, an illiterate will not be one who does not know how to read, but one who does not know how to learn.[13]

Arthur Combs, who gave us the term *self concept*, has his list of predictions and forecasts about the public schools.

- We can never have a single curriculum again.
- We must concentrate on process rather than subject matter. Our problem in education is that we are always trying to find answers to questions people don't yet have. The purpose of education needs to be one of training people how to confront problems and find solutions.

---

[12] op. cit., number 5.
[13] Estes, Nolan, Superintendent, Dallas, Texas, from a speech delivered at the Michigan Association of School Administrators conference, Detroit, Michigan, October, 1985.

- ◆ People must be able to enter the educational cycle at any time in their lives.

- ◆ Curricula must concentrate on human conditions. Most education deals with technical skills. We must emphasize responsibility in society.

- ◆ Education must become more individual and personal.

- ◆ We must regard schools as microcosms of society.[14]

Harold Grant, professor at the University of Michigan, looks at education in terms of ages in the history of mankind. He believes that we have gone through historical eras dominated by the military, the church, and economics. He believes that we are about to enter the age of education. In that age, schools will become the most important institutions in society. Success in that society will depend on the education of each individual.[15]

Mel Ravitz, sociologist at Wayne State University and city councilman in the city of Detroit, sees schools as the future political units in our society.

A comprehensive community organization program related to the schools would be of immeasurable benefit to a community. I know of no other single effort that could produce so beneficial a result. Were there only one thing I could do to strengthen a community and improve its educational and civic government, I would set up such a community organization with organizers in every school in the system and backed with sufficient auxiliary personnel. I would then await the heartening result of the gradual participation of the people in the building of curricula, in the shaping of civic policies, in the ordering of priorities, in their own involvement with the schools and with the city. From the view point of one who believes deeply in the democratic process and in the right of the people to know, to speak, and to organize,

---

[14] Combs, Arthur, Professor, University of Colorado, from a speech delivered at an Eastern Michigan University community education conference, East Lansing, Michigan, Fall, 1980.

[15] Grant, Harold, Professor, University of Michigan, from a speech delivered at the Mott Intern Program, Flint, Michigan, Fall, 1970.

nothing could he healthier for our society. That such action would pre-cipitate shock, dismay, some confusion and innumerable changes, there is no doubt. But that is precisely what our school systems and our communities require most at this point in their development.[16]

One of the most interesting and provocative futurists in education was Dr. Mario Fantini, who was the Dean of the College of Education at the University of Massachusetts. Dr. Fantini believed that education would become the dominant coordinating force in society and have a high priority in our post industrial society. He felt that we would move from a compulsory public schooling concept to a compulsory public education system. In this context, he saw schooling as basic literacy, knowledge, and vocational training. He saw education as personal growth, talent development, and competence in major societal roles. In his plan, the community would have far more involvement in the educational process. The quality of the education system would largely control the ability of the individual and group to grow.

He believed that the school has gone through two stages and will go through two more. In stage I, education was shared by the school, family, church, business, and community. We are in stage II, where the schools do everything or at least are expected to do everything, and are beginning to enter stage III. In this stage, schools will begin to delegate some of the responsibilities back to the appropriate places in the community. The ultimate education system will be stage IV in which the schools will become the brokers for all teaching and learning. All segments of the community will have educational responsibilities. The role of the schools will be as learner advocates. They will be the orchestrators of many educational opportunities. It will be their job to diagnose educational problems and prescribe solutions, using the many resources in the community.[17]

---

[16] Ravitz, Mel, Professor, Wayne State University and member, Detroit City Council, from a speech delivered at the Michigan Community School Education Association conference, Boyne Mountain, Michigan, Fall, 1972.

[17] Fantini, Mario, Editor, *Education in School and Nonschool Settings*, Eighty-fourth Yearbook of the National Society for the Study of Education, Chapter III, University of Chicago Press, Chicago, Illinois, 1985, p. 46.

All of these experts and futurists make us aware of one thing—we are greatly in need of a new philosophy of education. Dewey, Kirkpatrick, Cubberly, and Mort—indeed all of our educational theorists—made their contributions more that 60 years ago. They were giants in our discipline, but the rapid changes in our society require concepts and practices that are much more relevant to our times. Even *A Nation At Risk* prescribed changes to our system much more compatible to the ideas of these futurists than to what the current educators have recommended.

As we look at that document, we should be very aware of some of its recommendations.

◆ Education reform should focus on the goal of creating a learning society. At the heart of such a society is a commitment to a set of values and to a system of education that affords all members the opportunity to stretch their minds to full capacity from early childhood through adulthood, learning more as the world itself changes.

◆ Also at the heart of the learning society are educational opportunities extending far beyond the traditional institutions of learning. They extend into homes and work places, into libraries, galleries, museums and science centers, indeed into every place where the individual can develop in work and life.

◆ The search for solutions to our educational problems must also include a commitment to life long learning. In our view, formal schooling of youth is the essential foundation for learning throughout one's life.

◆ We must mobilize the voluntary efforts of individuals, businesses, parents and civic groups to cooperate in strengthening educational programs.[18]

---

[18] op. cit., number 1.

When we look at the status of education in the United States, it seems clear that this is a unique time in public education. We need to recognize that the circumstances of the times make major change in education more likely to occur than at any time since 1894. We must also recognize that if professional educators are going to have a major role in this change, they will have to expend some energy and come up with some creative ideas. This is more difficult than it sounds since paradigms are hard to alter, especially by those who built them in the first place. Change will occur. The question is, what will be the professional educator's role in it?

Only in rare instances are generations given the opportunity to make a major change in history. For current educators these are the "best of times" because these educators are in a position to influence the direction of education in the United States for the next 100 years. Education stands ready for a major alteration, and it is the purpose of this book to provide suggestions, directions, and alterations for such an effort.

CHAPTER II

THE HISTORY OF COMMUNITY EDUCATION—A CONCEPTUAL DEVELOPMENT

INTRODUCTION

Many chapters dealing with the history of a movement or educational development focus on the programs and people of significance to that effort. *This chapter will not.* Instead, an effort will be made to trace major ideas and concepts that have developed, showing the relationship between these ideas and the present community education philosophy. By looking at ideas and how they have changed and merged with other ideas, the reader's understanding of what community education is and how it developed should be enhanced.

ANTECEDENTS OF COMMUNITY EDUCATION

Ideas do not emerge from a void. They are, instead, a reconstruction and reordering of other ideas into new combinations of different patterns and expanded perceptions. The concept of community education is certainly no exception to this. In fact, a review of the history of education clearly establishes the ideas embraced by community educators as very old and consistently pursued by the great educators of the past.

James A. Dickenson, in Chapter XV of the Fifty-Second Yearbook of the National Society for the Study of Education, dramatically emphasizes this relationship with the past when he refers to the thinking of people such as Plato and Sir Thomas Moore.[1] Plato, in *The Republic,* for example, suggests a need for a continued emphasis on the establishment and maintenance of the community to assure the good life. The importance of the community and the positive force of education as a cultural mainstay dominated Plato's thinking. While some might feel that other aspects of Plato's concepts related to an all encompassing role for the state are inappropriate, certainly his ideas on the interrelationship between community and education are not.

In the sixteenth century, Sir Thomas Moore, in *Utopia,*[2] deemphasized the dominant role of the state as perceived by Plato while continuing to emphasize the importance of the community in the develop-

---

[1] Dickinson, James A., "Antecedents of the Community School Concept in the Utopian Theories," *National Society for the Study of Education Fifty-Second Yearbook, Part II The Community School*, University of Chicago Press. 1953. p. 241.

[2] op. cit., p. 243.

ment of the individual. The citizens of Utopia, Moore believed, had the dual responsibility of improving the community and themselves, with the idea that as people involve themselves in civic concerns a sense of social responsibility is created.

Brook Farm, which was established in Massachusetts in the mid 1800s in response to Moore's thinking, did gain some recognition as an experiment in true cooperative community life which was designed to enhance the individual. It failed for a number of reasons, but primarily for its over emphasis on the development of the intellect and its lack of responsiveness to the problems of life and other external influences that affect life.

Dickenson sums up what we as community educators should have learned from Plato, Thomas Moore, and the Utopian experiments:

> Each Republic theocracy, divinely ordained kingdom, or utopia offered a final, authoritarian solution of the innumerable problems of human association for all times. Coping with the problems of its own time, each unknowingly tried to make time stand still—to rule out new problems. Since every existing organization is a tentative solution of a social problem which the preceding form of organization could not solve, one cannot simplify new difficulties or existing ones by ignoring or deploring them, or yearning for archaic living conditions.—What may be adequate for today is inadequate for tomorrow.[3]

For this reason, the community school would propose no "social blueprint," even if it had one. Having learned that no plans last forever, community educators respond to the evolving needs of the community and, where possible, try to anticipate them. Goals and plans are cooperatively devised in terms of new developments. Change within the capacity of the individual to absorb it is recognized as a prime reality of the modern social scene. The final postulate is that the avoidance of reality is completely unproductive.

With the emergence of the industrial revolution, new educational problems and issues forced themselves on the thinking of the time. As

---

[3] op. cit., p. 249.

the society became industrialized, the need for a well trained work force became increasingly acute. The need to relate education to community life, and particularly to the labor needs of the industrial and business community, increasingly gained the attention of educators.

Out of this changing perception of the schools, the Fellenberg experiments emerged in the early nineteenth century.[4] Phillip Emanuel von Fellenberg, the son of a Swiss nobleman, purchased a 600-acre estate and developed a system of schools within this estate to aid in the solution of community problems. Since the primary activity of the estate was agriculture, the schools did much experimental work in this area, as well as involve the students in the improvement of the agricultural productivity of the estate. The experiment proved extremely successful, demonstrating that a relationship between education, community, and the world of work could be established.

Other schools were developed as success was achieved: an academy for the sons of other well-to-do farmers in the area, a trade school similar to present vocational schools, and a school of theoretical and applied science. All, however, followed the basic principle of relating what was taught to the life and needs of the community. In many ways Fellenberg created what might now be considered the first "modern" approach to community education. It is indeed unfortunate that upon his death his effort to relate education to the improvement of life did not continue. Fellenberg was 50 years ahead of his time.

It is quite natural that the United States would emerge in the avant garde of this developing direction in education. As a country that entered the industrial revolution early, and one without centuries of educational tradition, we accepted more easily new ideas regarding what education is and how it should relate to society. Henry Bernard, in the middle 1800s, wrote:

> It is a matter of vital importance to manufacturing villages, to close the deep gulf with precipitous sides, which too often separate one set of men from their fellows, to soften and round distinctions of society which are nowhere else so sharply defined . . . At least the elements of

---

[4] op. cit., p. 251.

earthly happiness and of a pleasant and profitable intercourse should be brought within the reach of all, be given to all through good public schools, and by other means of public education, good manners, intelligent and inquiring minds, refined tastes, and the desire and ability to be brought into communion with those who possess these qualities.[5]

Here Bernard expanded the thinking presented earlier. He is talking about the need to establish a meaningful relationship between the school and the community, as well as the need to use the school as a social equalizer. Bernard viewed the American school as an instrument of social justice whereby all people could have an equal opportunity to gain the best of life. Within that effort, he also viewed the school as being able to break down social, economic, and racial barriers.

Certainly, the most dominant thinker in American education was John Dewey. While much of Dewey's writing clearly incorporates many of the community education ideas we now espouse, two of his major books, *The School and Society* and *Democracy and Education*, deal almost exclusively in this realm. To attempt to deal with the breadth of his thinking in this chapter would be impossible. Let it suffice at this point to state that Dewey, more than any educator before him, perceived most clearly the intertwining of school and society—the interrelationship between a community and its schools to establish true learning. "The development within the young of the attitudes and dispositions necessary to the continuous and progressive life of a society cannot take place by direct conveyance of beliefs, emotions, and knowledge. It takes place through the intermediary of the environment. The environment consists of the sum total of conditions which are concerned in the execution of the activity characteristic of a living being."[6]

Before moving on to more recent developments in the emergence of the community education philosophy, one other individual's ideas should be considered—those of Ferdinand Tonnes[7]. Tonnes was a German sociologist who, in his book, *Gemeinschaft and Gesellschaft*, describes the

---

[5] op. cit., p. 256.

[6] Dewey, John, *Democracy and Education*, Macmillan Company, New York, 1963, p. 26.

[7] Tonnes, Ferdinand, as Translated by Charles Loomis: *Gemeinschaft and Gesellschaft—Community and Society*, Michigan State University Press, 1957.

difference between two types of communities and the subsequent impact on living conditions these differences bring about. The theory developed by Tonnes suggests that as communities become larger and more impersonal, relationships between people become more contractual and structured, more distant and impersonal. This he referred to as the Gesellschaft society. The Gemeinschaft society, on the other hand, is dependent on closeness and personal interaction based on a small community's natural interdependence.

Tonnes established four variables that interplay on human relationships, and these relationships were perceived as dependent on the nature of the society in which one existed:

1. Acquaintanceship vs. Strangeness
2. Sympathy vs. Antipathy
3. Confidence and Mistrust
4. Interdependence

1. *Acquaintanceship vs. Strangeness*—In a modern complex society, an individual might view an "acquaintanceship" as a friend, though the person may not be well known outside of work, or church, or a local organization in which membership is shared.

   The smaller simpler society demands a closer relationship for friendship than does the complex society. Ties must be deeper for a friendship relationship to reduce the "strangeness" and to move one beyond the levels of acquaintance. Friendship in a complex society can be a passing or temporary thing while in the smaller and simpler gemeinschaft society, more permanence is necessary.

2. *Sympathy vs. Antipathy*—Sympathy vs. antipathy is closely related to feelings of acquaintance or strangeness. The smaller the societal structure, and the more true acquaintanceship that exists, the more sympathy or antipathy are instinctive—based upon personal knowledge of the other. As society becomes larger—more impersonal—sympathy or antipathy are often determined by first impression, or by what we have heard about a person. Decisions are often not based on personal knowledge.

Both of the above come in different degrees and varying forms, as does the complexity of the societies in which they are found.

3. **Confidence and Mistrust**—Confidence and mistrust also interrelate with acquaintanceship and strangeness, and with sympathy and antipathy. The closer the personal relationship, and the greater the feeling of sympathy based on personal knowledge, the greater the trust (confidence).

Complex societies develop an impersonal confidence based on external criteria such as reputation, degrees received, etc.

4. **Interdependence**—Interdependence operates with all of the above and ultimately focuses upon the amount of freedom one is willing or required to give up for the security of an interdependent relationship. Simpler societies require greater interdependence, i.e., I help you because I may need your help. This necessitates a reduction in personal freedom. Complex societies allow more individual freedom, but at a price in cooperation and interdependence. To the extent we can operate without concern for others, we tend to separate our personal needs from requiring the support of others. Interdependence is reduced, as is cooperation.

To the extent we have "natural will" (based on personal relationships), we have a Gemeinschaft society. To the extent we have "rational will" (based upon structured relationships), we have a Gesellschaft society. Increased structure and complexity replace dependence on personal friends and community members with dependence on complex systems and unknown providers of services.

Fundamental principles have emerged from these early thoughts and efforts that directly affect the community education movement.

1. *School-Community Interaction is Crucial*

A common theme running throughout these writings is the importance of tying the community and the school together for good education. To the extent education separates from the community, both lose strength and quality.

2. *The Total Community is the Education Agency*

While similar to number one above, this concept recognizes the need not only to tie school and community closely together, but to use the entire community as a resource in the total education effort. By recognizing that learning does not take place in a vacuum, or only within the schools' geographical boundaries, one can begin using the entire community as a teaching and learning laboratory.

3. *Schools Have a Broader Role than Educating Only the Youth of the Community*

Through the review of the writings of these education leaders, it is increasingly clear that education is not and cannot be for the young alone. Educating a community means providing educational opportunities for all within that community.

4. *Education Must Relate to the Problems and Needs of the Community Being Served*

To the extent education closely relates to a community's problems and concerns, structuring itself to assist the community in resolving these problems and concerns through enlightened effort, it becomes more meaningful to its recipients.

5. *Education Must Relate to Smaller Communities or Community Sub-Groups for Maximum Effectiveness*

In that human interaction increasingly becomes more structured and formal, more impersonal and distant as communities grow larger, education agencies must struggle to maintain a relationship within that growing depersonalization with a smaller grouping. If learning and education is best achieved in a relationship of warmth, trust, and friendship, and this is best achieved by retaining the Gemeinschaft interaction described by Tonnes, the school must do what it can to retain this type of community structure.

MODERN DEVELOPMENT OF COMMUNITY EDUCATION

The preceding pages have been written to show that the ideas proposed by and pursued through community education are not new. While there may be variations and new combinations of past ideas, the fact is that most of what we believe was suggested long before the modern community education movement began. It is important to recognize that the conceptual framework we accept is the result of centuries of educational thought and development, and that we are involved in the support of that cumulative effort, rather than in the support of some recent fad or innovation. As we turn to the more recent developments of this concept, these conceptual bases should provide a common element.

Following John Dewey's writings in the late 1800s, a number of books and yearbooks appeared that dealt with the importance of establishing a close relationship between the community and the school. In 1911, the National Society for the Study of Education produced a yearbook dealing with "The City School as a Community Center." Concepts such as providing access to the school in the evening, expanding service to community residents, and broadening the use of school recreational facilities were suggested.

In 1913, Joseph K. Hart, in *Educational Resources of Village and Rural Communities*, also emphasized the importance of school-community interaction, but with a twist. He suggested the importance of using community resources in the school to expand and improve the educational quality of the school offerings.

In the mid 1930s, two experiments in community education were begun; one with the Tennessee Valley Authority (T.V.A.) and the other in Flint, Michigan, in cooperation with the Mott Foundation.

The T.V.A. community education project was a federally funded effort designed to improve conditions of life in the rural southern area served by the T.V.A. The effort focused on the need to provide lifelong opportunities in education that directly related to community needs and that served the entire community, not just its youth. Education, in this situation, was defined in the broadest sense, and efforts to improve economic and community living conditions were pursued. Dr. Maurice Seay was a major contributor to the T.V.A. community education movement, and many of his writings from that era are still community education classics.

Probably the best known community education program is the one begun in Flint, Michigan. Community education started in this city with a partnership between Frank J. Manley, a city recreation leader, and Charles Stewart Mott, a wealthy, local industrialist. The concept they promoted was simple: Give kids something to do, and they won't get into trouble.

As time passed, this simplistic approach to the reduction of juvenile delinquency expanded into other efforts to resolve community problems. Through the 1950s and 1960s, community education in this city expanded rapidly into hundreds and then thousands of courses, activities, and programs directed at community interests, desires, and needs.

During this developmental period in Flint and elsewhere, four principles emerged that became the foundation of the modern community education concept:

1. The school serves all of the community, not just its youth. As the educational center of the community rather than the educational center for the youth of the community, the school should provide all people extended learning opportunities.

2. The school facilities in a community are a major resource of that community, and maximum use should be had of that resource. Schools should not be limited to an 8:00 a.m. to 3:00 p.m. day, but should be available in the evening and on weekends for a variety of community activities.

3. Educational opportunities made available to the community should reflect citizens' interests and needs, not the perceived "appropriate" offerings established by the professional educators of the community.

4. The quality of education provided children is enhanced when a close relationship between school and community is established. Providing educational opportunities to the entire community is one of the best ways of assuring this close interrelationship.

These four principles became the nucleus of the emerging community education concept that began expanding across the nation in the 1950s and 1960s.

THE MOTT FOUNDATION

While the Mott Foundation became involved early in the Flint community education effort, it directed its efforts primarily to the local scene, assisting the city of Flint in developing and expanding its blossoming community education program. As more and more interest in this experiment developed around the country, the Foundation began accepting a larger and more expansive role. The Flint School system became a national model, and the Foundation began supporting efforts to help others view this model. A natural consequence of this effort were resultant requests for Mott financial support to assist other communities. The Foundation found itself being drawn further into the national scene and closely identified with community education.

While some school districts outside of Flint were supported with Mott funds to initiate the concept, the Foundation recognized that such assistance could only be provided to a limited degree. A major decision, made by the Foundation, occurred in the early 1960s when it decided to make a significant commitment to the training of leaders in education.

The Foundation accepted the concept of training carefully screened and selected educators in community education, with the belief that they would ultimately accept leadership roles in education and be able to establish community education in their own districts without Mott support.

This decision resulted in several important gains for the expansion of community education.

First, by separating itself from direct grants to local districts and moving to the training of leaders, the Foundation established itself at the core of the community education movement nationally.

Second, the opportunity for a true national community education movement was established as trained professionals left the Flint laboratory and returned to positions of leadership in education around the country.

Finally, by establishing this training program through a cooperative effort with the public universities in Michigan, an aura of prestige and respect was established for the concept that otherwise could not have been created.

With the establishment of this Leadership Center, followed by the inclusion of a National Center for Short-Term Training, other Foundation efforts directed to the further development of the concept nationally were pursued.

The National Community School Education Association was established in 1966, supported by Mott Foundation funds. This Association began with over four hundred members and quickly became a spearhead for the encouragement and support of the concept nationally. Shortly after this, the Foundation began supporting universities as community education centers with the goal of encouraging and developing the concept in their geographic areas.

From this, a network of regional and cooperating centers emerged around the country, working with local school districts to establish community education.

The Mott Foundation's efforts and the resulting impact on community education have been extensive. The rapid growth and acceptance of the concept is directly related to the Foundation's leadership, support, and commitment. To suggest that community education would not have emerged without the Foundation does injustice to the significance of the concept. To suggest that the rapid growth and acceptance that has occurred would have happened without the Mott Foundation does injustice to the foundation.

Some important developmental aspects also were occurring on other fronts during this same time. In 1938, the American Association of School Administration approved a position paper, "Purposes of Education in American Democracy." In this paper, public school administrators officially acknowledged that the role of schools had to be greatly expanded, particularly in the area of community service and involvement.

In 1953, two important publications appeared: one from the National Society for the Study of Education and the other from the American Society for Curriculum Development. Both provided a major exploration of the concept of community education, as well as an emphasis on the importance of school-community interaction.

Between the years 1945 and 1953, the Kellogg Foundation, in cooperation with the Michigan Department of Education, established numerous community school centers throughout the State of Michigan on an experimental basis. This cooperative effort was the culmination of the Kellogg Foundation's growing interest in rural community health programs, school camping programs, and continuing education. The 1952–1953 annual report of the foundation emphasized the need to help people to help themselves. This interest by Kellogg, tied in with the Michigan Department of Public Instruction's interest in encouraging schools to become a more integral part of their community, resulted in the establishment of eight community education experiments broadly spread throughout Michigan. The goal for these programs is best summarized in the proposal written by the Michigan Department to the Kellogg Foundation. "The community school idea is simple. It is the supposition that a local school system, well organized, well led, well supported, and working in cooperation with other agencies can by means of its services and executive energies contribute significantly to the goodness of living in the community."[8]

Shortly after the Kellogg project was underway, a similar effort was begun in Nebraska. The University of Nebraska, in cooperation with the Nebraska Department of Education, pursued a grant of almost $200,000 from the Carnegie Foundation to establish four community education centers in the state. The effort here was to establish the school system as a viable force in the development and maintenance of the community, as a total support system for the people within it. Services that were to emerge were broadly conceived, stretching from expanded cultural awareness to improved job and employment opportunities.[9] Like the Kellogg project, these projects were perceived as models of community involvement that could be emulated by other school districts.

---

[8] Seay, Maurice and Crawford, Ferris, *The Community School and Community Self Improvement*, Michigan Department of Education, 1954, p. 15.

[9] Bush, Donald, Professor of Educational Administration, Central Michigan University, Interview, January, 1979.

As community education has expanded across the United States, promoters of the concept have become aware of several other histories related to this concept. In Georgia, a program called "College in the Country" was begun in the 1920s under the direction of Collus Johnson. In Milwaukee, Wisconsin, Dorothy Enderis provided excellent leadership in the development of a community education program, beginning in 1910. This program gained national visibility and is likely the forerunner of the Flint program.

Other programs developed as well. Elsie Clapp organized an excellent community education program in Jefferson County, Kentucky. The program was so effective it attracted the attention of President Franklin Roosevelt, and Ms. Clapp was recruited by the President to start a similar program in Arthurdale, West Virginia in the 1930s.

During this time, similar programs were being implemented by Dr. Lloyd Tireman in Nambe, New Mexico, and by persons in other communities in the United States such, as Syracuse, and Buffalo, New York.

Programs also were being started in other places in the world. Henry Morris, the father of community education in England, was the director of education in Cambridgeshire, England and began his activities in 1923. At about the same time, the community school movement was being developed in the Philippine Islands.[10]

The interesting thing to note is that from 1900 through the 1940s, community education was developing throughout the United States and, indeed, throughout the world. There is a need in the community education movement to search out and examine these many histories to discover areas of commonness and interrelationship. It seems likely that there is some connection between these many separate programs developing at the same time. It also seems possible that there is some universal set of principles that develop within a community whenever the circumstances are just right. It would be helpful in the future growth of community education to have such information. One very possible conclusion, for example, is that the current receptivity of community education in the

---

[10] Bernardino, Vitaliano, *The Philippine Community School*, Phoenix Press Inc., Quezon City, 1958.

United States may be related to a natural and historical relationship to the concept and the principles involved.

RECENT ADVANCES IN THE COMMUNITY EDUCATION CONCEPT

As the concept of community education expanded in the late 1960s and early 1970s, confusion began to emerge over what community education really was, and whether or not it provided something unique in public education or merely offered a repackaging of existing school programs. Adult educators suggested, for example, that it was nothing more than adult education, while many recreation leaders considered it a school based form of recreation.

In retrospect, the confusion is understandable. As the concept expanded, limited budgets and the limited training of some community educators caused them to begin programs in school districts, emphasizing one or two components and virtually ignoring other aspects. The entire range of the program possibilities incorporated into the concept were usually not provided and all too often not understood. Thus, as efforts were established to serve the entire community, not just its youth, adult educators saw adult education programs being established. As school use was expanded, and school gymnasiums, pools, and other recreational facilities were used more extensively, recreation personnel saw recreation programs emerging. The fact that many of the people employed in leadership roles in community education had little or no training added to the confusion. Often they confused their role with that of other agencies or pursued programming based on their own limited training. The concept of community education was lost in the pursuit of specific programs and focused course offerings.

During this time, a small group of national leaders in community education began discussing an expanded concept of community education. It was clear that the meaningful involvement of people was crucial to the proper development of community education, yet this involvement was not emerging. While it was true that extensive citizen participation was occurring (through course attendance and pursuit of various program opportunities), this was not viewed as involvement. The distinction between the words *participation* and *involvement* assumed major importance.

The idea that people should have meaningful and extensive input in decisions that affect them also began to emerge as an additional principle of community education. Questions began to be raised regarding how community education could involve people in community problem solving, in decision making that affected their lives. In short, how could education help a community return to a form of active involvement and participatory democracy? This concern naturally led to discussions of expanded service to meet specified problems and the need to coordinate existing community services to meet specified community needs.

The net effect of this expanded concept resulted in the addition of two components to the four that were originally established. (See page 30 in this text.)

1. Community involvement in decisions that affect a community is crucial, with some form of community organizational structure deemed essential if meaningful involvement is to occur.

2. The coordination of community services is necessary, and the school can assist in that coordination by developing a delivery system based on relating identified needs to services available to that community. This implies that schools should not become the providers of all services—that other community agencies can better do this and that the schools' role should be one of facilitating and supporting those efforts.

Within the last few years, the concept as described has begun to achieve broad acceptance within the profession. The confusion that existed has subsided, and the new components that were introduced have been incorporated as an integral part of the concept. Community education is now much more than any addition to the education program—it has become an educational philosophy. When pursued to its logical conclusion, community education affects all of education, establishing an emphasis and purpose quite distinct from traditional structures now in existence.

With the establishment of the concept of community education, it is quite possible that American education has entered a new era and role. We have moved from the Latin Grammar School with its emphasis on literacy skills through the opportunity for a high school education for all and the establishment of the comprehensive high school with its expanded responsibility for preparation for life. We have now reached the concept of educating the entire community through a broad array of opportunities and cooperative interrelationships.

If we have accepted a new role—a new responsibility in American education—it is quite possible that community education will be the major modification. For when taking community education to its logical conclusion, we have established the concept that the school is responsible for assisting in the education of all citizens, that community school interrelationships should be held so closely that lines of distinction blur, and that education is a lifelong responsibility and opportunity.

CHAPTER III

COMMUNITY EDUCATION: WHAT IT IS AND IS NOT

The primary step in the examination of any subject is the definition of terms to clarify the guidelines of the inquiry and to assure that those involved are proceeding from a common base. Consequently, any discussion of community education should include an examination of the meaning of the term *community education*.

Unfortunately, the strengths and weaknesses of community education often have been examined without this basic step. As a result, community education has suffered more from misconceptions and misunderstandings than for any other reason. Many activities have been falsely labeled as community education, and many community education persons have promoted as community education things which fall short of the complete definition. Consequently, community educators have frequently had to defend their existence in the light of false conceptions and misunderstandings about the true meaning of community education and its potential.

Before attempting the task of defining community education, it might first be more appropriate to discuss some of the more popular misconceptions of community education and identify what community education "is not." In trying to point out the differences between community education and its misnomers, one thread of consistency is notable: in general, those things that are often called community education are usually only portions of it. Thus, proponents of community education often are settling for less than the total gestalt of community education without acknowledging this fact.

COMMUNITY SCHOOL

One of the key distinctions that need to be identified is the difference between the terms *community education* and *community school*. Generally stated, community education is a concept, and the community school is one of the most effective delivery systems for achieving that concept. Philosophically, community education is the belief that all communities have many problems and that these problems can best be solved through education. Germane to this belief, of course, is a much broader definition of education than the one most generally used by public schools.

Public schools tend to define education synonymously with "schooling." In community education, we define education in a much broader context. We perceive education much as John Dewey perceived it—as any experience which helps you deal with another experience.

If one can accept this definition, then it is not difficult to expand the perception of who the learners and who the educators are within a community. In a paradigm shift from a focus on schooling to a focus on education, at any one time everyone in the community is a learner, and at a different time, everyone is an educator. The process of community education then becomes one of matching all learning needs within the community with all resources. This would result in a shift from a school system to an education system. For the school system, this would mandate a shift from the dispenser of knowledge for a few members of the community to the brokers of education for the entire community.

In this broader sense, education becomes a means of solving identified human problems through the educative process. The educative process is the technique of applying human and material resources to groups and individuals in an effort to solve individual and community problems.

There are many groups and individuals involved in community education. Public schools, agencies, and government all have specific roles in the education of the community. Universities, community colleges, social welfare, recreation, churches, business, industry, unions, mental health, adult educators, and civic groups are also a part of community education. In fact, there are literally thousands of groups or individuals in every community that have both the expertise and responsibility for meeting specific community education needs.

The community school becomes a very important base for this concept. Granted that it may not be the only agency or model for the development of community education, but it does have some very specific advantages for performing such a role. The most defendable advantage has to do with location. A basic premise of community education is that in order to be carried out most effectively, the primary unit for effectiveness is the "gemeinschaft" or neighborhood unit. If this premise is true, and if, indeed, there is a desire to institutionalize the community education concept, then the school becomes one of the most effective agents for establishing a unique role within the concept of community education, since it is the only institution located on the basis of neighborhood relationships to our society.

There are other reasons for the selection of the public school as a delivery system or a catalyst in the community education concept. It provides an appropriate facility for many of the programs in community education. In addition, as a public tax-supported agency, it is the most acceptable, non-threatening institution to the citizens and other agencies within the community. Its strategic location also puts it in a position to most adequately serve workable portions of the population.

This topic will be dealt with more specifically in a later chapter. At this point, suffice it to say that the public school has proved to be the best organization for serving as the coordinating and facilitating device for the development and implementation of community education.

The main point to be emphasized here is that community education is the concept and the community school is the vehicle by which the potential of the concept is most effectively realized. As a concept, community education is based on the following basic beliefs:

1. Education is not synonymous with schooling and deals with an area much broader than technical training or vocational preparation.

2. Education is a lifetime process and is an integral part of the environment in which we live.

3. There are many groups and individuals involved in the education process, and every community has an abundance of untapped educational resources.

4. Education is our most valuable resource.

5. We should seek to maximize facilities and resources since collectively such resources can accomplish much more than they can individually.

6. Involvement of the community is a community right resulting in better decisions and better community support.

7. Improvement of the small community is the best approach in improving the larger community.

8. Services should be delivered as close as possible to where people live.

9. Education should be based on the needs and problems of those for whom it is planned.

10. The educative process (problem solving) is the most important means of meeting individual and community needs.

The school, then, becomes one institution's attempt to operate within the guidelines of these beliefs.

COMMUNITY EDUCATION PROGRAMS

The most frequent misconception is between the concept of community education and its programs. Community education is the over-arching conceptual base, while programs are the activities related to the solution of specific community needs. Thus, enrichment opportunities, recreation programs, cultural activities, avocational offerings, and political and civic programs are partial ways of resolving certain community problems.

> Too frequently, a well-intentioned program based on the concept of community education has culminated in evening activities for adults. This occurs because the personnel involved in such situations possess a vague understanding of the depth and ramifications of the community education concept. The most important aspect of community education is not *program* but *process*. It is the relationship between these two terms which is fundamental to the concept of community education. The ultimate goal of community education is to develop a process by which members of a community learn to work together, to identify problems, and to seek solutions to these problems. It is through this process that an ongoing procedure is established for working together on all community issues . . .

> Programs are those overt activities which are designed to resolve the issues identified by the process . . . Failure of community education efforts are often the result of excessive emphasis on programs with little or no attention to the process of community development.[1]

In fairness to those who do strive for total community education but end up with primarily programs, it should be noted that community education is generally achieved in two stages. The first stage is often highly program-oriented and comes about as a result of meeting the immediate, more obvious needs as perceived by the community. Local citizens and agencies will often demand to see programs in operation soon after community education is implemented. An abundance of programs will often meet some community needs through greater use of facilities, by providing activities, and by emulating what community members have seen in other communities. It will also help those responsible for community education to get people more actively and overtly into programs and provide additional access for getting them further involved. True community education is endangered when the community or the directors of community education become so obsessed and encumbered with programs that they are either unable or unwilling to proceed to the second stage—community process and community self-actualization.

NEIGHBORHOOD SCHOOL

Many people perceive community education and the neighborhood school concept as the same thing. The biggest problem with this misconception is the connotation that the term *neighborhood schools* has carried in the past. Schools do play an important part in the community education concept as advocated by most experts in community education; and the school building, as a neighborhood center, plays a key role in providing facilities and serving as a unifying force in identifying *community*.

The term *neighborhood school*, however, has been used frequently in the past in connection with racial segregation. It has been used to support segregation on the basis that students, due to convenience and other

---

[1] Hickey, Howard; Minzey, Jack; Van Voorhees, Curt; and Associates, *The Role of the School in Community Education*, Pendell Publishing Co., Midland, Michigan, 1969. p. 36.

advantages, should attend the schools in their immediate neighborhood. As a result, *de jure* integration was circumvented by *de facto* segregation on the basis of housing patterns. This usage of the term has negated its positive use with many minorities and, as a result, conjures up ominous perceptions that doom community education before it begins.

It is true that community education seeks to develop a sense of community in the neighborhood and to use the local schools for programs. Its success, however, is not dependent on the attendance of the school-age students at specific schools. Community education can function very effectively in a school district which has endorsed busing of students for integration purposes.

Many critics of community education have referred to it as a relic of the past—the neighborhood school concept with a new title. These same critics go on to state that, as such, it is not meeting the modern day societal problems that the education system must face and is, instead, an attempt to maintain the status quo.

The neighborhood school, in this traditional sense, is simply a school within a local community or neighborhood that is readily accessible to its constituents because of its proximity. It is normally perceived as an elementary school within easy walking distance of most children, its purpose being the education of these same children. This approach to education has become controversial, because some people believe that it is a means of maintaining segregation and a segregated education system. Because the school serves the surrounding community under this plan, and because segregation is usually most evident in housing patterns, the schools often mirror the ethnic distribution of the neighborhood and thus provide the basis for this criticism. As a result of present housing patterns, black communities tend to have black schools and white neighborhoods tend to have white schools. Critics believe this condition compounds the problem of segregation and tends to thwart attempts toward integration.

It is the contention of the authors that the concept of community education and the neighborhood school are not the same, and the two are similar only in that both use the local elementary school as the basic unit of the total education system. Further, it is our belief that because of the basic tenets of community education—citizen involvement, sharing of decision making, problem solving, and total community involvement in the education enterprise—the possibilities of true integration for the total society are greatly enhanced through acceptance of this philosophy. Further, the school integration of children must be viewed in its proper perspective. The year 1969 was the last in which the majority of the people in a community had children in the public schools. Today, that number is less than 20 percent. When one views community education in the context of education and involvement for all, then fully 80 percent of the people in a neighborhood community have needs for classes, programs, meetings, involvement, and use of neighborhood facilities. These needs exist regardless of which school the children in that community attend.

The very essence of community education is a belief that the school is most effective when it involves the people it is attempting to serve in designing the programs and opportunities that the education system is going to provide. Because large scale involvement is believed essential, the neighborhood school becomes the one unit that can be used as a base of operations. It is the one facility that all neighborhoods have in common. No other agency or government system has a structural framework that approaches the one available through the local elementary school, and it is the only government agency that exists in neighborhoods all over the country. This accessibility alone provides the very best opportunities possible for true grass roots involvement. Further, the education system is the one remaining unit common to all groups in our society that can bind and pull the very diverse elements within our society together and begin working toward some positive goals—goals perceived as worthwhile by a large number of people who are willing to work together to achieve them.

COMMUNITY CONTROL

Community control has become one of the controversial terms in education. The term is often used synonymously with decentralization and community involvement as well as community education.

Community control, as the word *control* implies, delegates the responsibility and the decision-making authority concerning the education system to the constituent citizenry—the grass roots, local residents. Lay citizens totally control the operation of the school and the education of their children and are responsible for all decisions, from trivia to major policy determinations.

The move toward an education system based on community control is based on several motivational factors:

1. There is a feeling, especially in large education systems, that local needs and local concerns are not only unmet by educators, but are being virtually ignored. Community control is perceived as a method of reversing this situation and providing individuals access to decision making within the education institution.

2. Many of the more militant factions of our communities believe that the polarization of races and their regrouping as an ethnic body must take place before meaningful integration can ever occur. One of the ways that this can be accomplished is through education systems controlled by the community and reflecting the education programs the community believes are necessary. Incorporated into this thinking is a total rejection of the involvement of the present structure, resulting from mistrust and past negative experiences.

3. There is a general belief that many of our social problems result from a highly bureaucratic, systematized, formalized operational pattern that stifles creative thinking and squelches disagreement and healthy dissent. This group generally believes that the answer to this problem has to be the elimination of the "system," replacing it with meaningful individual and group participation, the involvement of the lay citizen being the single most crucial need for the growth and development of a new, responsive system.

The problem with the recommendation of the community control proponents is that they fail to recognize the appropriate role of various groups with institutional decision making, and in their effort to overcome one discrepancy they introduce another. For any public agency to operate most effectively, and perhaps even legally, it is important to have three separate entities in operation—the professional, the legally responsible board, and the community. Each has a very specific role to play, which, if carried out appropriately, will result in maximizing the effectiveness of the organization. In the past, we have tended to emphasize the first two groups, the professional and the legal board, while excluding or at least not encouraging community input.

The people promoting community control, aware that they have been excluded as "community," tend to suggest that we should create a system that gives viability only to community and excludes or greatly minimizes the other two groups. Since all three are necessary, the result is a new model that also will fail to be successful because it too becomes a model built on exclusion rather than inclusion and cooperation.

Professional educators and boards of education must share the decision-making process in education programming and involve lay citizens in the process of formulating policies and procedures. This not only will avoid the past problems related to community control, but will also assure a more meaningful and relevant program. If we have learned one lesson from our past experience with community control, it is this: educators cannot afford to force people into extreme positions to gain a voice in the education system. When this happens, there is a tendency to eliminate both the professional educator and the board of education and the very valuable contributions they must make if high quality education is to be assured. Continued rejection of the community in educational matters will result in rejection of educators and school boards by the community. Community involvement must be a joint undertaking and approached on the assumption that lay citizens, boards of education, and professional educators have unique and valuable contributions to make and each, because of its uniqueness, cannot develop an adequate education program without the others.

In general terms, the phrase *community control* implies a truism that should exist in every school district. Legally, control of education is vested in the states, but most people subscribe to the idea that control of education should reside in locally-elected boards of education who are re-sponsive to the needs of the community. As a result of recent develop-ments, *community control* has tended to be associated with decentral-ization and more specifically with control over the educational operation of such things as curriculum, policy making, and employment of staff, rather than involvement of community in the decision-making process of schools. As a result, it does not seem to be a more viable method of in-volving community as much as one of substituting one special interest group for another to the exclusion of others who need to be involved. As such, community control does not deal with community involvement, community process, or problems diverse enough to be classified as com-munity education.

POVERTY AND DISADVANTAGED PROGRAMS

Many well-meaning social engineers attempt to relate community educa-tion only to the needs of the poor. Since community education has as a goal the solution of community problems, the assumption would seem to be that affluent communities have no problems. Few, if any, would acknowledge this, and, in fact, one could make quite a case to show that many problems of the poor (i.e., single parent families, drugs, juvenile delinquency, etc.) are equally prevalent in the affluent segment of our society, even if not for the same reasons.

There are needs in every community for community education. And whether it be for overt programs for children and adults, for a better un-derstanding of the cultural differences between segments of our society, or for the solution of community problems within the community, com-munity education has proved to be of value to all types of communities, regardless of the socio-economic factors of the communities themselves.

SOCIAL WORK

To compensate for the overemphasis on programs, some community edu-cators have promoted a technique which seeks to give more attention to community social needs and subsequently results in an exaggerated so-ciological orientation to local problems. While this may be a necessary device for solving some of the community's problems, it is not an adequate substitute for community education. The case study approach is not the same as community problem solving brought about through the community education process.

COMMUNITY DEVELOPMENT

The term *community development* has also become a substitute for community education. Part of the reason for this seems to be based on a feeling that community schools signify a rather mundane role relegating community education to programs and services. Community development, on the other hand, is regarded as a more noble purpose, leading to the improvement of society and the solution of community ills, and thus it is more emotionally rewarding.

The problem with this substitution in terminology is two-fold. First, its supporters have identified with a term that has had extensive and diverse prior usage. Community development is used by some groups to describe the physical development of a less than modern community in which the goals are development of public sewage systems, drilling of wells, building of schools and hospitals, and the use of modern farm equipment and fertilizers to improve agriculture. In other cases, community development has been used to describe urban renewal projects. Since there are already professionally trained community workers, peace corps personnel, and urban developers involved in community development, the terminology and the training of community educators who describe their activity as *community development* has become confusing.

The second problem related to community development is one of failure of those promoting this term to understand community education and the community school. Community development, either as physical development or human development, is an integral part of the community education concept. Since the concept deals with identifying problems and then using resources to help in the solution of these problems, community development takes place whenever the problem identified is a community development problem and some appropriate community development resource is brought in to provide assistance. To identify community development and community education as identical is to fall into the same trap as identifying community education synonymously with adult education or recreation. Community developers are valuable resources in the solution of community problems but are no different than any other resource in their relation to the concept of community education. To not see this relationship is simply an indication of an inability to comprehend the scope of the community education concept. Unfortunately, some community educators have engaged in a win-lose confrontation over the community education versus community development issue, and even though their arguments are primarily rhetorical, the emotion of their appeal has resulted in a division among the supporters of community education.

In summary, we have been looking at things that have been misconceived as community education. In some cases, the problem has been that portions of community education, such as programs, social work, or the community school, have been viewed as being synonymous with the total concept. In other cases, the label *community education* has been used to identify activities alien to the concept of community education, such as segregated neighborhood schools. The unfortunate result has been that many things that are not community education in its entirety have been promoted as community education, and this has culminated in misunderstandings and unjust criticisms about the concept of community education.

DEFINING COMMUNITY EDUCATION

To define community education, one should look first at the meaning of the words in the term. The word *community* must be viewed as a feeling as well as a geographical characteristic to effectively realize its potency. It is through the interrelationships in a community that community education realizes its power.

The point to be emphasized is that community is not merely a political unit or a geographic unit or a commercial unit; it is preeminently a social unit. Thus, ... we may say that a community consists of people who live in a more or less contiguous area and are engaged in such social processes and relationships as may normally arise in the pursuit of the chief concerns of life.[2]

The term *community* here is being used to refer to a local situation. It implies closeness which might be characterized by a neighborhood. It also implies people who have common problems and common goals. And looking at the word *common* one should note its relationship to this total discussion.

COMMUNITY EDUCATION: FROM PROGRAM TO PROCESS

There is more than a verbal tie between the words *common, community,* and *communication.* Men live in a *community* by virtue of the things which they have in common; and *communication* is the way in which they come to possess things in common. What they must have in common in order to form a community or society are aims, beliefs, aspirations, knowledge—a common understanding—like-mindedness as the sociologists say. Such things cannot be passed physically from one to another like bricks. They cannot be shared as persons would share a pie by dividing it into physical pieces. The communication which insures participation in a common understanding is one which secures similar emotional and intellectual dispositions—like ways of responding to expectations and requirements.

Persons do not become a society by living in physical proximity, any more than *a man ceases to be socially influenced* by being so many feet or miles removed from others. A book or letter may institute a more intimate association between human beings separated thousands of miles from each other than exists between dwellers under the same roof. Individuals do not even compose a social group because they all work for a common end. The parts of a machine work with a maxi-

---

[2] Olsen, Edward G., *The School and Community Reader*, The Macmillan Co., New York, 1963, p. 362.

mum of cooperativeness for a common result, but they do not form a community. If, however, they were all cognizant of the common end and all interested in it so that they regulated their specific activity in view of it, then they would form a community. But this would involve communication. Each would have to know what the other was about and would have to have some way of keeping the other informed as to his own purpose and progress. Consensus demands communication.[3]

To properly fulfill the complete analysis of the term *community education*, we must also give scrutiny to the word *education*. Dictionary definitions tend to place education in a very structured, traditional setting of a combination of teaching and learning. Such a limited definition, however, does not display the potential of the term in bringing about change. A more relevant definition by H.G. Wells states, "Education is the preparation of the individual for the community,"[4] or one by John Dewey, who defines education as "that reconstruction or reorganization of experience which adds to the meaning of experience, and which increases ability to direct the course of subsequent experience."[5]

It is from the conceptualization of community as a feeling rather than a geographical boundary and education as a means of understanding experiences and directing new ones that we may now proceed to a definition of the term *community education.*

The defining of the term *community education* has been attempted by many persons over the years. It would seem logical that a proper definition might be developed by analyzing these many definitions and establishing a composite that represents a consensus of those who are experts in the field. In considering the many different definitions, however, one cannot give equal weight to each since some fall short of achieving a definition that includes the complete potential of the concept. For example, the National Association for Public School Adult Education limits its definition by focusing on the community school component of community education.

---

[3] Dewey, John, *Democracy and Education*, The Macmillan Co., New York, 1963, p. 26.
[4] Wells, H.G., *The Outline of History*, Garden City, New York, Garden City Publishing Co., 1929, p. 1089.
[5] Dewey, op. cit., pp. 5–6.

> When a school stays open in the morning, afternoon, and evening . . .
> up to twelve months a year . . . with programs geared to the needs of
> the total community which it serves . . . for boys and girls, men and
> women . . . involves representatives from the entire community in its
> policy formulation and its program planning—this is a community
> school.[6]

The problem with this definition is that it conveys the idea that community education is centered around programs in the school setting. In a similar way, the definition adopted by the State of Michigan in 1969 seemed to place its emphasis on the school and its program. It defined community education as:

> . . . the composite of those services provided to the citizens of the community by the school district, excepting for those services provided through regular instructional activities for children aged 5 to 19 years. Such community school programs may include, among others, preschool activities for children and their parents, continuing and remedial education for adults, cultural enrichment and recreational activities for all citizens, and the use of school buildings by and technical services to community groups engaged in solving economic and social problems.[7]

While this definition also tends to imply that the regular school is not a proper part of community education, the often quoted definition by Elsie Clapp goes to the other extreme by equating community education with extensive interaction between the regular school and its community. Miss Clapp states that community education is identified by the following characteristics:

> First of all, it meets as best it can, and with everyone's help, the urgent needs of people, for it holds that everything that affects the welfare of the children and their families is its concern. Where does school end

---

[6] National Association for Public School Adult Education, Washington, DC, "Community School Education—A Comprehensive Concept," Vol. XIV, No. 5, March, 1968, p. 3.

[7] Michigan State Board of Education, "Policies for the Distribution of Monies to School Districts for Community School Programs in 1969–70 in Accordance with the Provisions of Act 307. PA of 1969 (as adopted by the State Board of Education on October 1, 1969.)"

and life outside begin? There is no distinction between them. A community school is a used place, a place used freely and informally for all the needs of living and learning. It is, in effect, the place where learning and living converge.[8]

In a similar fashion, other writers have arrived at definitions that are less than adequate for conveying the total concept. Consider the following:

The school as an embryonic, typical community is one of the earliest forms of the community school concept. Its central feature is that the school, in all its internal aspects, should represent the kinds of human relationships and moral ideas that ought to characterize society.[9]

Any school is a community school to the extent that it seeks to realize some such objectives as the following: (a) educates youth by and for participation in the full range of basic life activities (human needs, areas of living, persistent problems, etc.); (b) seeks increasingly to democratize life in school and outside; (c) uses community resources in all aspects of its programs; (d) actively cooperates with other social agencies and groups in improving community life; (e) functions as a service center for youth and adult groups.[10]

Community school is the term currently applied to a school that has two distinctive emphases—service to the entire community, not merely to the children of school age; and discovery, development, and use of the resources of the community as a part of the educational facilities of the school.[11]

It should be emphasized that these examples are not rejected as much for being inept as for providing a very limited perception of the scope of community education.

---

[8] Clapp, Elsie, *Community Schools in Action*. The Viking Press, New York, 1939, p. 89.

[9] Smith, Othanel B.; Stanley, William O.; and Shores, Harland J., *Fundamentals of Curriculum Development*, Harcourt, Brace and World, Inc., New York, 1959, p. 535.

[10] Cook, Lloyd Allen, "A Community School," *Encyclopedia of Educational Research*, 1st Edition. The Macmillan Co., New York, 1941, p. 1002.

[11] Seay, Maurice F., "Two Distinctive Emphases," *Forty-fourth Yearbook, Part I*, National Society for the Study of Education, University of Chicago Press, 1945, pp. 209–228.

Some definitions are felt to be more accurate in their attempt to clarify the meaning of community education, and these are submitted as being more germane to any discussion of the concept. While some of these appear to be more appropriate than others, they all contain the essence of true community education and are not stated here on any priority basis.

> Community Education is a process that concerns itself with everything that affects the well-being of all citizens within a given community. This definition extends the role of community education from one of the traditional concept of teaching children to one of identifying the needs, problems and wants of the community and then assisting in the development (or the identification) of facilities, programs, staff and leadership toward the end of improving the entire community.[12]

In April, 1968, the Board of Directors of the National Community Education Association adopted the following definition:

> Community School Education is a comprehensive and dynamic approach to public education. It is a philosophy that pervades all segments of education programming and directs the thrust of each of them toward the needs of the community. The community school serves as a catalytic agent by providing leadership to mobilize community resources to solve identified community problems. This marshalling of all forces in the community helps to bring about change as the school extends itself to all people.[13]

Here is still another definition:

> Community Education is an attempt to marshall all the educational resources within the community to create a laboratory for the management of human behavior . . . Community Education is a theoretical concept—a way of viewing education in the community, a systematic way of looking at people and their problems . . . It is based upon the premise that education can be made relevant to people's needs and that the people affected by education should be involved in decisions

---

[12] Minzey, op. cit., pp. 31–32.

[13] *Second Annual Directory of Membership*, National Community School Education Association, Flint, Michigan, 1969, p. 6.

about the program. It assumes that education should have an impact upon the society it serves. It requires that all who are worthy of the name 'Community Educator' are involved in all facets of the community at large.[14]

The broader, more inclusive aspects of community education have been identified in more recent definitions.

Community Education is a process that achieves a balance and a use of all institutional forces in the education of the people—all of the people of the community.[15]

> Maurice Seay
> Professor of Education
> Western Michigan University

We come to the conclusion that community education was the process of a community assessing its needs, also its resources, deciding which resources it could use to meet specific needs, assigning a priority to the needs; and in our project theory, we assumed that the greatest resource of any community for meeting its own needs and for its own improvements is its educational system.[16]

> Walter Beggs
> Dean of the School of Education
> University of Nebraska

As a philosophy, Community Education concerns itself with everything that affects the well being of all citizens within a given community and the dynamics of relating the problems of people to community resources. It allows people to experience success in resolving their community problems, meeting their goals, and making institutions more responsive to community needs and wants.[17]

> Wilson Riles
> Superintendent of Education for
> the State of California

---

[14] Weaver, Donald C., "Community Education—A Cultural Imperative," *The Community School and Its Administration*, Pendell Publishing Co., Midland, Michigan, January, 1969.

[15] *Statement on Community Education*, U.S. Government Printing Office, Washington, DC, 1977, p. 48.

[16] Statement on Community Education, op. cit., p. 48–49.

[17] Statement on Community Education, op. cit., p. 49.

> Community education brings community members together to identify and link community needs and resources in a manner that helps people to help themselves raise the quality of life in their communities.
>
> Duane Brown
> Director
> National Center for
> Community Education

> Community education is an opportunity for local citizens and community schools, agencies and institutions to become active partners in addressing education and community concerns.
>
> National Community Education
> Association

In its simplest form, community education is the education of the entire community but with a broader, more expansive definition of education beyond that of schooling. In addition, it is now possible to more specifically identify those activities and programs that can result in the implementation of the more general and esoteric nature of community education definitions.

In analyzing the differences in these definitions of community education, and in trying to look objectively at the characteristics of those that seem most complete and descriptive, the following ingredients seem to be necessary in developing a proper definition. The definition must include both the traditional and extended programs of education—for both children and adults. It must suggest impact on the entire community and stress community process as well as programs. Finally, it must project the catalytic role played by the school while recognizing the contributions of other groups and agencies. Taking all of these factors into consideration, the following definition is submitted in an effort to combine these many ingredients into one definition:

> Community Education is a philosophical *concept* which serves the entire community by providing for all of the educational needs of all of its community members. It uses the local school to serve as the catalyst for bringing community resources to bear on community problems in an effort to develop a positive sense of community, improve community living, and develop the community process toward the end of self-actualization.

This definition was developed by the authors in 1971. During the ensuing years, it has been frequently quoted by many community educators. This definition, or some form of it, can be found in many other publications, including books, brochures, articles, dissertations, and position papers. Since it seems to have withstood the test of time and analysis by many experts, it still appears to be a viable definition of community education.

It should be pointed out that the preceding definitions used the terms *community education* and *community school* interchangeably. In our definition, we have sought to emphasize again that community education is a concept and that the school has a vital role to play in carrying out that concept. The following references to community education are made with the role of the school in mind. While we are completely aware of the many roles of others in community education, it is the public school's role we are attempting to define and describe.

OBJECTIVES OF COMMUNITY EDUCATION

A philosophical presentation of community education is incomplete unless an attempt is made to describe the objectives that will, we hope, be achieved. Since objectives are related to needs, it seems that before one can enumerate objectives, one must first examine the needs that mandate the development of community education.

One of the first of these needs for community education relates to the expanded educational needs of our society. The inadequacies of the programs are apparent at several levels. They can be found in what might be termed the typical programs related to the kindergarten through twelfth-grade offerings or in the needs for education by other groups in the community who are denied access to publicly supported education programs.

In the case of the children in the community, one great need is in the area of early childhood education as it relates to pre-school experiences. Most educators agree that in terms of both education and attitudes, the first few years of life have a tremendous impact on a youngster. Yet, few school districts provide education programs prior to entrance into the traditional school at age five, and in many states this does not occur until about age six. While federal programs have recently provided funds for encouraging such an educational opportunity to the community, there are still many districts that tolerate these programs as long as funding is available rather than view them as a responsibility of the school district.

For the child already in school, the need is one of relevancy—relevancy to the community in which he or she lives. Schools which were designed to meet the education needs of the community now frequently perform as though there was no community to be served. They have become institutions unto themselves, performing without regard to the student's environment or the influence the community is having on the student. Schools continue to operate as though they represent 100 percent of the child's educational input despite the fact that the child is actually in school less than 11 percent of his or her yearly clock hours. There is a need for the school to be aware that the child is a product of his or her total environment and to be cognizant of the words of Dr. James Conant who said:

> The community and the school are inseparable. It has been established beyond any reasonable doubt that community and family background play a large role in determining scholastic aptitude and school achievement. Anyone who thinks differently simply has not visited widely among American schools.[18]

For still another group in the community, there is a need for the traditional education services of the schools. This group is the adult population—those persons who have passed the legal age at which they may avail themselves of the services of the public schools. Included in this group would be persons in need of basic education skills, adults who need or want a high school diploma, persons who need vocational skills, and community members who desire other programs related to avocational interests, health, physical activity, or personal problems. We have convinced our communities of the need for education, but in many instances

---

[18] "The Community School—Past and Present," Editor, Clyde Campbell: *The Community School and Its Administration*, Pendell Publishing Co., Midland, Michigan, December 1963.

we are not providing such programs. Too often we proceed as though public education is a terminal thing despite our lip service to the concept that education is a lifetime process.

The second need for community education has developed as a result of our changing society. In the historical development of our country, it is easy to trace our community structure from one of small communities to large cities to that gargantuan society we call the megalopolis.

To put this in perspective, we note again the distinction made by the German sociologist, Ferdinand Tonnes. He describes two kinds of culture: the gemeinschaft and the gesellschaft. The gemeinschaft is the type of community which is small and simple. It is characterized by:

A. A relationship between persons largely based on kinship
B. People who know most of their neighbors
C. Continuity brought on through informal controls
D. Little division of labor
E. A self-sufficient community
F. People with a strong sense of community identity
G. A general absence of special interest groups

In this type of culture, behavior is usually well-defined for all.

The gesellschaft is characterized by:

A. A community tie based on territory rather than kinship
B. Division of labor with great specialization
C. Proliferation of society and organization
D. Lack of acquaintance with others, even neighbors
E. Formalized social controls set by laws and enforced by police
F. High interdependence with other communities
G. Anonymity of many persons, where few associate with community life[19]

---

[19] American Association of School Administrators, "Todays Community," *Educational Administration in a Changing Community 1959 Yearbook*, National Education Association, Washington, DC, 1959, pp. 35–53.

This type of society tends to foster a loss of sense of belonging, a loss of personal identity, a lack of concern for others, and creation of an environment which in many ways is abnormal for people. Thus, according to Tonnes, the old gemeinschaft community of our forefathers has disappeared, and in many communities the primary group has been disarranged.

> The result has been a considerable degree of cultural confusion. Most of us today may be likened to a traveler in a strange land where the crossroads are many, and the signboards few . . . In short, the community and especially the urban community, is no longer the highly integrative force it once was.[20]

With this kind of social change has come a number of social problems. One may question the idea of cause and effect, but there seems to be a strong indication that there is a direct relationship. These social problems include such things as a change in moral values, poverty, racial and social unrest, increased crime, dangerous increases in population, unemployment, lack of concern for our elderly, health problems, and the deterioration of our environment. These problems grow increasingly acute in our society and demand immediate attention in order to develop appropriate and timely solutions. While the inferences suggested may appear questionable, and the solution simplistic, it would seem logical that if these societal problems have been intensified with loss of a real sense of community, then the solution might lie in the recapturing of this feeling. And while it may be impossible to return to the gemeinschaft society, it may be possible to incorporate its strengths into our existing society by reorienting the existing social organization.

The third need for community education, and one closely allied with the second, is related to the failure of our existing social agencies. In the past, we have relied on traditional institutions, such as the home, the church, and the school, to solve our social deficiencies.

---

[20] Edwards, Newton, *The School and the Urban Community*, University of Chicago Press, 1942, p. 196.

But these deficiencies are systematic, not local and specific, and specialized institutions seem unable to get at them. Our city homes have largely become places where we go to sleep. Our churches are centers of retreat from life. Our city schools are buildings where we study, not problems, but examples.[21]

The number of new agencies in our social setting has been increased over the years so that for every problem there is a multitude of social agencies designed to act on it. A myriad of federal and state funded projects also have attempted to focus on our social needs. But these agencies, along with our traditional institutions, have failed to meet the increasing needs of our society.

The lack of coordination, the development of empire building, and the failure of our social agencies to perceive the real nature of the problems in other than a segmented fashion, have resulted in an inability to cope with the social issues. In fact, the school, the one institution on which we are predicating our greatest hope for change, is perhaps the institution that is most misdirected from its rightful role in society.

> Many schools are like little islands set apart from the mainland of life by a deep moat of convention and tradition. Across the moat there is a drawbridge, which is lowered at certain periods during the day in order that the part-time inhabitants may cross over to the island in the morning and back to the mainland at night. Why do these young people go out to the island? They go there in order to learn how to live on the mainland.
>
> After the last inhabitant of the island has left in the early afternoon, the drawbridge is raised. Janitors clean up the island, and the lights go out . . .
>
> Such, in brief, is the relation of many American schools to many an American community.[22]

---

[21] Hart, Joseph K., *Social Frontier*, 3, December, 1936, pp. 73–75.

[22] Carr, William G., *Community Life in a Democracy*, National Congress of Parents and Teachers, 1942, p. 34.

With this as a background, let us look at the objectives of community education. Many writers have attempted to enumerate the things that typify community education. There are some differences in content and points of emphasis, based primarily on differing definitions. There are also, however, many similarities and the following is an effort to compile these general areas of agreement.

First, it is necessary to restate that community education is a philosophical concept and not a set of programs. This means that in the implementation of community education, programs become one of the devices in its development. The problem that arises is that it is difficult to refer to community education in operation without calling it a "Community Education Program." This dual use of the term program leads to misunderstandings, and persons pursuing an interest in community education must maintain an awareness of this double use of terms.

It should also be stated that community education does not imply the elimination of current educational endeavors by the public schools in order to substitute something else in their place. It means instead, an expansion of the existing K-12 programs generally in progress. In addition to an expanded role for the public schools, it means scrutiny of current curriculum practices to be sure that maximum effort is being made to have high quality traditional programs and that these programs profit from the positive inputs of community education. The extended hours of the school, integration of educational services, addition of staff, and community involvement should serve to enhance the traditional program rather than harm it.

Let us now look at an enumeration of the objectives of a community school within the philosophy of community education. It should be noted that this compilation is an attempt to list the objectives in a general rather than a specific way, and there is no attempt to put these objectives in any order of priority.

1. *A community school attempts to develop a number of community programs.*

The term *program* here means specific activities aimed at community participation. The techniques for effectively accomplishing this will not be detailed here except to state that it is important that such programs be based on community needs and desires. These programs would include, among others, adult education, high school completion, enrichment classes for school-age students, avocational activities, vocational training, basic education, recreation, citizenship, cultural offerings, and special programs aimed at solving community problems. These programs will be an acknowledgment of the importance of developing a concept of education as a lifetime experience.

> We are going to replace the obsolete scholastic establishment of the past with a true educational system, a system which maintains only schools that are for all, young and old, true community schools.[23]

Certain precautions should be taken in the organization of programs. First, one must not lose sight of the traditional day program in planning other programs. An integration of effort should be made rather than the creation of a separate operation. Second, it is important to look at both individual needs and community needs. And third, it is easy to fall into the trap of allowing all your energies to be used up in program development with the end result that a series of programs, serving a small portion of your population, becomes the total community education operation.

2. A community school attempts to promote interaction between school and community.

This goal may be accomplished in the more overt and simplistic way of opening the school for more hours of the day, days of the week, and weeks of the year. Merely opening the school, however, does not insure the proper school and community relationship for making schools the relevant places they should be. The purpose of an improved relationship is to cause the traditional school programs to do those things for which they were intended—to reflect the ideals of the society and to prepare young people for living in that society.

> A school that reflects the needs, interests, and highest educational and social ideals of its own immediate community (and the larger state, national and world communities of which it is a part) provides a bet-

---

[23] Melby, Ernest, "Community Education, America's Social Imperative," *The Role of the School in Community Education*, Pendell Publishing Co., Midland, Michigan, 1969, p. 13.

ter education, academically and socially, than the school which stands apart. A public school is simply not doing an effective job unless the life of the school is integrated with the life of the community. Brief reference to a few of the basic principles of learning and curriculum construction will make this clear.

A. Children learn best when they are interested in what they are doing; what better well-spring of interest can we find than the life and activities and environment in which the child himself lives.

B. Learning is most effective when there is a chance to experiment and find out and verify facts, individually and in groups; what better laboratory for identifying and solving problems than the community itself?

C. We must start in the learning process where the learner is now, building on these past experiences and devising new learning experiences; how can we know where he is now unless we know the environmental and experimental background the community has given each learner.

D. We must teach the whole child, most of us would agree. How is this anything but an easy platitude to which we give meaningless lip service, unless we can know the whole child in the light of his whole background?

E. The good modern school is the adaptable school: How can the school adapt to changes in the life of society unless the school is constantly being made sensitive and responsive to what goes on in the community?[24]

The education process must strive to take the students into the community and bring the community into the school. We have drifted away from the purposes of education, and our debate over the relative merits of book-centered and child-centered education has caused us to forget our responsibilities to education and its relation to the community.

The conventional belief . . . is that the young must be shielded from contact with the unpleasant and amoral aspects of the universe and

---

[24] Hensen, Kenneth H., *Public Education in American Society*, Prentice Hall, Inc., Englewood Cliffs, New Jersey, 1955, p. 260.

that they must be kept in an ultra-conservative environment . . . the less the discontinuity between the life of the school and the life of the world outside, the better will be the training for life which the school gives to its students.[25]

It is from this need to identify with the community that schools can best provide for their particular students and also begin to develop information to further expand the concept of community education as a total education program.

As a result of their interest in the child and his total environment, school personnel initiate contacts with the community and consequently become aware of not only family-centered problems, but also other problems which hinder the community in its development as an ideal living center.[26]

From this concern for students and their problems, there should develop an interaction with parents and techniques for bringing about community involvement. It is only through such techniques that education can become relevant, and schools can play the role for which they were created.

3. *A community school attempts to survey community resources and to assist in their delivery.*

These resources will be both formal and informal, institutional and individual. In every community there are untapped resources of assistance that can be useful in both the traditional and community education programs. Industry and business have facilities, programs, and activities that can be converted into educational aids and community assets. They are good sources for field trips, speakers, and teachers, and can often provide assistance, both political and financial, for community projects. In addition, the human resources in the community can be of great help. There are many talents, professions, and backgrounds in any community waiting to be used once they have been identified.

---

[25] Waller, Willard, *The Sociology of Teaching*, John Witey & Sons, New York, 1932, pp. 33–35.

[26] Minzey, op. cit., *Role of the School*, p. 34.

Such resources are not only of tremendous use to community education and its various programs, but by recognizing and using these resources another by-product accrues to the education programs. For as community members are more involved in assisting in the education and community programs, they gain a personal satisfaction, and the result is often a more positive attitude toward the education system and its personnel.

4. *A community school attempts to bring about a better relationship between social and government agencies.*

In most communities, there are a myriad of agencies designed to cope with community needs. There are also many differing organizations and institutions that make up the environment of each community member.

> Bill Jones is in *Junior High School*, he goes to a *Sunday School;* has a home in a certain *neighborhood*; he is a member of a *scout troop* and frequents a certain *playground* from time to time; goes *camping* in the summer and attends *movies* twice a week. Those dealing with Bill in those different settings, know very little or nothing of each other.[27]

5. *A community school attempts to identify community problems and ferret out the needs of the community.*

Ability to perform this function is dependent on successful communication between the school and the community. It also implies a different role and responsibility for the school than the traditional teacher-pupil-subject role. If the communication channels are clear, then it becomes the responsibility of the school to assess the nature of the problem and decide what role it should play. It may refer, coordinate, or provide the entire service itself, depending on the situation. The school is not all things to all people, but is instead an expediter, a facilitator, or an ombudsman whose main concern is solving community problems.

---

[27] Hunt, H.W., "Relation of the School to Other Educative Forces in the Community," *Junior-Senior High School Clearing House*, 8, May, 1934, p. 526.

6. A community school attempts to develop a process by which the community can become self-actualized.

The many problems plaguing our societies are compounded by the apathetic resignation of those who live within them. Action is dismissed by a feeling of powerlessness or by the attitude embodied in "you can't fight city hall." The solutions to problems and the changes required to improve our society can be meaningful and long-lasting only if such change comes from the community itself.

In community education, members of the community are made aware of the "community power" they possess. They are shown how, by following a particular process in problem solving, they can cope with the needs of their community and bring about change. As they proceed, step by step, through cooperative ventures, they are able to recapture the feelings of involvement and a sense of community feeling, motivating them toward further joint efforts with like-minded persons.

It is through this process that a community can develop real community identification and begin to solve community problems. And it is by this means that we can bring about the changes needed by our society.

> The traditional view of the school as an intellectual skill center cannot be expected to produce solutions to the critical problems which we face in this century. When viewed within the context of the modern social milieu . . . the Community Education approach to problems can be viewed as a cultural imperative.[28]

---

[28] Weaver, op. cit., p. 2.

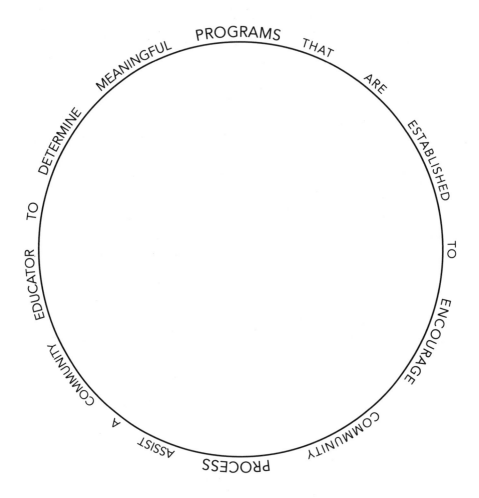

CHAPTER IV

MOVING FROM PROGRAM TO PROCESS: BEYOND DEFINITIONS

One of the topics most frequently debated by those involved with community education deals with the difference between *programs* and *process*. To many, the difference is not apparent because in many schools, community education and community education programs are identical.

To those who have a better grasp of the concept, however, there is a vital difference between the terms *program* and *process*, and an understanding of this difference is critical to the development of meaningful community education. In fact, this difference is so important that without an awareness of the meaning and potential of each term, community education will probably not make the significant changes in the community of which it is capable. Therefore, let us first attempt to identify the differences between *programs* and *process* to which we have alluded and then present a rationale and evolutionary context for the sequential development of each.

The misunderstanding related to the term *community education program* becomes more apparent when one realizes that the phrase is often used indiscriminately to describe different aspects of community education. On one hand, the term refers to overt activities of participation by community members. Therefore, adult education, roller skating, town hall meetings, recreation, and enrichment classes are examples of community education programs. The term is also used, however, to describe the entire operation of community education in a community. Therefore, when a school district adopts the concept of community education and implements it in the community, it is described as having a community education program. Thus, the term has been used to describe the specific activities of community education as well as the total concept. For the purpose of this discussion, the term *program* will be used to describe specific activities. The term *process* will be used to deal with more extensive community involvement and interaction.

THE ROLE OF THE SCHOOL IN COMMUNITY EDUCATION

In the previous chapter, community education was defined in various ways, and the difference between community education and a community school was discussed. While it is true that there are many possible models for the development and implementation of community education, it appears that the public school model is by far the most prevalent, popular, and successful. Therefore, while there are many groups and agencies involved in community education, the model described here will be the public school model, and thus, the description will relate to the role of the public school in relationship to community education.

We have already pointed out some of the problems in defining community education, but it might be well to repeat some of the points of the discussion. As the idea of community education continues to grow and expand to more and more school districts across the country, the arguments about its nebulous nature and the lack of a precise definition continue to be heard. Both supporters and opponents of community education point out that there is a great disagreement regarding the definition and meaning of community education. In general, they emphasize the fact that there is a vast difference between the philosophical goals of community education and the actual programs in operation. More specifically, they acknowledge that much of what is called community education is, in reality, programs in adult education or recreation, and as such, is neither unique nor capable of accomplishing all that community educators claim can be accomplished through the community education concept.

Whether there is a greater divergence in community education between philosophy and practice than exists in other disciplines is questionable, but the fact that it is still an idea seeking acceptance makes it more susceptible to scrutiny and criticism than more established programs and practices. It is, therefore, the intent of this chapter to explain some of the reasons for the existing confusion about community education and to place the concept in a different perspective in hopes that it will establish a clearer understanding of community education and the role of the community school.

A CHANGE IN THE MEANING

Part of the misunderstanding that has developed in community education can be traced directly to its historical development. Community education did not begin at the stage at which it currently exists. It is an idea that has evolved over the years and has only recently taken on the aura of a philosophy of education. During its developmental stages, community education was at various times synonymous with extra activities for children, adult education, and recreation programs. Unless observers are either aware of the developmental aspects of community education or of the less observable components of community education, they will get a false sense of what is actually happening and consequently, will develop false perceptions of the ramifications of the community education concept.

To best describe the current status of community education, one must take into account the dramatic change in the concept over the past few years. Community education has moved from programs, which were added on to the regular school schedule, to a philosophical concept that has changed the role of the public schools.

In the past, community education and community schools had been used interchangeably. When asked to define community education, people were likely to make little difference between conceptual and actual operation. To best show the changing nature and the mingling of terms, it might be well to look at community education as it evolved in Flint, Michigan, a model used for the development of many community education programs throughout the United States during the 1960s, 1970s, and 1980s.

When community education was first started in Flint in the 1930s, it had a distinct recreation flavor. If Frank Manley, the father of the community education in Flint, had been asked in 1935 to define community education, it is likely that he would have described it as a recreation program for children, taking place primarily in the public schools. And this is what a person would have observed as they visited the Flint Community Education Program at that time.

During the following years, the definition was to undergo a change. This change was the result of challenges to the limited nature of the existing programs. Critics argued that the needs of the children were much broader than the typical "ball and bat" activities of the typical community education program.

As a result, a new community education orientation took place in the 1940s. During that time, it is likely that Mr. Manley would have defined his community education programs as all activities for children and youth, over and above the traditional school, and taking place primarily in the public schools. Here again, no difference was made between community education and a community school when referring to the program in operation.

In the 1950s, the program in Flint was to change again. Flint had been challenged to show why the community education program was oriented primarily toward the child. It was pointed out that adult needs were also of concern to the community. As a result, a visit to Flint during the 1950s would have revealed a community education program that would have been defined as a program for all members of the community, over and above the regular school day, and taking place primarily in the public schools. This 1950 definition of community education (also called community schools) became the focal point of the programs which Flint exported to hundreds of school districts throughout the United States and to several foreign countries.

In the early 1960s, the Mott Foundation, the main financial contributor to community education in Flint, began another program that was to have a major impact on community education throughout the United States, and indeed throughout the world. The Mott Foundation started a program called the Mott Inter-University Clinical Preparation Program for Leaders. The intention of this program was to identify potential leaders from throughout the United States, train them in leadership, provide them with university degrees, develop in them a high level of sophistication in community education, and have them return to their homes to promote and influence the development of community education.

This program was extremely effective. Over a period of eight years, it trained over 750 persons, many of whom did dedicate their professional careers to community education and would be perceived as the "fathers of community education" in their states and communities.

An unplanned outcome of this program greatly influenced the future direction of community education. These new promoters of community education, professionally known as Mott Interns, became critics of community education, but critics with loyalty to the concept. As loyal critics, they devoted themselves to improving and expanding the ideals of community education, indeed moving it toward a more conceptual framework. Under their direction and influence, the community education movement, during the 1970s and 1980s, evolved toward a philosophical and conceptual orientation. Community education became a concept based on a set of principles identified previously (pages 42–43). A community school was identified as one institution's attempt to implement these principles.

Schools, which were primarily responsible for the limited education of the children of our communities between the ages of five and sixteen, have now recognized an additional responsibility of providing for the educational needs of all members of the community. In addition, these community education oriented schools have addressed themselves to the problems of community service and community involvement. This does not mean that schools are to be "all things to all people." It does imply that community schools should provide a catalytic and coordinating role for the community, acknowledging a responsibility to see that community needs are identified and dealt with more effectively.

THE COMPONENTS

On the surface, such a responsibility seems awesome, and to speak in generalities about the potential of community education tends to make the concept overly idealistic and suspect. Therefore, to more appropriately put community education in perspective, let us focus on the ingredients of community education via the community school. While the specifics of the community school's responsibilities will differ from community to community according to the characteristics of each community, certain basic components are necessary to all community school programs.

I. *An Educational Program for School-Age Children*
This program is the traditional program offered by all school districts. It is frequently referred to as the K-12 (kindergarten through twelfth grade) or day school program. This is listed as an ingredient of community edu-

cation for two reasons. First, it is a vital part of the education program of any community, and second, it is often excluded when we describe community education, leaving the impression that community education is nothing more than an addition to the regular program. The important point is that while the regular program is a key part of education, it is not the only part, and it should be integrated into the total community education effort. It should also be mentioned that in community education, attention should be given to relevance, community involvement, and the use of the community to enhance classroom teaching.

This component can be more dramatic than it might at first seem. Community involvement has long been a part of schooling. Students have been taken into the community and the community has been brought into the classroom through field trips, speakers in the classroom, student-public official exchanges, guest teachers, job shadowing, teacher aids, lunch room supervisors, community volunteer programs, and student community service projects. But since one of the axioms of community education is brokering of community resources and identifying who can best perform particular education services, the school is now in a position to pass some of its current roles on to others in the community while spending more of its time on tasks it does best. This offers some interesting opportunities.

Schools can now evaluate who might best perform some of their functions. While each school and each community will have to determine how this might happen in the community, there are some possibilities to consider. Perhaps physical education, in some communities, could best be taught by the recreation department. Some of the arts might be taught by local artisans. Health education related to contraception, abortion, AIDS, etc. might best be handled by those in our community most knowledgeable in such subjects—the professionals in the health fields. Driver education might become the responsibility of the insurance companies, and vocational education might best be handled by local business and industry.

While these suggestions will raise some consternation and a great deal of uneasiness, they are important possibilities to consider in a new education system. There is more than enough for everyone to do in a community education system, and it becomes necessary that all do what they do best if the community is to reach its potential educationally. If we can get beyond the "turfdom" and the emotion, then there is a great deal of logic to moving in this direction. Issues such as training, certification, organization, liability, finance, authority, and the like are only problems to be solved, not reasons for maintaining the status quo.

II. *Use of Community Facilities*

It has long been a contention of community educators that school buildings are used only a fraction of the time that they could be used. Many communities build additional facilities such as recreation buildings, community centers, and boys clubs to be used while the school buildings stand idle. There is often an abundance of unused space in most communities in school buildings, fire halls, churches, city buildings, and recreation facilities, and maximum use should be made of these facilities before new ones are constructed. School buildings, in particular, should become a focal point for community activities and services. Under community education, the definition of a school building is that it is a community center sometimes used for the education of children.

III. *Additional Programs for School-Age Children and Youth*

This aspect of community education presumes that there is an ever increasing need for additional activities and education for youngsters. Despite the fantastic growth in the amount of recorded knowledge, students are receiving a decreasing amount of time exposed to the formal school day. Additional information, activities, and experiences can be provided by expanding offerings to students before school, after school, on weekends, and during summers. Enrichment, remedial, and supplemental education activities can be offered as well as recreational, cultural, and avocational programs. This dimension of community education also offers a fine option for year-round schools, since it makes maximum use of educational facilities on a voluntary basis and truly is "year-round" education rather than a rotating vacation period typical of most year-round plans. This aspect of a community school becomes particularly important in light of the research relative to time on task.

Since the beginning of established education institutions in the United

States, schools have measured the degree of a child's success on the basis of each child's ability to perform scholastic work as observed by the teacher. Measurement starts in the first grade and continues on through formal education in the form of letter grades, numbers, smiling faces, percentages, or some designation as "the blue birds." Despite the fact that a total education should consist of learning human, technical, and conceptual skills, students spend most of their time on the technical aspects of education and are rewarded for their successes in how well they do at these skills as perceived by the teacher.

In 1905, some new experiments began to give insight into another way of measuring students. These experiments were refined by a Frenchman named Binet, and in 1916, the world became aware of a method of measuring potential mental ability through tests that would determine the intelligence quotient (IQ) of children. We were now able to measure children's educational potential (scholastic aptitude) as well as their performance in school, and we have locked ourselves into this system of assessing potential and performance ever since. Most of us now accept the fact that we can effectively reflect innate talent through standardized IQ tests and ability to perform through teacher grades.

In the past few years, researchers have found another ingredient in learning regularly neglected in American education—*time*. Simply stated, these researchers have discovered that there is a strong relationship between the amount of efficient time spent on a learning task and how well that task is achieved. Furthermore, these studies support the finding that the amount of *time* spent on a task is at least as important as intelligence.

The fact is there are really four things that result in effective learning for our children: intelligence, quality of teaching, motivation, and time allocated to learning. Public schools tend to look primarily at the first two, pay some attention to the third, and completely neglect the fourth aspect—*time*.

We approach *time* as though it were a constant. Classes are the same length for everyone. The school year, week, and day are the same for all students, for every grade, and for every subject.

Yet such an approach defies not only educational studies, but our own logic. Actors, musicians, coaches, and artists all believe that they can improve their abilities and surpass others if they devote more *time* to their competencies. Many of us interpret the weaknesses in our golf or tennis games to a lack of time to work on our skills. Most people would express a belief that if you increase the *time* dedicated to a task, you will improve in that task.

Now the researchers have corroborated these premises. Benjamin Bloom of the University of Chicago has found that if given the proper amount of *time*, 80 percent of all students can achieve as well as the top 20 percent. We have tended to think that slow learners are the result of a low IQ. Now it is believed that a low IQ score is simply a way of identifying students who need more *time* to learn. The slowest five percent of the learners take five times the length of *time* to learn the subject as the faster learner. Therefore, we must give these students five times as much instruction and practice *time* to bring them up to the average level of the class. As J.B. Carroll, another noted researcher in the area, has stated, *time* is really the central variable in school learning. Scholastic aptitude is the measure of the amount of *time* it takes a student to reach some basic criterion.

We have known this information about *time* for the last century and yet have done nothing about it. If *time* is the central variable and the necessary *time* is provided, then the attainment of desired learning is possible for all students who can be properly motivated to use the *time* appropriately. In fact, *time* is the basis for the heralded "mastery learning" so frequently supported by leading educators. If you provide the help, the motivation, and the *time*, all can learn.

Unfortunately, in the operation of the public schools, *time* is not being increased, it is being decreased. Teacher strikes, budget cutbacks, the energy crisis, half-day sessions, and increased time for teacher planning have contributed to reduced education *time* for our children. There are a number of research findings related to education *time* that should give parents and educators reason for alarm. A summary of some of these includes:

- ◆ The number of hours of schooling for public school ranges from 710 hours per year to 1,150 hours.

- In a six-and-one-half-hour elementary school day, students spend less then half of their time on actual instruction.

- In a 35-hour high school week, students spend less than 17 hours on instruction. The rest of the time is spent on announcements, passing out materials, assemblies, lavatory trips, discipline, waiting for instructions, lunch, recess, etc.

- A fifth grade in one school spent 140 minutes per day on reading while another fifth grade in the same school spent only 60 minutes on the same activity. This results in one fifth grade having 240 hours more reading time per year than the other.

- Teachers often do not teach on Friday or the day before a holiday.

- A class of 263 high school students lost over 61,000 hours of instruction in four years of high school through absenteeism.

- In one major city, the teachers studied used 44 percent of their class time for non-instructional activities. This was equal to the loss of two days per week of teaching time.

- The amount of time allocated by teachers to a specific subject area is as much as three times greater by one teacher than another (i.e. one teacher may spend three times as much time on science or on the teaching of the Civil War as does another teacher).

- In some school districts, the school year has decreased the equivalent of 50 days per year during the past 20 years. This has resulted in a loss of 3,600 hours of education time during a child's 12 years in school or the equivalent loss of four school years of instruction when compared with the current 900-hour school year.

- The fact that Asian American children do better in school than do other ethnic groups in America is probably due to the fact that they spend twice as much time on homework as do other ethnic groups in the American schools.

- In every case studied, the percentage of gain in achievement exceeded the percentage of increased time in schooling.

◆ Private high school students do twice as much homework as do public high school students.

◆ A one-half-hour increase in the school day resulted in a 13 percent increase in math achievement and a 26 percent increase in reading comprehension.

◆ The number of minutes of classroom instruction are directly related to student performance.

◆ The student who comes to school regularly has higher grades than the student who does not attend regularly.

One might have anticipated that such studies would have produced an outcry from the public. Instead, we continue to ignore the findings. More alarming is the fact that some professional educators are suggesting that the school year and the school day should be shortened even further. Not so with education systems in many other industrialized countries. The length of the school week in Japan is 59 hours, in Russia 53 hours, while in the United States it is 30 hours. The school year in Japan is 240 days, in America 180. Japanese students also spend twice as much time on homework as do American students; however, polls by Gallup in 1982, 1983, 1984, and 1985 show that Americans do not want to increase the school year. In fact, these same polls show that our public does not want to increase the school day. A partial explanation for the findings of this poll probably lies in the economic realities of increasing school time. It has been predicted that increasing the school year by one day throughout the United States would add approximately one billion dollars to school costs. Another factor probably has to do with our lack of information and awareness of the importance of *time* to education. The end result is that *time* appears to be so valuable, and yet, there seems to be no movement by either educators, the legislators, or the public to support a move toward longer days, weeks, or years for students. There are, however, some things community members can do to address this concern in a constructive way.

1. Insist that the board of education hold administrators and teachers accountable for using the existing *time* more effectively and efficiently.

2. Protect the existing school day and year and do not allow it to erode further.

3. Get the state board of education and the local school board to at least make modest increases in the school day and year.

4. Encourage your schools to experiment with varying schedules so that some classes might be taught over longer periods of *time* rather than be limited to the one-semester, one-hour orientation of the current schedule.

5. Become a "parent-teacher" and use some of your time to teach your children.

6. Provide children with learning *time* at home with a place and *time* for homework.

In addition, community education has some suggestions for dealing with the concerns related to time.

1. Find other learning activities for your child in the community through other agencies and private learning entrepreneurs.

2. Encourage schools to provide enrichment and remedial activities for students beyond the regular school day (before and after school, week-ends, summers).

Education *time* is too valuable to waste, and once lost, cannot be reclaimed. We should not let the schools erode children's learning *time* in the name of motivation, attention span, administrivia, or teacher negotiations. Furthermore, we should not let the schools continue to ignore the research and imply that students with a low IQ cannot be helped and are destined to spend the rest of their lives without the maximum benefits of education. Certainly innate ability accounts for something, but far more children are capable of growing educationally than are currently succeeding if given the right amount of *time*.

It has been fairly well established that the future of a person, a city, a state, or a country is dependent on the educational successes of the individual. Each person's future, and indeed our nation's future, is dependent on the degree to which we maximize our children's education. There are vast differences in people's ability to learn and become educated. *Time* is a great equalizer, and, if properly used, will allow most children to realize the benefits of the great American Dream.[1]

IV. *Programs for Adults*

This aspect of community education provides the same services to the adult population as are offered to school-age children and youth. Included would be such things as basic education, high school completion, and recreational, avocational, cultural, and vocational education. The needs of the adults would be recognized as being as important as those of the school-age student, and the students would be perceived as all of the people who reside in that community.

In addition, there is one very valuable aspect to this part of a community education program that will have far reaching effects on the school-aged population. Despite arguments to the contrary, there is little evidence to show that our schools have an impact on anything but the cognitive education of our children. More affective characteristics such as attitudes, responsibilities, and human skills appear to be much more influenced by the community, including the family. We have admitted that language patterns are primarily the result of home and community influence, and it seems likely that such things as personal perceptions and values are governed in the same way.

In fact, Joseph K. Hart noted this fact more than 50 years ago when he stated:

> No child can escape his community. He may not like his parents, or the neighbors, or the ways of the world. He may groan under the processes of living, and wish he were dead. But he goes on living, and he goes on living in the community.

---

[1] Minzey, Jack D., *Are the Public Schools Stealing Our Children's Educational Time?*, Center for Community Education, Eastern Michigan University, 1991.

The life of the community flows about him, foul or pure; he swims in it, drinks it, goes to sleep in it, and wakes to the new day to find it still about him. He belongs to it, it nourishes him or starves him, or poisons him; it gives him the substance of his life. And in the long run, it takes its toll of him and all that he is.

The democratic problem in education is not primarily a problem of training children; it is the problem of making a community within which children cannot help growing up to be democratic, intelligent, disciplined to freedom, reverent of the goods of life, and eager to share in the tasks of the age. A school cannot produce this result; nothing but a community can do so.[2]

Therefore, this aspect of the community school's responsibility to community education seems to have great potential for influencing our youth in a more positive manner. If attitudes are formed in the community, then changing or molding youthful attitudes will only be done well by affecting the attitudes of the community.

There is one additional factor to be considered in relation to this component. As stated earlier, about 80 percent of the adult population in most communities does not have children in the public schools. These people have neither an emotional nor a personal relationship to the schools. They often have negative perceptions about many of today's youth and are not moved to support schools based on students' needs or teachers' salaries. In fact, they are often on a fixed income with a major tax obligation for schools coming through their property taxes. They often wonder what's in it for them and are very aware that schools are not serving their personal needs. If schools do not pay more attention to their education problems, then they are not likely to provide the financial support to the schools' kindergarten through twelfth-grade functions.

V. *Delivery of Community Services*

In most communities, it has been found that there is not a shortage of community services, but there is a woeful lack of coordination. As a result, a specific community agency's services are generally provided to only

---

[2] Olsen, Edward G., by Phillip A. Clark, *Life-Centering Education*, Pendell Publishing Co., Midland, Michigan, 1977, p. 116.

a few of those in the community who either need or qualify for such services. In addition to the lack of coordination, most community services are organized and delivered on a community-wide basis rather than in the neighborhoods where people can avail themselves of such services. The school, by means of its school buildings and community school personnel, can help identify problems and resources and provide the coordination necessary to bring these two together. The key role of the school is catalytic, and the school would not provide programs or services which are either already provided or capable of being provided by other agencies. Only when existing agencies are unable to provide services would the community education coordinator assist in the development of new programs. The coordinator actually acts as a broker, relating problems to resources and making referrals to the appropriate sources. By making existing resources aware of the many problems that exist in the community but that are not being accommodated, agencies will find it necessary to coordinate their efforts in order to effectively provide the services needed.

Basic to this component of community education is the law of subsidiarity. This law states that no matter how effective the system for providing services to clients, unless the service is fundamental to the survival of the individual (food, shelter, clothing), never as many as 10 percent of the people who need or qualify for the service will be receiving it. Under the law of subsidiarity, services can increase their effectiveness to 25 percent by simply taking the service to the client rather than asking the client to come to where the service is located.

This should not be surprising to those of us who have been involved in services since this has been the technique agencies have been using for many years to increase their service to their clients. The library, for example, has increased its circulation through the book-mobile. Cooperative extension offices at land grant colleges have become more effective in serving their clients by placing their offices in every county in the United States. Inoculation programs conducted in schools or senior citizen centers have proved to be more effective than those conducted in central locations serving a larger geographic area. Programs for fluoridation of teeth and the administering of polio shots proved to be more successful when conducted at local schools rather than at citywide locations. In fact, the idea behind the success of party-type stores is tied to their handy location in the neighborhood.

If one can accept the logic of the law of subsidiarity, then another logic follows. There is a publicly-owned building, used less than 11 percent of its clock hour time, and located within walking distance of 93 percent of all the people who live in the United States. It is the elementary school. The importance of this facility as a resource for delivering services to the community seems obvious and compelling.

VI. *Community Involvement*

This phase of community education often has been described as the effort to return to "participatory democracy." The idea is to help persons who live in a particular neighborhood participate in identifying local problems and developing the process for attempting to solve such problems. In areas the size of an elementary school attendance area, the school assists in the development of a community council whose membership is based on community representation and two-way communications. Community education personnel assist this council in its organization and development until it is able to continue on its own as a viable organization.

In order to look at this component more completely, we must look at the whole notion of democracy. We pride ourselves as being the great democracy of the world. If we analyze definitions, however, we are really not a democracy but an oligarchy. The definition of an oligarchy is a government run by a few people, and as long as roughly three percent of our communities elect our boards of education and five percent elect our city councils, we are really not even a representative democracy, let alone a participating one. In fact, since the president of the United States is elected by less than 25 percent of our voters, one can see that even in the most popular elections, we fail to involve a majority of the population.

Three entities make our democratic system work—the legally elected board, the professional administrator, and the community. For much of our history, only the first two functioned, and the community was effectively not involved in the processes of democracy. Some of this was due to lethargy, and some was intentional. Whatever the reason, community members were minimally involved in the governmental processes. In the

1960s, there was great concern about this obvious injustice, and during the next few years, the community members were involved at the expense of the professionals and the legally elected boards. The results did not lead to more effective or efficient processes and seemed to prove that all three are necessary in the operation of a democratic government.

The addition of community is not an argument for having the community take over the functions of the other two members of the trilogy. The community should carry out the functions that rightfully belong to it and that, if executed, will make it the major player in the political process. These functions include voting, recall, protest, petition, initiative referendum, economic sanction, and problem solving (using group process to identify community problems and seek solutions to these problems).

Democracy is not attained through osmosis. It works because people recognize their responsibilities in it and put forth the effort to make it work through their actions. The purpose of this component is to make people aware of their role in a participatory democracy, to teach them the skills to carry out these responsibilities, and to give them experiences in the democratic process so that they can see the results of their efforts. By showing them how such things can be accomplished in the public school setting, it is then possible to make the transfer to the larger democratic arena.

ANOTHER PERSPECTIVE

To this point, much of what has been said has been discussed extensively among community educators without absolute agreement or acceptance of the ingredients mentioned. To provide a better understanding of the community education concept and the relationship of its components, the following models are presented.

If one were to try to diagram the ingredients of community education they might look like Figure 1 opposite.

FIGURE 1—The Ingredients In Community Education

Component I	Component II	Component III	Component IV	Component V	Component VI
K-12	Use of Facilities	Activities for School Age Children and Youth	Activities for Adults	Delivery of Community Services	Community Involvement

Historically, the ingredients in community education have tended to develop on a continuum (from left to right as shown in Figure 1), and most school districts seem to follow the same pattern. This is probably true for several reasons. For one thing, those on the left represent the part of the model most school districts have implemented, and neophytes seeking information on community education are most exposed to these phases of community education. Second, components I through IV of community education are the most dramatic and traditional, and school boards and administrators are relatively comfortable in working in these areas. Components V and VI are less understood, less traditional, and more threatening, consequently they are not often perceived as appropriate roles for the schools to play.

While not all school districts develop community education in the same manner, there does seem to be a similarity in the way that the majority of school districts implement the concept. This is true because, as mentioned before, the school decision makers are more receptive to the first four components of community education. In fact, in order to get beyond the fourth component, there is an extra effort and commitment necessary to move on to the total concept of community education. After community education has been introduced into a school district, there seems to be an almost immediate and automatic development of com-

FIGURE 2—Blockage of Community Education Development

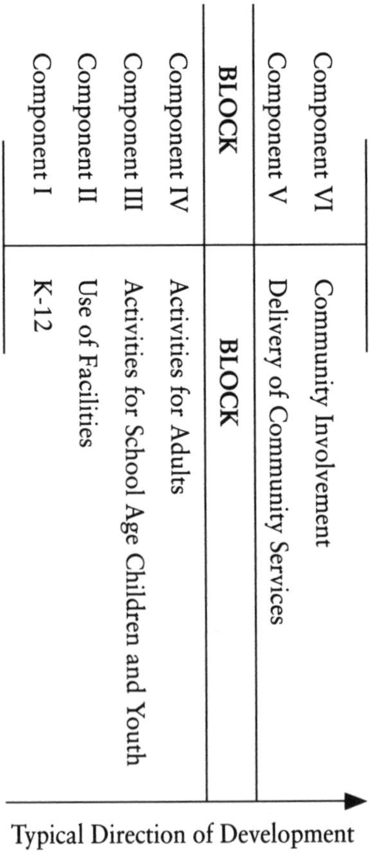

Component I	Component II	Component III	Component IV	BLOCK	Component V	Component VI
K-12	Use of Facilities	Activities for School Age Children and Youth	Activities for Adults	BLOCK	Delivery of Community Services	Community Involvement

Typical Direction of Development

munity education up to a point, and then the growth slows down and, in some cases, terminates.

This blockage is the result of several things. In some instances, the school districts perceive community education as dealing only with the first four components and feel that these encompass community education in its entirety. In other cases, school districts would like to move on in their community education development, but they are unwilling or unable to commit the additional staff and money necessary for components V and VI. As a result, most community school programs stop somewhere short of the goals involved in true community education.

PROGRAM AND PROCESS

The development of the previous model is an outgrowth of an attempt to portray two aspects of community education—*program* and *process*. The parts of community education involved in components I through IV are primarily program-oriented and tend to be comprised of those activities that are combinations of various programs for different clientele within the community. Components V and VI tend to be more process-oriented; they tend to provide a means for the involvement of community resources and community members toward positive change. The introduction of these terms, *program* and *process*, has introduced a degree of controversy which has tended to confuse rather than clarify the relevance of these terms. As in most arguments, the discussion has tended to become an either-or confrontation in which community educators are asked to be either program community educators or process community educators.

The preceding models do present a continuum that appears to flow from program to process and leave the impression that if you have programs, you do not have process, and if you have process, you do not have programs. The model has also been interpreted to imply that components on the left of the model are not as valuable as those on the right, and consequently, that programs are less important than process.

FIGURE 3—Program and Process

	PROGRAMS					PROCESS	
Component I	Component II	Component III	Component IV	BLOCK	Component V	Component VI	
K-12	Use of Facilities	Activities for School Age Children and Youth	Activities for Adults	BLOCK	Delivery of Community Services	Community Involvement	

Typical Direction of Development

CHRONOLOGICAL DEVELOPMENT OF COMMUNITY EDUCATION

Perhaps a further explanation of program and process would be in order at this point. The program aspect of community education will certainly meet many needs of the community. There are concerns in every community, however, that cannot be met by the program approach to community education alone. First, all people are not equally motivated to attend programs. Through timidity, suspicion, antagonism, lack of awareness, lethargy, and for numerous other reasons, many community members will not attend programs they may want or need. In fact, many times community members are not aware of those things that may be of most benefit to them, and often, those most in need of services are least willing to avail themselves of existing opportunities. Therefore, programs, at best, will serve a small percentage of the total population.

Second, many people in the community have problems that are individual in nature. These problems are extremely difficult to identify and require different techniques to resolve. The solution of these problems will require a personal approach, and the prescription for these problems may result in participation in community education programs, a referral to existing social or government agencies, or a solution designed especially for the person by an appropriate person using available resources. This phase of community education is much more personal and might be construed as individualized programming.

Third, there are some basic assumptions related to community education that demand further development. These assumptions are:

A. Communities are capable of positive change.

B. Social problems have solutions.

C. One of the strongest forces for making change is community power.

D. Community members are desirous of improving their communities and are willing to contribute their energies toward such ends.

These assumptions relate to the ultimate goal of community education: the process aspect resulting in self-actualization. The term *community self-actualization* is here used to mean the ability of a community to become the best that it is capable of becoming. In essence, community self-actualization is aimed at community development to the point that community members are involved in identifying problems and working through a process that enables them to plan courses of action and carry through on possible solutions.

If these assumptions are true, communities are capable and willing to become self-actualized. The solution to the problems inherent in triggering this self-actualization is the organization and encouragement of community groups until they have achieved community identification, have been motivated, have mastered the techniques of a community approach to problem solving, and have experienced success or failure with these techniques to the degree that they see the potential of their joint efforts.

When a community is capable of the initiative and sustained action necessary for attacking and solving its own problems, and when it is moving in the direction of the fulfillment of individual and community needs and community potential, then it can be said to be self-actualized.

With this as a background, let us now look at the evolutionary development of a community education program in a school district. There is no absolute best development formula, but there is impartial data available to indicate that an evolutionary step-by-step process is usually the way that community education begins and matures in a community.

PROGRAM DEVELOPMENT

The fact is that both programs and process are important to the total concept of community education. And while the development of community education does tend to be from program to process, it is possible for it to develop in a reverse fashion, and in such cases, the process without the program aspect of community education would be as limited as programs without process. Also, most school districts have all aspects of community education to some degree in their communities, and the implementation of community education is more one of identifying these aspects and fixing responsibility than of creating something new. This can best be shown if the preceding model is made bi-dimensional rather than uni-dimensional. Thus a school district, even without subscribing to community education, might look like the following in respect to the ingredients of community education.

Under Component I (K-12), a typical district is probably doing more than it is in any other part of community education. It is also usually concentrating most of its efforts for improvements in this area even though this will be the most advanced and most highly developed component of community education.

FIGURE 4—Community Education Components in a Typical Community

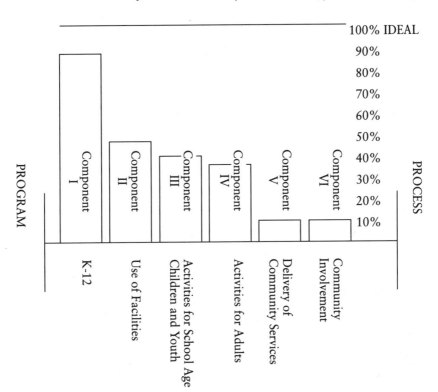

Component II (Use of Facilities) will likely have had some degree of development. There will be at least limited use of school facilities by community groups under a policy developed by the school board. This policy will generally have a fee structure, and traditional school activities will be given a high priority. There usually will have been little effort to make maximum use of school facilities or coordinate their use with other facilities and agencies in the community.

Component III (Activities for Children and Youth) will also show some development but will be perceived as an extra which the school provides only if there are enough financial and personal resources. This program will often be recreational and usually will not be integrated with the traditional activities of the school.

Component IV (Activities for Adults) will also be perceived as an add-on program. It usually will concentrate on traditional programs, such as Adult Basic Education and high school completion, and will provide other programs only if they are self-supporting. This program, too, will not be viewed as an integral part of the day program or an absolute responsibility of the schools.

Component V (Delivery of Community Services) will probably be going on in the community, but not with any assistance from the schools. There generally will be some community-wide attempts at coordinating services and some type of directory of services is usually available. Any coordination is strictly voluntary, however, and the degree of successful coordination is very limited. Generally, people are expected to come where services are offered. Services are not taken to where the people are. Success of service agencies is measured in terms of the busy schedule of the agency rather than community need.

Component VI (Community Involvement) is also an area that is not influenced to any degree by the schools. This component of community education is usually done on a larger basis than the neighborhood community, and the people involved are often representative of the status- and power-based people in the community. In general, such groups are neither representative nor attuned to the problems of the neighborhood.

While this profile has been described as typical, it is possible that many communities will vary extensively from the profile presented. In all communities, Component I (K-12) will be better developed than all other phases. But it is possible to find other communities in which coordination of services is quite well developed, while use of facilities may be minimal. In like fashion, different phases may be in different relative stages than those described in the model.

The point is that all communities have all dimensions of community education to some degree. In the implementation of community education, the school district must first be willing to accept responsibility for all dimensions of community education. The district does not provide all programs or services to the community, but it does agree to provide the leadership necessary to assist, encourage, and sometimes initiate the various aspects of community education. This acceptance of responsibility is in essence the difference between a district with community education and one without it.

BLOCKAGES TO COMMUNITY EDUCATION

If school boards do agree to accept community education as the undergirding philosophy of their schools, then the data necessary to prepare their own profile must be collected in order to evaluate where their communities are in the development of community education. The community education program then becomes one of deciding what priorities will be established, what resources will be allocated, and what time line will be followed in the development of total community education in the community.

There is no one plan of development appropriate for all communities. Some communities may develop delivery and coordination of community services first and leave programs for adults and youth until later. The most frequently employed approach is to implement use of facilities and adult and youth activities first (the program aspect) and leave the process components until later. In any event, two cautions should be considered.

First, the same problem of program emphasis is still inherent with the bi-dimensional model, namely that school districts tend to allow a blockage of their community education development in the form of a plateauing of their programs.

Second, community education occurs in stages, and the level of sophistication depends on the direction of development and the time schedule in each community. Thus, in a district just starting, community education use of facilities or programs for adults may be a very appropriate community education program, while in another community, which has been a community education district of long standing, such a program dealing only with facilities and adult activities would not represent satisfactory community education development.

FIGURE 5—Plateauing of a Typical Community Education Program

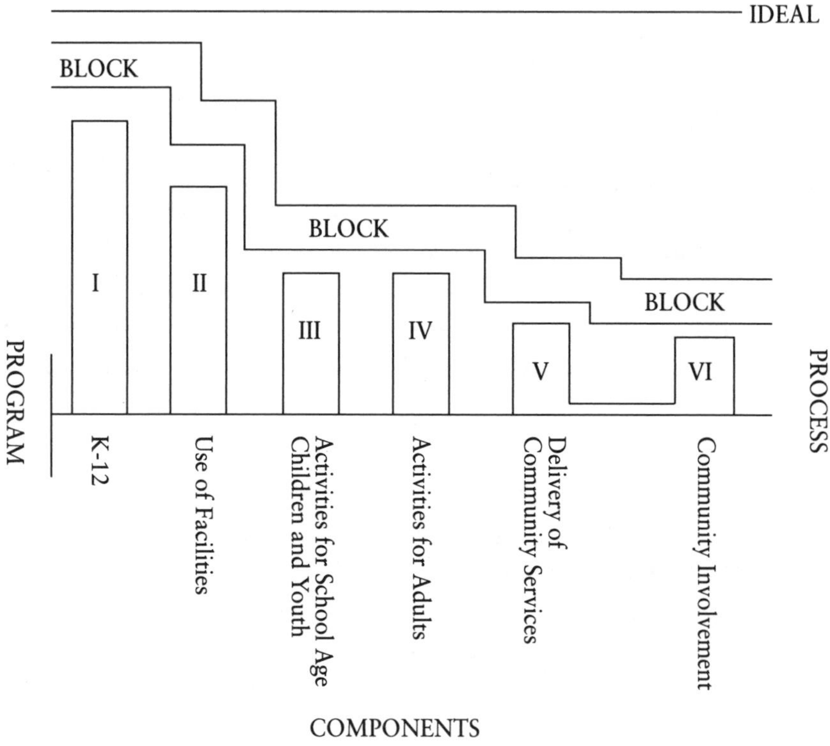

The point is that community education is a concept composed of various elements. The ultimate goal is to achieve the total concept by maximum development of all of the components. To have only one aspect of community education, such as adult education, is appropriate when this effort represents the first steps in community education. Thus, the content of a community education program for one district may not be the same as for another, depending on the stage of development. Real community education is a product of time and the development of the components of community education, and in order to measure successful growth, one must not only assess what the community has in operation, but also the direction in which the community is moving in the development of the concept.

CHAPTER V

WHY THE SCHOOLS?

The concept of community education has been one of the fastest growing phenomena in recent years. It has widespread support from many organizations and agencies, government support at the local, state, and national level, and its principles permeate professional and contemporary literature. The tenets of community education are logical, socially defendable, fiscally sound, and emotionally appealing. As such, the question is not, "Should we have community education?" but rather, "Who should bear the primary responsibility for carrying it out?"

TWO SIDES

One of the most frequently asked questions in community education is, "Why the schools?" This is usually followed by arguments about the bureaucracy of the schools, their past failures, their inability to cope in new areas, and the indictment that they are "trying to be all things to all people."

These accusations and concerns are understandable when viewed in the context in which they are usually made. Most groups dealing with community education tend to view the concept in terms of programs or services. They do not have a sound understanding of the fundamentals of community education and are not able to discriminate between the community education concept and the role of the community school within that concept. Thus, they perceive that the schools are going to expand their activities into the specialties of other agencies and will infringe on, disrupt, interfere with, and even eliminate other organizations. It is a typical case of "turfdom" of which we are all sometimes guilty, and the resulting uneasiness in our comfort zone is transmitted into quarreling over what is "mine" and who will get the credit.

The schools are not without fault in this disagreement. School people are notorious for implementing a "community education program" without a thorough knowledge of the concept. And they do, indeed, begin to carry out functions already better done by some existing agency. Under the guise of a community education program, many schools have actually created an adult education program, an enrichment program, a recreation program, or a community development program. Often, other

groups may be absolutely accurate when they charge schools with dupli-
cating services and carrying on programs outside the school's area of
expertise.

A CASE OF ROLE DEFINITION

There have been several attempts to resolve this conflict between schools
and other agencies dealing with community education. The question usually asked is, "Can the schools and other agencies cooperate in community education?" The general response is a resounding, "yes!" followed
by joint meetings, mutual planning, position papers, and written agreements of cooperation.

The result has been a coming together of those affected by the community schools with the usual agreement that for the benefit of all concerned, there will be the establishment of guidelines of cooperation, a
"splitting of the pie" so to speak, so that cooperation comes to mean
that territory will be identified, and each will stay within the boundaries
of agreement.

Thus, with regards to adult education, for example, the community schools might provide all non-credit courses, while the regular adult
education program provides high school completion and adult basic
courses, and the community colleges provide all post twelfth-grade classes.
In the case of recreation, the community schools may provide for certain
age groups and programs, while the city or township recreation personnel provide for the balance of the program. The ideal program then becomes one in which the various groups providing the programs have been
able to divide the problems along some kind of agreeable guidelines, and
then, each continues to offer services to its target group without inter-
ference from the others. If such agreements prove to be operable, then
the entire program is promoted as an ideal situation, and each group
proudly advertises that its community is a prime example of how the various components of community education can be brought into a harmo-
nious existence.

This approach to cooperation in community education is most common, and yet it is fraught with problems, the primary one being the em-

phasis on cooperation. It is not that cooperation is in itself bad. The problem lies in what the term implies. To be sure, it signifies together-ness, moving toward a common goal, a joint venture. And the very use of the word brings about positive connotations. But the word *coopera-tion*, as it applies to community education, has come to mean compro-mise, splitting the take, carving out turf, cooptation, delineation of ser-vice. It has not helped to increase the numbers of persons served or to provide a more effective attack on community problems. In fact, there is a great deal of evidence to show that the primary motivating force in such cooperation is based on fees, income, or reimbursable student head count. Attacking the needs of the community seems less important than determining who will get the credit and subsequently the dollars that ac-company the program.

Because the past practices of cooperation have not resulted in the most positive benefits to the community, it might be appropriate to sug-gest that the primary problem facing community agencies and commu-nity schools is one of role definition. The potential contribution of com-munity schools in community education is not one of cooperation in which the population is divided among various institutions for services, but one of providing a system through which others, such as adult edu-cators, recreation personnel, or community colleges, can do a better job of what they were intended to do. This responsibility separates the schools in function from those of the other groups. All of these agencies, institu-tions, and groups are resources for providing programs to meet the vari-ous needs of the community. Community schools are the vehicle by which these institutions, with their programs, are brought in contact with com-munity needs.

To more effectively view this situation, let us again look specifically at the reason for creating a community school and the responsibilities implied therein. In all communities, there is a need for certain functions to take place that assist in the viability of the community. These func-tions include education activities for all members of the community (edu-cation here is used in the broad sense of implying not only basics, but recreation, citizenship, health, vocations, and avocations), facilities where these activities can take place, provisions for effectively offering community services, and community involvement. In most small communities where personal interaction and community identity are strong these functions usually seem to happen naturally.

FIGURE 1—Impact of Community Education Components on a Small Community

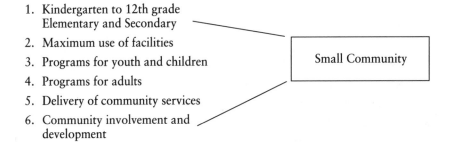

1. Kindergarten to 12th grade Elementary and Secondary
2. Maximum use of facilities
3. Programs for youth and children
4. Programs for adults
5. Delivery of community services
6. Community involvement and development

Small Community

It is not unusual for the schools in this type of community to take a leading role in regard to these functions and often without benefit of calling themselves community schools. Many of these smaller districts have adopted "community schools" as a way to more directly focus the role of the schools on these responsibilities.

FIGURE 2—Impact of Community Education on The Larger Community

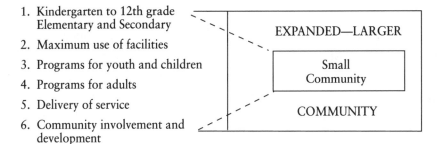

1. Kindergarten to 12th grade Elementary and Secondary
2. Maximum use of facilities
3. Programs for youth and children
4. Programs for adults
5. Delivery of service
6. Community involvement and development

EXPANDED—LARGER

Small Community

COMMUNITY

In larger communities, however, while the functions continue to be prevalent, they have expanded to the larger community with the resulting effect that the smaller parts of the community no longer benefit from such functions to the same degree that they used to.

The role of the community schools in the larger community is to restore to the smaller community the benefits of community education.

Thus, there appear to be differing reasons for the adoption of community education in different size communities. For the smaller community there is the desire to better coordinate and preserve the components of community education, while in the larger community, there is the desire to recapture the benefits of community education at the neighborhood level. In this latter instance, the local elementary schools are seen as a way of breaking the larger community into a number of smaller communities through which the components of community education can then be provided.

This entire concept is based on the premise that "smaller is better." It follows the ideas stated by Tonnes that "gemeinschaft" societies are capable of interacting because they are small and have the potential of face-to-face contact larger communities do not have. If this premise is true, then the most successful social interaction can be accomplished only if the communities do not exceed a certain size.

In today's society, we have attempted to deal with community without a great deal of reference to size. It is suggested here that size is very important and that there is a kind of sociological geometry which implies that the whole is equal to the sum of its parts. Thus, if we could take large communities and break them down into small "gemeinschaft" communities, we could develop the social interaction which would make each of them more viable and thus make the total large community more viable.

This logic has been further expanded by a concept called *synergy*. This idea supports the same thinking. It makes the analogy that when you attempt to combine several good small communities into a larger community, the end result is similar to that of combining several ingredients to form an alloy. The end product is something stronger and better.

Thus, through synergy, the whole is greater than the sum of its parts, and the large communities are therefore greater than the sum of the qualities and morale of all the small communities.

In the case of both the large and small community, the community school plays a particular role, one that might be described as catalytic, facilitative, or even coordinative. The role is best carried out if the community has a population base and a geographic size that allows for community interaction, involvement, and two-way communications. In some communities it may be a village, in others a subdivision, in yet others, a neighborhood. The staff of the community school may involve professionals, paraprofessionals, or volunteers. The school may vary in organizational structure, but its function will be the same—to relate community problems to community resources, avoiding duplication whenever possible and creating new programs when needed. This, simply, is the function of a community school and is shown in Figure 3.

A community school becomes the brokerage operation for relating problems to resources, the coordinating system for helping community resources respond to community needs.

More specifically, a community school would tend to operate as follows. The community school staff, through various techniques, would identify community problems. They would also identify community resources. It should be pointed out that this process is not meant to imply

FIGURE 3—Function of Community Schools

arbitrary or capricious decisions by a few people in respect to either community problems or resources. Inherent in this process is community involvement in both problem identification and use of resources to solve these problems. Again, it is stressed that the community school personnel are to play a catalytic role.

When a problem is identified, it is to be referred to the appropriate resources for solution. Therefore, an adult education problem may be referred to the adult education division of the school, or to the community college, or to any other agency created for that purpose. It then becomes the responsibility of these agencies to service the need with existing programs or create new programs where none exist. This aspect of community schools tends to place the responsibility for solution of problems where it belongs—on the existing resources, and it forces both cooperation on the part of these resources and accountability for meeting the needs of those they are supposed to serve.

In the case of a community problem that has no agency or resource to deal with it, the community school is then in a position to develop its own program by means of its local resources. For example, a needed adult or student program which no existing resource can or will provide can still be developed locally by the community itself.

The role this description of community schools depicts is meant to illustrate that community schools and other agencies, groups, or institutions are not in the position to cooperate as equals in community education since their functions are quite different. Community colleges, adult education, business, industry, libraries, unions, hospitals, recreation, social agencies, universities, other government units, and even individuals are resources created to solve particular problems in their communities. Community schools provide a system by which these services can be more adequately delivered. The resources cannot replace the schools in this system; they have the neither the staff nor the facilities necessary for the system to work in the smaller community. The community schools, by the same token, do not have the capability for providing programs or services comparable to those provided by the various resources and should not attempt to duplicate the operations of others. The only time a community school should provide programs outside its specific area of expertise, whether credit or non credit, adult or recreation, is when no other agency or institution can or will provide the service appropriately.

Thus, the problem of relating community schools to any other resource in the community is not one of cooperation, if cooperation means a compromising position of sharing as it has in the past. It is one of role definition in which both the resources and community schools recognize that the function of the community school as a delivery system can serve to identify community problems of such a magnitude that the demand on all community resources will increase beyond the capability of all of us to provide for such community needs.

CURRENT STATUS

The arguments continue, and several attempts have been made at creating models other than public schools. The literature on community education often makes suggestions on this issue. In fact, it has become fashionable to search for that perfect model presumed to be other than the public schools almost with the fervor of seeking the "Holy Grail." And there are a limited number of other models to look at. A few community college models have received national publicity as have some recreational models. There has also been a limited attempt to develop some models on new structures such as consortia, neighborhood organizations, or "model cities" types in order to more effectively involve the "grass roots" and avoid the bureaucratic entanglements of existing institutions.

While these various models have certainly contributed to community education in their respective communities and have provided some alternative ways of developing community education, the public school model still dominates as the most successful means of bringing community education to the community. Statistically, of the thousands of communities committed to community education, and the even greater number of neighborhoods seeking to develop the concept, all but a very few have used the community school model as a way to best achieve the benefits of community education.

WHY THE SCHOOLS?

Unfortunately, when this question is discussed, it often results in win-lose arguments, because the answer seems to imply that one group of professionals is more capable than another. The logic of roles is lost in the emotion of the issue, and the end result is often based on *who* is right rather than *what* is right.

The choice of the schools for this role has little to do with their past failures or successes, the quality of the personnel, or the motivation or training of their staff. In fact, the most frequent rejection of the introduction of the schools into community education is on the part of the education establishment—the board of education, the administrators, the teachers, and the staff.

The choice of the schools for this role is based on some defendable factors other than the pressures of one group attempting to outdo another. Granted that community education has been promoted primarily by educators over the past 80 years, and there is some obvious bias inherent in such a situation. This is also observable in individual programs in which recreation leaders who develop community education programs often end up with recreation programs. Adult educators who develop community education programs often emphasize adult education, and social workers who develop community education often tend to have programs with a heavy social orientation. The undergirding idea of community education, however, is to attempt to improve particular things within a community. Basic to this idea is the belief that thousands of groups and persons are involved in community education, but some system needs to be used to maximize the efforts of all.

There have been many attempts in the past to develop such a system, but frequently these attempts were in the form of operations, such as Jane Adams and Hull House. These systems worked very well, but they were unable to develop immortality—when the individual passed on, so did the system.

It seems logical to assume that one way to guard against the demise of efforts like those of Jane Adams would be to institutionalize such a system—to make it the responsibility of some existing institution which would assure the permanency of such an idea. Such an institution would take on responsibilities related to the following premises:

1. Services to the community should be delivered at the neighborhood level rather than community wide.

2. Agencies and institutions have a responsibility to "reach out" to clients and encourage them to take advantage of their services rather than wait for clients to come to them.

3. Services to the community should be based on the needs of the community.

4. Existing facilities, programs, and resources should be used before new ones are created.

5. Conditions in the total community are improved as conditions in each of its neighborhoods are improved.

When one identifies the purpose, the goals, and the need for the neighborhood operation of such a system, and if there is a desire to institutionalize such functions, then the public schools stand out as perhaps the best means of accomplishing this.

Another way to look at this issue is to recognize that we are talking about something broader than adding a set of programs on to the public schools. Community education is not to be an accretion to the public schools; it is to be a change in the basic philosophy of the schools themselves. Our major error is probably our continued use of the term *community education* to describe this new role for schools when we should be talking about the role of the school in community education. The school is not and can never be the wherewithal in community education. Its role is distinctly as an energizer, or perhaps we should say synergizer, and we are in need of another term to describe this new area of responsibility and accountability, or we must constantly use the word community school when referring to community education to describe this relationship. The point is that we, in the community education movement, have not clearly delineated the difference between the promoters of community education in its broadest sense and those who believe in the axioms of community education but are really attempting to identify the role of the public school within the community education context.

The thrust of this text is based on the community school approach to community education and thus, the belief that the school should be expected to change its role and accept some new responsibilities over and above those for which it previously was accountable. Those new roles are directly related to the community education concept. More specifically, the schools, in addition to their traditional K-12 functions, should maximize their facilities for community use; provide extra programs over and above the traditional offerings but "mainstreamed" into those offerings; provide for the education needs of all community members, not just school-aged youth; provide a system for identifying community problems and relating community services to them; and take the leadership to develop community councils and other techniques to promote community involvement in problem solving and decision making.

There are many who would say that these are not the responsibilities of public schools and that it is inappropriate to expect schools to be so involved. A part of the basis for this thinking has to do with our tendency to develop paradigms. Paradigms are models we develop based upon our assumptions of what something should be. Over the years (and generations), the popular model takes on the appearances of law and truth and soon becomes almost invulnerable to change. For centuries the Ptolemaic view of the universe with the Earth as the center was so well accepted that even Galileo was forced to denounce his own beliefs.

> All of us, scientists or not, share the assumptions of the paradigm. If something comes along that doesn't fit the paradigm, it makes us feel uncomfortable, and it sounds bizarre and kooky.
>
> Obviously, paradigms have great utility. They provide us a ground for communication, so we don't have to start over each time, and they make the world seem continuous and stable and somewhat predictable. But they also limit us, especially when we forget that we make up the paradigm in the first place.[1]

---

[1] Smith, Adam, *Power of Mind*, Random House, New York, 1975, p. 21.

But for those of us promoting community schools, we are suggesting a new paradigm for public education as a way of accomplishing some of the goals of community education and making them more relevant to our current communities. Our logic for such a recommendation is based on the following:

1. The community school model has proved to be the most effective model for maximizing community education in the community.

2. If we are going to institutionalize certain aspects of community education, the school appears to be the most appropriate institution for this purpose.

3. The schools have facilities which are frequently available for community use and most adaptable for a wide variety of community uses and programs.

4. The school is the only organization with a neighborhood base and is located to be most accessible to community members.

5. The school is publicly supported and has the potential for raising funds for expanded responsibilities.

6. Schools have strong community identities, and people often select their place of residency on the basis of the school.

7. Schools are the least political units and are often most free from the abuses of politics.

8. Schools have an entree into communities through children who provide an effective and emotional tie with the families in that community.

9. School boundaries cross political boundaries, and schools usually can unify communities where there are embedded political divisions.

10. Schools are the most trusted institutions within the community. They are more highly supported by community members than any other institution, and other agencies tend to trust the schools more than they trust each other.

11. Community members developing community education
    programs will invariably select the schools as the institution
    to develop their community education program.

When reviewing the logic of such a role for schools, it seems that the question is not, "Why the schools?" but, "Why not the schools?" And yet, the argument will continue because of the lack of understanding of the concept, the school's role, and the emotional implications of the term *school based*. The interesting point is that even this term has added to the confusion. Scrutiny of many of the non-school-based models indicates that non-school-based means that salaries are paid by other than the schools (even though sometimes paid through the schools), that there is another advisory or policy board other than the school board, that there is overt cooperation with other agencies, or that the major programming is done by other than school people. If school-based refers to having the primary functioning component in the local community, however, then all of the effective models are school-based since they do use the local school as a part of their delivery system. Again, our problem seems to be one of semantics. The key to success is the neighborhood component, regardless of the structure for actualizing, organizing, or financing that component.

Finally, one last point on this whole issue of why the schools in community education: there is a need for the public schools to accept some new responsibilities in our modern society. A major part of this new role is in the area of community education. That there are many other groups, agencies, and individuals in community education there is no doubt, and they should be encouraged to carry out their responsibilities in the most effective ways possible. The question we are dealing with is not who should control community education, but rather should the schools take on the new roles as described by community school parameters. The functions of a community school can greatly enhance the programs of all in community education by providing for a systematic method of relating problems to resources. It would seem that every group or person in community education would welcome the addition of a staff in every neighborhood to ferret out problems and refer them to the proper agencies. The method suggested is meant to be facilitating, not mandatory, so that if such a system was not most effective for a particular group, it could devise its own means of operation.

Should the schools carry out this role? Will the schools carry out their role? Community members tend to answer this question in the affirmative. Some school districts say "yes;" some say, "maybe;" and some are noticeably quiet. Agencies and institutions also are reacting in a mixed fashion. There is strong evidence, however, that state legislators and state and federal governmental agencies are taking their cue from community members and are moving in the direction of new roles for the public schools as community schools. Schools have changed before, but with the same reluctance that other institutions change. Perhaps we are arriving at the place where 80 years of effort are about to be reflected in our educational paradigm.

> The establishment is always invested in the old paradigm. So the new paradigm does not get adopted just because it is neater and works better than the old one. The old crowd wins the first few battles, and in fact the paradigm doesn't change until the old crowd dies and new young crowd grows up and rewrites the text books and becomes the establishment itself.[2]

---

[2] Smith, Adam, op. cit., p. 21.

CHAPTER VI

COMMUNITY
EDUCATION
PROGRAMS

Terms such as community education, adult education, and recreation are often used interchangeably and perceived as merely different names for the same thing. Adult educators, for example, look at community education and see programs for adults designed to enable them to complete high school, to gain literacy skills, and to develop new interests and talents. Because the programs are identical to ones offered through their own education system under a program called "Adult Education," it is understandable that the conclusion drawn is that they are one and the same.

Recreation directors also observe many recreational programs in schools and see a variety of sports activities being both taught and made available for general participation. Comparing these activities to their own offerings, little difference is observed, and the conclusion, again, is understandably the same as that drawn by the adult educator—that there is no real difference between community education and school-based recreation programs.

There is a very basic difference between community education and the programming available through adult education, recreation, and the like. This difference is primarily a conceptual one, a difference in goals and objectives, rather than specific differences in existing programs. Community education is the philosophical base, the others are programmatic components designed to achieve the broader goals of the philosophy.

Adult education leaders and other program directors develop programs to provide people with activities, skills, new experiences, interests, and a general opportunity to improve and upgrade themselves so that they can live and enjoy life at a higher level. These programs are often highly successful, involve large numbers of people, and often do meet the program objectives. Community education accepts the value of these goals and incorporates those concepts into its general framework. Beyond this, however, another dimension is added. Community educators believe that this initial participation is one means of developing and encouraging deeper involvement of people in improving the community in which they live. The programs that are designed are not an end in themselves, but they become an entree to a greater individual involvement and contribution to the community. It is an unfortunate fact that many community educators often do not perceive this differentiation and thus offer a variety of programs that truly are distinguished from adult education or recreation in name only.

It is important to again recognize here that true community education is not achieved in a few years. It is a process that must develop slowly and steadily. New community education programs often are a number of activities and programs, nothing more. The crucial test, however, is the direction that is being taken. Are the programs being planned to assure deeper involvement later, or are they planned to provide a service to the individual with no further objectives? Participation in classes is not involvement, as is evidenced daily in colleges and universities. Students attend classes but are not necessarily involved in the life and destiny of the university. Community education should use classes and activities as a springboard to social action and to get people accustomed to using their schools and being partners in their community's education process. The individual growth that results from the class activity is only one part of a broader program objective.

From class activities, adults can become involved in helping plan their education program and that of their children, and finally become involved in working toward a better community for both themselves and their neighbors. The dimension community education adds is one of concern for the betterment of all people, not just the individual.

ADULT EDUCATION

HISTORICAL OVERVIEW

Adult education in America can be traced back to Benjamin Franklin. In 1727, he initiated discussion clubs to explore moral, political, and philosophical problems. C. Hartley Grotten refers to Franklin as the "patron saint of American Adult Education."[1] From this very early beginning, the adult education movement expanded in very diverse and creative directions. This diversity, however, was unified in purpose. The first task of

---

[1] Knowles, Malcolm S., *The Adult Education Movement in the United States*, Holt, Rinehart and Winston, 1962, p. 11.

adult education in this nation was the transformation of an entire people from being subjects to being citizens, from perceiving themselves as subservient to an acceptance and understanding of freedom and a democratic form of government. This first attempt at adult education in this nation was obviously successful and assisted the nation in its efforts to become an independent democracy.

By approximately 1810, evening schools were beginning in many of the large public schools. They were unstable in that they were often started, dropped, and started again. While evening schools today are generally accepted as the domain of the adult, the early evening schools were established primarily for working children over twelve years of age. The curriculum was usually a repeat of the day program, stressing reading, writing, and computational skills. As these schools began to stabilize, the age of the student population being served gradually shifted to older teens and young adults. This gradual expansion established the foundation for today's adult education programs in the public schools.

From this, specific programs were established to meet specific adult needs, such as Americanization classes, vocational training courses, high school completion programs, and special interest courses. The state and federal governments began exhibiting some interest in the education of the adult population and began making their presence felt. The state governments began by establishing permissive legislation giving local schools the authority to operate evening schools. This late entry is especially interesting since the governments, in effect, gave permission to do something that had been going on for a number of years. This legislation was followed by mandatory requirements regulating the adult education offerings.

Following this entry into adult education, several states began legislating financial assistance. While most states providing adult education did not establish legislative programs until after 1920, a few earlier notable exceptions do exist. The New York Legislature authorized an expenditure of $6,000 per year in Adult Education, and the Rhode Island Assembly appropriated $5,000 in 1873 for the same purpose. Once legislation was passed, the fourth stage in the developmental process of state involvement was the establishment of statewide assistance and services through the state departments of education. This fourth stage is extremely important because it incorporates the concept of adult education into the statewide education structure.

The federal government's first real entry into adult education was in agricultural education. This was initiated with the Hatch Act of 1887 which established agricultural experimental stations within the land grant colleges. This act was followed in 1914 by the Cooperative Extension Act. The Cooperative Extension Act was intended to educate farmers to improve crop yield and farming techniques. Today, this effort is heralded as this nation's greatest single adult education venture and its most successful.

More recently, the federal government established the Adult Basic Education Act in an attempt to reduce and ultimately eliminate adult illiteracy. This act and the funding it makes available is having a major impact on the adult education movement in this country.

In reviewing the growth and establishment of adult education in this country, certain basic principles have emerged in public education:

1. Public schools have a responsibility to assist the citizenry in keeping abreast of change within the society. Adult educators have recognized that the society requires not only a literate population but an intelligent one that is willing to share responsibility for social progress.

2. Public schools have an important role in training for the wise, purposeful, and enjoyable use of leisure time. The ill effects of enforced idleness and expanded time for leisure can be offset by creative, wholesome, recreational activities and educational opportunities.

3. Public schools have a responsibility to provide second chance opportunities to those individuals in the society who, for a variety of reasons, did not complete high school. The problems faced by the non-high school graduate are severe and will become increasingly so. Adults must be given the opportunity to obtain the basic high school credentials that are required in the society.

4. The public schools should expand the use of their facilities, personnel, and leadership. They should become more active within, and available to, the community they serve.

5. Because of technological advances and expanding job automation, the public schools should become increasingly involved in vocational training, retraining, and readjustment.

6. Adult education provides the means for accomplishing the goal of creating a learning society—for establishing learning as a lifetime process rather than some activity that concludes at age 18 or 22.

In addition to these six principles, community education is in the process of establishing a seventh for the public school—that of coordination. It is clear, through any cursory review of adult and continued education efforts, that literally thousands of agencies and organizations are involved in the process. A crucial role that has emerged is the need for some coordination and cooperative activity, some analysis of overlap and duplication with a corresponding determination of remaining need and potential areas of service. Community education, with its broadened service role in public education, naturally leads the adult education component to this very critical coordinating responsibility. This last principle is at some risk of achieving fulfillment, as many adult educators focus on taking all responsibilities rather than working with and through others.

While it remains clear that public school adult education will and should remain the provider of a variety of continuing education opportunities, its role in assisting others to provide these services too is equally important. The coordinative function may well, in fact, become far more important in the future than the present role of providing courses.

While adult education encompasses a variety of specific programs and activities, this chapter will deal only with those three most often found with the public schools: Adult Basic Education, Adult High School Completion, and Adult Noncredit Special Interest Programs. There are several areas of concern that apply generally to adult education and encompass all three of these areas.

ADULT BASIC EDUCATION

We are rapidly moving to a point in time where the undereducated adult in the United States will have virtually no opportunity to survive in the society on his or her own. At a time when over 90 percent of the jobs are already available only to the skilled and educated, it takes little imagination to assess the future potential of our illiterate adult five or ten years from now. Adult illiteracy is a very real problem in our society. According to the 1990 census, there are 58,868,435 persons of age 25 and over. Of those adults, 16,502,211 have less than a ninth-grade education and were termed functionally illiterate.[2] These figures do not include the substantial numbers of adults completing more than eight grades of formal education but still functioning below the eighth-grade level. They also do not include those adults unwilling to admit to an education level of less than eight grades. While the total number of adults today estimated to have less than a grade eight education level has been reduced, the problem remains significant and the devastating results far reaching.

In an attempt to encourage education institutions, and specifically public schools, to solve this problem, the United States Congress passed the Adult Basic Education Act. This act provides funds to "encourage and expand basic educational programs for adults to enable them to overcome English language limitations, to improve their basic education in preparation for occupational training and more profitable employment, and to become more productive and responsible citizens."[3] Initially, this act was Title II-B of the Economic Opportunity Act and was a part of the much heralded "War on Poverty." In 1966, it became part of Title I of the Elementary and Secondary Education Act, administered through the Department of Health, Education, and Welfare, and became "The Adult Education Act of 1966" under this legislation.

Funding for adult basic education programs is almost completely obtained through this federal enactment. It is supported through a 90/10 funding plan, with the federal government providing 90 percent of the costs and the state providing or assuring the other 10 percent. In most

---

[2] Department of State, Census Bureau, Detroit, Michigan.
[3] *Compendium of Federal Education Laws*, Prepared by Committee on Education and Labor, House of Representatives, May, 1967, p. 335.

states, proposals must be submitted to the State Department of Education describing the local situation faced by the school district, plans for effectively serving that segment of the society that functions at less than an eighth-grade level, and a proposed budget that indicates how the district plans to spend money granted to it. Each state has its own plans and some specific regulations to be met. Anyone planning to initiate adult basic education programs should spend some time learning about the program as it operates in his or her state and the program established by the State Department of Education.

While funding is extremely important to any education program, it is not the crucial problem faced in adult basic education. The crucial problem in adult basic education is the recruitment and retention of the illiterate adult. This problem increases with the adult's need for literacy training. These adults generally have not had positive experiences with the school. They did not succeed as youngsters and usually have many misgivings about going back into the same situation in which they previously experienced failure.

While fear is often one important reason why adult illiterates avoid basic education, there is another phenomenon interjected into this avoidance. Phillip Jackson refers to this as the development of a closed-minded system resulting from personal alienation from the society. He feels there are levels of personal alienation toward the world and toward specific things in the world and that as people move through these levels there is an increasingly greater tendency to reject societal values and the values held within societal institutions.[4] This phenomenon is often found among the undereducated, underemployed, and unaccepted portion of our society, and one of the negative results is the closing of the mind against the value of education and education and societal goals, with those most in need being the most alienated.

Encouraging students to participate in these programs is extremely difficult. Most mass media and traditional approaches don't work. Tech-

---

[4] Puder, William and Hand, S.E., "Personality Factors which may Interfere with the Learning of Adult Education's Basic Education Students," *Adult Education*, Vol. XVIII, No. 2, Winter, 1968.

niques that focus on one-on-one relationships and personal caring are the most effective. Interrelationships between people are primary in overcoming the rational reluctance of "going back to school."

Once students are attracted to adult basic education, they should begin a program that provides them with much personal satisfaction, a feeling of growth and potential, an ability to better handle problems that are presented daily, and a steady observable growth in literacy skills. Obviously, a program of this type takes much planning and consideration. It cannot be done by simply selecting a textbook and a teacher. Like the development of any curriculum, the adult basic education curriculum should be the result of the thinking and study of all teachers involved, the program administrator, and any school service personnel that will be either directly or indirectly involved with the program.

Once the program has been established and is in operation, continuous evaluation is crucial. A later chapter will deal specifically with evaluation. It is sufficient to say at this point that the evaluation system must provide continuous and instant feedback to allow program changes whenever it is evident that such changes are warranted.

Adult Basic Education is certainly one of the most difficult areas to program in all of continuing education. One can seldom justify its existence on the basis of extensive program enrollments. In very basic terms, it is the core of what adult education is all about. It is providing service to those most in need—individuals whose entire lives are dwarfed and diminished by an inadequate education, who often do not realize the cause of their dilemma, and who sometimes actively oppose any attempt to assist them.

ADULT HIGH SCHOOL COMPLETION[5]

Adult high school completion programs have been established to provide second chance opportunities for adults who have not completed high

---

[5] Many of the ideas presented in the Adult Education section of the chapter are the result of the thinking of a committee established by the Michigan Department of Education. This committee was chaired by Dr. Clyde LeTarte. Committee members were: Mr. Don Arsen; Mr. Walter Cooper; Mr. William Dietzel; Mr. Bruce Jacobs; Mr. Kenneth Lane; and Mr. Charles Porter. Appreciation is expressed for the time and effort expended by these committee members.

school. This group of adult citizens, along with those adults previously discussed who are in need of basic literacy skills, present many problems to the society in addition to the personal problems they encounter in their daily lives. The Michigan Committee on Post-Twelfth Grade Community Education stated the problem this country faces with undereducated adults very well:

A. As workers, undereducated adults are less and less able to meet the rising levels of skill demanded by our improving technology. They are inevitably the last hired, the first fired, and the perennial consumers of our welfare budgets. They lack the basic educational means to take advantage of vocational retraining programs and become an increasingly larger and harder core of chronically unemployed.

B. They are less and less able to provide the parental guidance their children need in the face of growing complexities of modern urban life, and, under these circumstances, their lack of education diminishes the stability and the beneficial influence of our nation's families, whose vigor undergirds our national virtue.

C. They are less resourceful in using, wisely, the increasing hours of leisure which improved technology and increasing longevity are providing.

D. They are readily exploited by those who prey upon the ignorant and the gullible. They find it difficult to protect themselves, their families, and their communities from irresponsible or malicious propaganda.

E. They provide a weak and shifting element in the foundation of citizen understanding upon which our national leaders depend for support in the complex decisions of the day.[6]

High school completion programs for adults, like any other education programs, must be carefully planned and initiated to attain maximum success. This planning must concern itself with curricular and course

---

[6] Michigan Department of Education, "The High School Completion Program for Adults and Out of School Youth," Bulletin No. 370, 1967.

content, scheduling, counseling, financing, administration, facilities, faculty in-service, and marketing. This total program should be planned to assure integration into the total school program. To be successful, school districts considering a high school completion program for adults should make provisions for one person to be responsible for the program and to assure that person an adequate amount of time to properly meet responsibilities. At its inception, this individual often is the person responsible for community education in the district. As the program matures and expands, it often becomes necessary to employ a director whose total efforts are dedicated to the high school completion aspect of the community education program.

GENERAL EDUCATIONAL DEVELOPMENT (GED) PROGRAMS

No discussion of adult high school completion programs is complete without mentioning the ever-increasing trend toward high school equivalency programs. In most states, it is possible to obtain high school equivalency through the General Educational Development Test (GED), which is certainly the most common test in use today. Many programs have been established to assist adults in the preparation for this test. These programs vary extensively, from brief cram courses covering only the test material to programs that are more broadly based, providing basic knowledge in a variety of academic areas. These equivalency programs are viable alternatives to the more traditionally structured programs and are extensively available through public school adult programs. When done well, they focus on expanded knowledge, skill development, and improved abilities to cope with the environment. When done poorly, they focus on successful completion of the test.

ADULT NONCREDIT SPECIAL INTEREST PROGRAM

The general area of special interest noncredit programs for adults is often the most maligned program area in which adult educators are involved. Derogatory references to "underwater basket weaving" and other noncredit courses of nonacademic stature are often suggested to the adult educator by other more traditional educators. There seems to be a general feeling among many that the "fun" type course offerings or the non-academic self-enrichment courses are somehow beneath the dignity of the education establishment and that education, by offering the nonacademic, will be reduced to meaningless trivia—that the "academic standards" of the institution will become sullied and the education program will become somehow less valuable.

To state that there is room within the education system to meet the varied interests of an adult community is certainly not novel. To imply that public schools are justified in providing enriching activities also is not unique. In 1918, the NEA Commission on Reorganization of Secondary Education established seven basic principles of education.[7] These "Seven Cardinal Principles" have been stressed in university education courses ever since. In fact, they have become an important keystone in our entire education philosophy. Five of these seven principles include "worthy use of leisure time," "health," "worthy home membership," "citizenship," and "ethical character."

Each of these can be accepted as part of a basic ingredient in a non-academic activity for adults. Certainly, the education system in this country has not become so stifled and traditional that any hint of enjoyment of learning is perceived as unworthy of public support. It is imperative that adult educators recognize the value and worth of special interest courses designed to meet a variety of individual interests and that they perceive these courses as an important integral part of the total adult education program.

Paul Bergevin's statements on the goals of adult education incorporate special interest programming:

A. To help the learner achieve a degree of happiness and meaning in life;

B. To help the learner understand himself, his talents, and limitations, and his relationships with other persons;

---

[7] Commission on the Reorganization of Secondary Education, "Cardinal Principles of Secondary Education," Washington, DC, U.S. Government Printing Office, 1918.

C. To help adults recognize and understand the need for life-long learning;

D. To provide conditions and opportunities to help the adult advance in the maturation process spiritually, culturally, physically, politically, and vocationally;

E. To provide, where needed, education for survival, in literary, vocational skills, and health measures."[8]

To attempt to meet these five major goals exclusively through the academic credit activities would be impossible.

While it is very difficult to categorize the thousands of noncredit special interest courses and activities that are taught daily, an attempt will be made to limit this discourse to seven major areas:

1. Programs for the aging
2. Programs in economics and money management
3. Programs providing recreation activities and learning opportunities
4. Programs in public affairs and community development
5. Programs to support and improve the home and family
6. Programs in the arts
7. Programs for providing and expanding vocational competency

RECREATION

Recreation programming within community education, like any other well-planned program opportunity, requires much thought and planning. The establishment of objectives and an understanding of why opportunities for recreation are important to the health of a community is even more important than in most other program areas we have discussed. This is true because using tax money for "fun and relaxation" seems somehow frivolous to many people—especially to those who do not participate in recreation events.

---

[8] Bergevin, Paul, *A Philosophy for Adult Education*, The Seaburg Press, New York, 1967, pp. 30–31.

It is the purpose of this section to establish a basic philosophy of recreation and then present some general guidelines for the establishment of recreation programs. The concepts and guidelines presented will not be all-encompassing because of the unique and individual recreational requirements and existing opportunities in any given community.

ESTABLISHING A PHILOSOPHY OF RECREATION

While writers in the field of recreation tend to disagree on which agency or agencies should provide the bulk of recreation opportunities in a community, they do seem to agree on the reasons for providing them:

A. Our society is increasingly becoming a sedentary one. This is most evident in the spectacular rise of spectator sports over participatory activities. For very basic health reasons, the human body requires physical activity. A person is a total unit, and for the unit to operate at peak performance, all parts must function properly. To reduce the effectiveness of any one part of that unit reduces the effectiveness of all other parts. As a person's physical capacity deteriorates, it directly and indirectly affects his or her emotional and intellectual capacities. Various recreation activities provide an opportunity for physical fitness and offer encouragement for a more active use of leisure time.

B. As the society becomes increasingly complex, individual tensions and strain increase. People must have a release from the many pressures modern society places on them. Recreation opportunities can provide this release either through physical exertion or through the expansion of interests that make it possible to get away from everyday troubles and concerns.

C. Much has been written about the depersonalization of the society. As our society has grown larger and more complex and we are forced to live in closer and closer proximity to our fellow beings, we have tended to build, emotionally and intellectually, more barriers between ourselves and those living and working around us. Recreation provides a positive opportunity to reverse this trend and improve a community's chances to have positive personal interaction. Socialization opportunities can be provided through recreation, and, as a result, individuals get to know their neighbors.

D. From the beginning of the human race, people have sought to achieve new skills, new thoughts, and new and better ways of living. They have always been interested in growth. While some may call this instinct natural competitiveness and others a person's desire to grow as an individual, the fact remains that human beings do have a normal desire to achieve that which is beyond their present level of proficiency. A good recreation program provides an opportunity both to learn new skills and improve existing ones.

E. Technology has brought a mixture of blessings and problems. One of the negative aspects of technology is the suppression of individual identity. Human beings become an integral part of a larger, complicated process and often feel stifled and anonymous as a result. Recreation provides the opportunity each person needs to excel in something—develop some unique skills or talent that sets him apart from other people. This uniqueness, this positive individualism, provides a counterbalance to the depersonalization of the society and gives individuals a better chance to perceive themselves positively.

DEFINING RECREATION

Within these five basic reasons for providing opportunities for recreation rests the basic philosophy of a good recreation program. Most writers in the field generally seem to concur about the nature of recreation.

. . . recreation is looked upon as activity voluntarily engaged in during leisure and motivated by the personal satisfactions which result from it. Recreation can be physical, mental, social, or a combination of all three. It can be organized or unorganized, planned or spontaneous, undertaken by individuals or groups, and stimulated, sponsored, or provided by public, private, voluntary, or commercial interests. In any event, it is always a form of human expression and an influence on personality development.[9]

Recreation is defined as a field of activities, freely chosen, possessing potentialities for the enrichment of life through the satisfaction of certain basic individual needs and the development of democratic human relations.[10]

. . . any activity pursued during leisure, either individual or collective, that is free and pleasureful, having its own immediate appeal, not impelled by a delayed reward beyond itself or by any immediate necessity. Recreation includes play, games, sports, athletics, relaxation, positiveness, certain amusements, art forms, hobbies, and avocations. A recreational activity may be engaged in during any age period of the individual, the particular action being determined by the time element, the condition and attitude of the person, and the environmental situation.[11]

There seem to be five general characteristics shared in each definition. They are:

A. Recreation is a freely chosen, voluntary activity. People participate because they want to.

B. Recreation provides personal satisfaction to participants and immediate gratification for their efforts. People feel good while they are participating and afterwards.

C. Recreation is comprehensive in that it includes a variety of activities—physical, mental, or social.

D. Recreation provides opportunities for personal growth and development.

E. Recreation is all-inclusive. No age group is specified as a primary target group, and no age group is excluded.

---

[9] *The Recreation Program*, The Athletic Institute, Chicago, 1954, p. 1.

[10] Danford, Howard S., *Recreation in the American Community*, Harper and Brothers, New York, 1953, p. 120.

[11] Newmeyer, Martin H. and Newmeyer, Esther, *Leisure and Recreation*, The Ronald Press, New York, 1958, p. 17, a quote from (by permission of) Dictionary of Sociology, edited by Henry Pratt Fairchild, pp. 25–52, copyright 1944, Philosophical Library, New York.

The scope of recreation as defined by people dedicated to the field indeed seems extensive. Far more extensive, in fact, than the role usually ascribed to it by community educators. This difference in role perception is a crucial one for the community educator to understand in working with various community recreation leaders interested in serving the recreation needs of the community. The recreation leader's perception of recreation is often broad and encompassing. The community educator's ideas of recreation tend to be more focused because the diversity and scope of other programming areas tend to overlap into recreation. Because of the responsibility for many activities other than recreation, there is a tendency to narrowly define the limits of each program. Because many community educators have a general area of responsibility titled, "Recreation," along with several other categories of responsibility, they tend to narrow their concept of what recreation is to fit general program descriptions. While there is nothing basically wrong with this, very real problems can develop if this limited perception of recreation is held as a school begins working with other agencies in establishing good community recreation. As a director with a limited perspective of recreation begins working and discussing shared recreation programming with agencies that have a much broader concept of what recreation is, a discrepancy in the perceptions of which programs and responsibilities should be shared may well result. The recreation director will perceive a responsibility for activities in many areas which the community educator might designate as adult education or student enrichment. Perhaps an example would help at this point.

One community educator, in establishing a community education program in a city where an extensive recreation program previously existed, met with the recreation director to discuss mutual interests and possible joint planning. As a community school director, the individual had established the concept of recreation programs as those programs involving participatory physical activity and had excluded physical activity resulting from learning situations. For example, a golf match was considered recreation, but a class in golf designed to teach basic rules and to improve skills was considered adult education. The recreation director's perception incorporated both activities under recreation. When discussion began, the terms *recreation*, *mutual planning*, and *comprehensiveness* had entirely different meanings for each of the participants. Because of these initial conceptual differences, as discussions continued, mistrust developed. The recreation director began feeling that he was being ascribed a rather minuscule role, and the community educator began feeling that the recreation director was empire-building and attempting to establish himself in the field of adult education. It was fortunate for the community that the two men had known each other previously and could state their concerns frankly, or it is very possible that two agencies that should naturally operate in close harmony would have been separated by misunderstanding and a lack of trust.

The important point is not that one definition is inherently better than another, for they both served the purposes of the individuals involved, but that community educators must understand there is often a broader, more encompassing view of recreation than their own, and they must be willing to accept and respect this as they begin planning recreation programs for the entire community. The best recreation programs are those incorporating as many agencies as possible. Great diversity and choice in recreation offerings is best achieved through diversity in the groups and agencies providing the services, each coordinating its efforts with the others. The community educator should perceive his or her role as an initiator and coordinator as well as a recreation provider. The more programs provided by other agencies, the more extensive the resources the community educator has for other areas of need.

Meyer and Brightbill discuss five basic principles in establishing recreation programs in a community:

1. That anything and everything that is done should have its base in the community;

2. That there should be ample recreational opportunities for all the people—children, youth, and adults—in all economic and social strata;

3. That the talents of people and the natural resources of the community should be used to the fullest extent;

4. That the program should function through all types of agencies, public, private, and commercial;

5. That recreation should be recognized as an essential force in the life of the people for what it contributes to social well-being.[12]

STUDENT ENRICHMENT

The third general program area normally considered an integral part of community education is student enrichment. This term generally encompasses a variety of special activities available to school-age youth preceding or following the regular school day, on weekends, and during the summer. While most community educators accept this program phase as a legitimate part of community education, few ever attempt either to establish reasons for its existence or goals and objectives to be accomplished. Student enrichment has tended to be that programming phase done primarily because everyone else seems to be doing it, rather than because of its legitimate value and pre-defined purposes.

It is clear that the potential value of this effort is greater now than ever before. Knowledge is now doubling every few years, and great quantities of additional information are being created that should be disseminated through the schools. While this is occurring, the amount of school time offered students has regularly and continuously decreased. A study conducted in one school district comparing school time in 1964 to that in 1981, for example, showed the following:

1. A reduction in the school year from 193 days to 180.

2. A reduction in instructional time from seven hours per day to five and one-half.

3. An inclusion of ten professional days in 1981. Three existed in 1964. This resulted in a loss of seven additional instructional days. While this study is dated, few would suggest that time in school has increased since 1981.

---

[12] Meyer, Harold D., and Brightbill, Charles K., *Community Recreation, A Guide To Its Organization*, Prentice Hall, Englewood Cliffs, New Jersey, 1986, p. 46.

The net effect of this reduction in days and daily schedule is the loss of 50 days of instruction per year. Based on a five-day week, this is a loss of three months of instruction.[13] Thus, at a time when we are in the midst of a knowledge explosion, we are reducing by one-third the amount of instruction provided as compared with that offered 17 years earlier. Student enrichment provides an opportunity to regain some of that lost time and to provide new opportunities for learning that may otherwise be lost.

To initiate any discussion on student enrichment, it is necessary to begin with the students themselves—to look at their needs, concerns, desires, and problems and to attempt to then review the existing curriculum and analyze how well these needs, concerns, desires, and problems are being met by the education institution.

Earl Kelly, in his book, *In Defense of Youth*, believes that more than anything else, youth needs a bona fide place in our society. He further states that as a result of the expansion of technology and resulting expanded requirements for participation in society, the only bona fide place that can be provided—be assured—is in the public schools. Somehow the public schools must provide youth an opportunity to feel that the school is theirs—to meet their needs and to serve them.[14]

While one may or may not agree with Mr. Kelly's basic assumption, it is difficult to disagree that there is something underlying our present youth alienation that has resulted in a youth drug culture, a rejection of social norms, and the establishment of a youth subculture possessing an embryonic revolutionary character. If nothing else, Mr. Kelly's observations do lead one to consider today's youth in light of the school's responsibility to them and to attempt to look at existing curriculum and assess it in light of relevance to youth. While one may argue that the school should or should not be youth's new reason for being, it is difficult to debate the need for expanded relevance and the establishment of new concerns for meeting educational needs.

---

[13] Minzey, Jack D., "The Purloined School Year," *Michigan School Board Journal*, February, 1981, p. 24.

[14] Kelly, Earl, *In Defense of Youth*, Prentice Hall, Englewood Cliffs, New Jersey, 1962, pp. 30–37.

In reviewing the existing curriculum in most schools, it becomes evident that, at the very least, change and innovation in education have not kept pace with social change, and that some degree of disparity exists between what is taught and what is needed to successfully cope with living in our modern society. The traditional curriculum has been patched, twisted, added to, and subtracted from, but has not basically changed. This has resulted in an attempt to present increasing amounts of knowledge in a time span that has remained constant and sometimes shortened in subject areas that often are outdated and of little real concern to the student. The consequence of this is the establishment and entrenchment of an intellectual rather than an education institution with a resulting imbalance favoring the academic aspect of learning at the expense of the social, cultural, and vocational.

It is not the purpose of this section to present a critical review of American education, but instead, to recognize some serious shortcomings, attempt to discuss them, and offer some suggestions for improvement. American education has often stressed the importance of developing the social and moral character of students as well as the academic. This need exists today more than ever, especially with the increasing complexity of our society and need for citizens to know how to relate to each other. It seems important, then, that community educators attempt to answer several questions when planning student enrichment activities:

- ◆ What can be done in planning student enrichment programs to broaden the existing curriculum—to expand the limited concept of a six-hour education day and a nine-and-a-half month education year?

- ◆ What can be done through special programming to attempt to balance the academic side of education with a more socially-oriented approach—to provide opportunities for cultural enrichment, recreation interests, and expanded education enrichment?

- ◆ How can students and community be incorporated into program planning to assure the establishment of a program relevant to their needs and concerns?

These questions can best be asked in relationship to the existing curriculum provided in a given school district, the nature of the local community being served by the school, and the nature and needs of the student group to be served.

PLANNING A STUDENT ENRICHMENT PROGRAM

Based on the preceding statements, there are several reasons for providing students with an extended voluntary program. These include:

1. Providing an opportunity for youth to expand and improve their social skills. These skills include the ability to cooperate in following group rules, to learn the give and take of everyday living, and to learn to better relate to other human beings. These skills are often ignored in the traditional classroom setting where greater stress is placed on more academic concerns.

2. Provide students with an opportunity to pursue their own goals and to expand their abilities in areas of their own choice, as dictated by their personal interests. This includes providing an opportunity to try out new courses and new techniques, and to have the opportunity to fail without feeling like a failure.

3. Provide an opportunity for extensive recreation activity. The need to release excess energy is felt by youth more than any other group, and, certainly, recreation equipment and facilities owned by the public school should be used as extensively as possible for this purpose.

4. Provide a school that assures a positive force in the students' lives. Extended programs help improve attitudes toward school and develop positive feelings toward education.

5. Provide an informal, friendly atmosphere, free of academic structure, where teachers and students can get to know each other on a personal, one-to-one basis. The establishment of this relationship should carry over into the regular academic program.

GENERAL ACTIVITY CATEGORIES

There are five general categories for most student enrichment programs. Each of the five provide very specific benefits to the participants and expand the education program in rather diverse and unique ways.

1. Many, if not most, of the student enrichment programs provided through public schools are based solely on one premise: they must be fun. Within this fun category, a host of recreation programs are possible. Some of these include: badminton, teen dances, table games, ping pong, basketball, football, arts and crafts, swimming, and roller skating. And there are thousands more.

    While students participate in these activities only because they enjoy them, many subtle but very real educational benefits accrue. One of the most important of these is the establishment of a more positive feeling toward the school. The more a child enjoys being at school, the more positive the feelings he or she develops for the entire education program. Human beings establish positive or negative feelings toward something by weighing the good against the bad and then generalizing either a positive or negative feeling about the whole. The more positive experiences that educators can provide within the education framework, the better the chance of assuring a generalized "good" feeling about the total education process.

2. A variety of student enrichment programs are designed primarily as skill development programs. While these activities are also perceived as fun by the students, they do provide an additional dimension. They give the student a chance to learn or improve a skill and add breadth to his or her scope of interest. Many of the skills learned in this type of activity can be carried over into adult life. Some courses providing these skills might include sewing, cooking, woodworking, model building, knitting, etc.

3. Many student enrichment activities are designed around existing curricular offerings in the regular day program. These activities attempt to provide an additional dimension to a specific subject

area through approaches quite different from those used in the regular program. Math for fun, for example, might be developed around math games and puzzles, and an elementary science for fun activity might be centered around laboratory experimentation the day program is unable to provide. Often this type of student enrichment activity expands and encourages students' interest in specific subject matter areas. It also provides an opportunity for students who were forced to choose one subject over another during the regular school day to now obtain both.

4. Activities that have not been developed as completely as some, but certainly possess an exciting potential, are student service-oriented programs. While a variety of successful programs do exist, a good example of what can be done by getting students interested in assisting others was demonstrated by a teen service club called the Pacemakers. Some of the activities sponsored by this group include:

   ◆ sponsoring three disadvantaged children to a camp;
   ◆ providing a summer field trip for 60 youths;
   ◆ providing free babysitting services and a car pool to aid people in voting;
   ◆ providing and showing educational movies on crime and narcotics;
   ◆ replacing or paying for new nets on all outdoor basketball courts;
   ◆ making a down-payment on a halfway house for ex-convicts and assuming the mortgage. Once the house was purchased, club members contributed time and effort to recondition the house themselves.[15]

---

[15] Ollie, Leslie, "Study of Selected Aspects of the Community Education Program in Benton Harbor, Michigan," States Human Resources Council, Lansing, Michigan. Unpublished.

5. The fifth general category of student enrichment includes those programs established to assist students with special problems. These programs, while focusing on learning difficulties, might also be developed to assist in the physical or emotional development of children with special problems. An example of this was the establishment in one community of a tutorial program for disadvantaged youth with average intelligence but very low achievement scores and grades. The tutoring was done in the homes of the children. Tutorial groups were established, when possible, among existing friendship groups, and these groups were hosted by parents. They met three times a week for a study session with a teacher. Afterwards, parents provided refreshments. This approach not only assisted the children academically and socially, it also helped the parents learn what was required to assure success for their children and provided them an opportunity to participate in their children's learning. As a final reward, the tutorial groups were treated to a professional baseball game and a visit to a museum.

It is important to note that this program was designed for a very specific purpose—to help under-achieving children with average intelligence improve their achievement level. Many programs can be designed to meet the unique, specific problems of other school-age youngsters.

Programming for student enrichment is an extremely difficult and important process, yet one that is often ignored, or, at best, given only cursory attention. This is unfortunate because student enrichment better than any other program segment provided through community education can tie the community education program of the public schools to the existing curriculum and achieve a first step toward positive curricular change.

CHAPTER VII

MARKETING AND MANAGEMENT IN COMMUNITY EDUCATION

In recent years marketing has moved from business to the nonprofit public sector. Colleges and universities in the 1980s staved off a predicted dramatic enrollment decline by implementing marketing strategies. Numerous nonprofit fund-raising organizations have built extensive national networks by using these techniques as well. In fact, public education seems to be the one significant arena where this has not occurred. This is surprising in that the concepts that undergird marketing are very consistent with good education, and in particular, good community education. Marketing incorporates three primary foundations or building blocks:

1. A consumer-needs orientation which reorients an organization from looking inward at its own needs to looking outward at consumer needs.

2. An integration of activity that recognizes that all parts of an organization must work together in a complimentary and integrated way. Everyone in the organization must share in the responsibility of caring about the people he or she serves and must accept responsibility for enhancing the organization's ability to provide that service.

3. A focus on consumer satisfaction and a concern for long-term consumer benefit and welfare. These are built into the organization's thinking.

How different are these three foundations from the goals we profess as community educators? Certainly we have a community-needs orientation, with the community as our "consumer" or "customer." We know that community education does not work well if all responsibility is given only to the community educator. Where good community education exists, broad organization support and involvement are present. And finally, our end goal is a satisfied community. We develop programs, services, and activities with the end goal of building a better community, and, in doing that, of assuring a supportive community that is pleased with its schools.

The reality is that the basic principles underlying marketing are very consistent with community education. Therefore, much that we can learn from marketing professionals is applicable to our programs and activities if we are willing to open our minds to knowledge and skills gained outside the traditional education system. This chapter will focus on some of the key ideas developed by marketing experts over time that are applicable to education, specifically to community education.

WHAT IS MARKETING?

The American Management Association Board defines marketing as "the process of planning and executing the conception, pricing, promotion, and distribution of ideas, goods, and services to create exchanges that satisfy individual organizational objectives."

Phillip Kotler, author of *Marketing for Non Profit Organizations* and co-author, with Karen Fox, of *Strategic Marketing for Education Institutions*, has defined marketing somewhat differently.

> Marketing is the analysis, planning, implementation and control of carefully formulated programs designed to bring about voluntary exchanges of values with target markets for the purpose of achieving organizational objectives. It relies heavily on designing the organization's offerings in terms of target markets' needs and desires, and on using effective pricing, communications, and distribution to inform, motivate and service the markets.[1]

This definition seems more applicable to the nonprofit, public sector than that of the AMA, but both are remarkably consistent when analyzed. Kotler's definition breaks down into five major components:

1. Analysis, planning, implementation, and control of programs. The "product" we offer—our programs and services—must be carefully developed and controlled to assure high quality service.

---

[1] Kotler, Phillip, *Marketing for Non Profit Organizations*, Second Edition, Prentice Hall, Englewood Cliffs, New Jersey, 1982, p. 6.

2. Carefully formulated programs designed for target markets focused on the needs and desires of those being served. We must design programs around the needs of those we serve, and we must really understand those needs with each unique group with which we work.

3. Programs and services that create an appropriate exchange of values. This means that both parties (those providing the service and those receiving it) must walk away from the relationship satisfied that good value was received.

4. Effective pricing, communication, and distribution of the programs and services built into the planning. Part of all thinking regarding the offering of anything must include consideration of pricing that assures adequate revenue and good value for the purchase, a means of effectively communicating the service or program and its benefits, and an appropriate and convenient means of providing that service.

5. A match created between the organization's objectives and the programs and services offered by it. And this needs to be an assumption in the nonprofit sector—that organizational objectives are built around public need and appropriate public service for the organization.

THE FOUR "P'S" OF MARKETING

Phillip Kotler also is known for his "Four P's" of marketing—the basic ingredients of any good marketing plan. Building on the basic principles described previously, Kotler suggests that all marketing planning is built on:

Product
Place
Price
Promotion[2]

---

[2] Kotler, Phillip, *Marketing for Non Profit Organizations,* Second Edition, Prentice Hall, Englewood Cliffs, New Jersey, 1982, p. 108.

PRODUCT

He suggests that the first effort pursued by any organization is to carefully think through and analyze the program or service that will be offered. This must be done in relationship to the organization's strength and ability, a careful analysis and understanding of those to be served, and a match between costs and the value of the service to be offered.

PLACE

Place is where or how the product will be offered. From a retail perspective, the best clothing line in the world will not succeed if a good distribution system is not in place. From a public school perspective, our service must be available at a time and location and in a sequence that makes it easily accessible. This might mean remote locations, applications of technology, or unique "packaging" that meets the time constraints of those being served.

PRICE

At some point in the planning process, a decision has to be made about the relationship between the program offered and the relative value of that program to the cost incurred, and to determine what your "customers" are willing to pay for that program and still feel that the "exchange of value" was appropriate. Good business is built around a relationship with customers that assures each transaction (relationship) between the business and the customer concludes with the customer feeling good about the relationship and the business receiving adequate compensation for the service. Nonprofit organizations must build the same relationship. When we provide a service, those receiving it need to feel good about it, and the program offered needs adequate funding to continue. This relationship should hold true whether or not the receiver of services pays directly for those services or indirectly through taxation.

PROMOTION

The last of the "Four P's" is perhaps the most misunderstood and most misused in community education. "Promotion" or "advertising" has become synonymous with marketing rather than a component of it. Many community educators skip past the need for careful analysis of program, location, and pricing and move immediately to promotion. Slick brochures, newspaper ads, or radio spots are often viewed as acceptable and appropriate marketing. This is not the case and, in fact, when pursued can cause more damage to the program than if nothing at all had been done. Good marketing is built around the creation of a relationship of trust between the individual and the organization. Advertising that does not build in careful program planning and analysis will invariably create a difference between what is promised and what is provided. This leads to ultimate distrust of those offering service.

MARKETING TERMS

A number of marketing terms exist that, when understood, help to relate both the importance of marketing to community education and the match between the philosophies undergirding marketing and community education. While this is not intended to be an inclusive presentation of marketing terminology, it is intended to present some of the key ideas.

NEEDS ASSESSMENT AND PERCEPTION ANALYSIS

Very sophisticated methods exist for analyzing the needs and desires of those we serve, going far beyond the traditional questionnaire. It is incumbent on professional community educators to learn and use these techniques. Part of the process is not only improving our understanding of those we serve, but also of getting constant feedback on our organization—how it is perceived and how it could be improved.

PRODUCT LIFE CYCLE/PRODUCT MOTIVATION

In business, every product has a life cycle, a time frame within which the product remains desirable. Hoola Hoops, Pet Rocks, and Cabbage Patch Dolls had a relatively short life cycle, popular one season and gone the next. Computers, specific modes of transportation, and communication devices, for example, have longer life cycles. In all instances, however, change will occur, with newer products and services replacing older ones. Products and services mature and decline, and the life cycle of that service peaks, declines, and ultimately ends.

Organizations, like products and services, also have life cycles. This shouldn't come as a surprise, as organizations are the providers of the goods and services, and all possess life cycle limitations. The company that created pet rocks as its single product had a life cycle matching that of the rock. Computer companies producing computers that did not keep pace with the changing demands of the work place shared the fate of their product.

Schools, just like other organizations, face the same reality. As their service becomes less meaningful to the general population, or fewer people find their service important, maturity and decline set in, both for the service provided and for the organization providing it. Chart I illustrates the life cycle principle.

CHART I—Product and Organizational Life Cycle

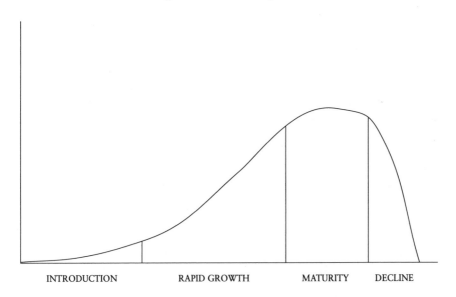

| INTRODUCTION | RAPID GROWTH | MATURITY | DECLINE |

A normal product-organization life cycle usually has a slow start-up as a new, untried innovation and then picks up and grows rapidly as the service becomes viewed as important. At some point, the need for the service is saturated and decline sets in.

While specific services and products face this process as an inevitable end, organizations do not have to accept that same end. Most organizations provide multiple services. To the extent that they are continually involved in innovation and change, with shifts from old and less needed services to new and needed ones, organizations' growth and maturity can continue indefinitely. Chart II demonstrates how new innovations, built on already existing products and services, extend the life cycle process. This can be repeated as long as the organization reflects and incorporates services that reflect changing needs.

CHART II—Product and Organizational Life Cycle—Extended Life

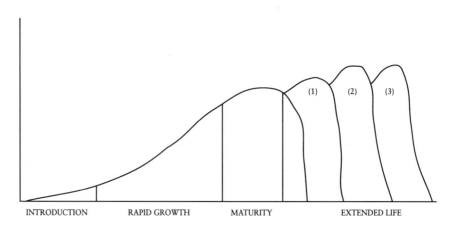

INTRODUCTION   RAPID GROWTH   MATURITY   EXTENDED LIFE

MARKET SEGMENTATION AND TARGET MARKETING

Community educators serve a very broad and diverse population. We often serve elementary children, teenagers, and adults. We serve rich and poor, men and women, the employed and the unemployed, and many races and cultures. The mixture of needs that can be combined is virtually inexhaustible. Often, people planning programs in community education do not consider these many variables and attempt to program for all people in one program. How can we believe that the needs of a young mother have any relationship to those of a recently retired senior, or, for that matter, the needs of a wealthy young mother to one who is raising a child in poverty? Market segmentation is a process that allows for a structured differentiation of who we are serving and recognizing the needs of those we try to serve. Target marketing takes market segmentation one step further, breaking down the broad spectrum of those we want to serve into reasonably-sized groupings with common needs and concerns. This provides the base for program planning that matches service with unique need.

ENVIRONMENTAL SCANNING

This concept encourages organizations to keep aware of what is going on in the environment in which they operate. All organizations are affected by the changing world in which they operate. Keeping aware of those changes and building an analysis of them and their potential impact is an important part of planning and marketing. As our society becomes older and the wealth of the society increasingly shifts to our senior population, what impact does this have on our planning and programs? As our schools increasingly struggle with a youth population that is more violent, rejecting traditional societal values, how does that affect our programming and planning? By analyzing demographics and a variety of studies and simply becoming more aware of environmental influences, we improve our ability to provide effective services.

MARKETING MIX

Marketing mix refers to how the "Four P's"—Product, Place, Price, and Promotion—are interrelated in a plan. At some point in the development of a service, where and how it will be provided and advertised is tied together with cost and how that cost will be met. This combination is referred to as a "marketing mix."

As new programs and services are developed, built around community and individual needs, this is one of the great unrealized potential opportunities for community education—keeping our schools relevant.

With the preceding offered as a brief overview on marketing and its potential application, it is suggested that a new arena and a new opportunity for community educators is the development of a marketing plan within each school district, a plan that will provide an essential service to our schools and for our communities.

CREATING A MARKETING PLAN

Marketing plans are built around the following structure:

1. Defining a general goal (for the organization, those to be served, or the service to be provided);
2. Segmenting the market and creating a target market;
3. Developing an appropriate marketing mix that defines service, location, cost, and promotion;
4. Evaluating, eliciting feedback, and making revisions to the programs or services.

Community education can become the research and development component of our education system. We must first redefine the skills, roles, and responsibilities of community education professionals. And we must build in the concept as an integral part of education, not the "add on" it often becomes with the possibility of being eliminated whenever financial difficulties arise.

EMERGING MANAGEMENT CONCEPTS

THE QUALITY REVOLUTION

In the last decade there has been a fundamental shift in American management thinking. Ideas about management that started in Japan and the Far East have been increasingly embraced by American business and industry. While the change started with business and industry, it is increasingly being picked up in public and nonprofit organizations. Just as education built its management system in the past around business concepts, so, too, is it incorporating this "new" management concept.

The new concepts go by many names—Total Quality Management, Continuous Quality Improvement, Total Quality Improvement, Total Quality Process, and Continuous Improvement Process. Regardless of the name, they all represent a fundamental shift in focus toward quality, they all share common principles, and they all are part of a worldwide shift commonly referred to as "The Quality Movement."

AN HISTORICAL PERSPECTIVE

Many management fads have come and gone in this country over the past decades. Most have failed because of either a fundamental flaw in the concepts or a misuse or misunderstanding of the ideas presented. Continuous Quality Improvement (our favorite term for education) is unlike past changes in two significant ways. First, it is not new. It began in Japan after World War II and has since been refined and improved as a system. It was introduced to the Japanese by an American, Dr. W. Edward Deming, so it is also not uniquely Japanese. It has been introduced into other countries over the past several decades where it has also shown success. It is a proven concept that works. Second, it is built on fundamental management concepts that have been accepted for years. While it combines these concepts in different and often complex ways, Continuous Quality Improvement brings us back to the basics. The three major thinkers in the Quality movement are all Americans: W. Edward Deming, Joseph Juran, and Phillip Crosby. In fact, much of the early writing in support of the management concept was done by Americans for American business and industry.

CONTINUOUS QUALITY IMPROVEMENT PRINCIPLES

Many writers have attempted to distill the key elements in this concept. Most will include, in some fashion, the following:

1. Quality is defined by the needs and expectations of those served.
2. Continuous improvement becomes a way of life in an organization, and it is never ending.
3. Decisions are made based upon data and facts, and processes are in place to assure good information.
4. Continuous Quality Improvement is systems focused, incorporating vision, mission, goals, methods, and action for constant improvement.
5. Continuous Quality Improvement is team-based, built around a shared respect for all in the process.

These principles become the framework for organization structure and activity. It is important to note that principles that focus on service, respect for others, and team-based structures are far more consistent with educational values than are older hierarchical structures. And yet, education is only recently discovering and incorporating this concept.

CONTINUOUS QUALITY IMPROVEMENT

To understand how truly revolutionary this concept is, the following comparison demonstrates the difference between old organization thinking and newer thinking.

Comparison of New and Old Organization Thinking

Old Organization	New Organization
Top Down Control	Local Control United by Purpose
Focus on Each Operating Unit	Focus on the Whole System
Units Organized Hierarchically	Flat, Mobile Flexible Structure
Competition Between Units	Cooperation, Teamwork
Change is Disruptive	Change is Expected
Information is Controlled	Open Information Systems

For community educators, reform and school restructuring are wonderful opportunities. We have always been in the forefront of change, new direction, and new service focused on community needs. We have done that in an organization structured around the education of children within a narrowly defined concept of education.

Suddenly we have the Carnegie Commission's call for reform and America 2000 (now Goals 2000), a national response demanding change in our schools, committed to by virtually every state governor. And from the local level, we see a virtual revolution in our constituent base demanding change and reform in our schools. To accomplish the changes demanded, we cannot possibly hope to move forward with an organization structure based on 1920s and 1930s thinking.

And for community educators, a system has emerged that closely fits their beliefs. Concepts such as respect for all in the process, listening to what your community (customer) wants, building programs and systems around what is needed and wanted by those you serve, are all basic parts of the new concept. Community educators need to learn as much as possible about the new concept and then help bring it forward in their own schools. We can help create change not only in the communities we serve, but within the institutions that provide that service.

CONTINUOUS QUALITY IMPROVEMENT GENERALIZATIONS

While the principles described earlier provide the foundation of the concept, the following generalizations help to assure that it is implemented successfully.

1. Management commitment is key to success. Top management must understand, be committed, and provide long-term leadership.

2. Systems and systems thinking are the core of the effort. Structure and strategy that are clear and communicated well throughout the organization are essential.

3. The Continuous Quality transformation depends on the knowledge, skills, and abilities of people at all levels of the organiza-

tion. It requires an ongoing commitment to learning through never ending training and staff development. Leaders must model, coach, and reinforce the new behaviors required.

4. Quality is measurable and definable. Decision making and focused improvement must be built around good data and information.

5. The initial focus of CQI is problem prevention. It allows an organization to identify its most important problems and opportunities and to systematically address them.

6. Prevention is not enough. The focus must shift over time to continuous improvements and innovation. The organization expects constant improvement and the staff is committed to it.

WHY CHANGE?

Change has always been with us, and for those who forget this basic truth, here are numerous embarrassing examples to help us remember:

"Everything that can be invented has been invented."

—Charles H. Duell, Director of U.S. Patent Office, 1899

"Who the hell wants to hear actors talk?"

—Harry M. Warner, Warner Bros. Pictures C. 1927

"Sensible and responsible women do not want to vote."

—Grover Cleveland, 1905

"There is no likelihood man can ever tap the power of the atom."

—Robert Millikan, Nobel Prize in Physics, 1923

"Heavier than air flying machines are impossible."

—Lord Kelvin, President, Royal Society, C. 1895

"Ruth made a big mistake when he gave up pitching."

—Tris Speaker, 1921

While change has been a constant part of the human experience, the generations living today never have experienced the kind of change we now face.

We are undergoing a fundamental restructuring that is different from anything we have known. In fact, some historians have suggested that the extensive change we are now facing occurs only once every few hundred years.

The last change of this magnitude was the transition into the Industrial Revolution. That move was basically one from farm to city, from agriculture to manufacturing. And the impact of the change affected everything—from where we live and how we work to how we think and act and what we believe to be important or unimportant. As we look back on that period of history and trace its impact, we realize the advantages and disadvantages that fundamental change brought. Whatever the value we place on change, the fact is we were drastically changed.

As we look at our current time, we recognize that as a nation we have become used to change, or, perhaps, immune to it. The expression, "The only constant is change," has become a hallmark of American society. It is important for us to recognize, however, that change itself is changing and that the changes we have experienced in the past are not the same as the change we are experiencing now. We need to differentiate between fundamental and incremental change.

Incremental change is the type we have been experiencing—change that builds upon previous change but doesn't modify basic structures. A school, for example, can modify its curriculum by modifying courses within it, adding or substituting a course, or shifting an emphasis. Change is clearly present, but the fundamental curriculum structure remains.

Fundamental change occurs when the curriculum itself is deemed unacceptable, and, therefore, the concepts behind the course work offered are no longer accepted. At that point, everything changes and many of the old rules, those past unquestioned concepts, are no longer valid. When we decided to go into space, we didn't try to rethink the jumbo jet, looking for ways to improve wind design or increase jet engine power. Space presented an entirely different environment, and the ship that could successfully navigate it had to be fundamentally rethought.

Alvin Toffler, in his book, *Learning for Tomorrow*, has a marvelous story that demonstrates this important difference. Toffler talks about a tribe of natives who lived in an Amazon jungle, disconnected from civilization. One of the tribesman was thinking about how to prepare his son for the future. So, in thinking about the future, he began to contemplate things. He thought about how his father before him had always lived there on the river, and about how he, himself, lived on the river. Thus, he concluded that it would be very important for him to educate his son in how to live on the river—how to fish and build boats and swim, and so on. His conclusion was a perfectly logical one. His vision of the future was based on what is and what has been, on what he knew and understood. What he didn't know, though, was that 500 miles upstream there was another tribe that had developed a technology enabling the tribesmen to build dams. And they were busily engaged in building a giant dam across the headwaters of this river. In the Spring, the river would no longer be there.[3]

The tribe in Toffler's story didn't face incremental change—how to better live on the river. They faced a fundamental restructuring of their lives—how to live when the focal point of their lives no longer existed. We are now living in one of those transitional periods called by many names—"The Second Industrial Revolution," "The Knowledge Revolution," or "The Third Wave." They all suggest fundamental restructuring.

Our advantage as a society is that we have advanced enough in our knowledge and understanding to know that it is happening, and, in knowing, to be able to make some choices for our future. By knowing, we can't change the trends, but we can modify them to reduce their negative effects and expand the positive opportunities they bring.

We are now in a worldwide competitive restructuring that will determine the new "have" and "have-not" nations of the twenty-first century. We have watched our auto industry ignore this trend at its peril. Advanced technology that we once owned is now dominated by others, and basic manufacturing is being closed in this country to be started elsewhere with better and cheaper goods.

In the early 1980s, Michigan, so dependent on the auto industry, was one of the first states to feel the impact of this change. The industry's dramatic struggle to learn to compete worldwide had a wrenching im-

---

[3] Toffler, Alvin, *Learning for Tomorrow*, Random House, New York, 1974, p. 3–4.

pact on the state. A group of economists was brought together to define the problem and propose a policy for dealing with it. The result of the group's effort was a paper, "Path to Prosperity." Though it was focused on Michigan and is now out of print, the conclusions presented in the paper are appropriate for a much broader and current review. Three options were presented: think poor, think different, or think smart.

Think Poor.   This option was to attempt to compete and not make changes. As cheaper labor in other parts of the world drove prices down, this choice meant lowering costs to match. The problem, of course, was that by continually lowering wages to match those elsewhere in the world, we would destroy the social structure and quality of life that Americans enjoy and expect. This was not viewed as a viable option but was suggested as a realistic result if change did not occur. It was, in fact, the natural result if other choices were not made.

Think Different.   This option suggested that by fully embracing the most advanced technologies, making rapid and constant change at the most advanced level of the competitive spectrum, we could sustain current life styles and worldwide competitiveness. It meant that the industry would have to leave Michigan's manufacturing base for whatever technological option had the greatest potential. While this was viewed as a potential choice, it brought with it extremely high costs, high risks, and the need for an exceptionally advanced and highly educated workforce. It also meant high unemployment levels for those in the society that could not or would not reach the necessary levels of education. While parts of this concept could be incorporated into any new plan, it left large segments of the society unable to participate.

Think Smart.   This option suggested that the focus needed to shift from the idea of capital investment to one of human investment. By building on the natural productivity and talent of our workforce through constant training, education, and skill development, we could create an exceptionally competitive society. Building on the manufacturing base that was already in place would make tremendous capital costs manageable, and the focus would be one of productivity with high wages. The focal point of a society that "thought smart" had to be knowledge institutions— schools, colleges, training centers, etc.

The conclusion of the report, of course, was that the only real option was the "Think Smart" option, and it required a rethinking, a "fundamental" change in how we looked at what is most important to the society.

As educators, we now have moved to center stage as our democracy attempts to cope with the worldwide shifts now upon us. Make no mistake, we are experiencing a fundamental shift in thinking, and the easy answers we have provided to deal with change in the past no longer are acceptable.

THE PUSH FOR SCHOOL REFORM

As we think about the fundamental restructuring we are experiencing, with its critical need for a "smart" workforce, the demand for education reform comes into focus. At the core of it all is the fear of the public that our schools are not good enough to meet these very new and different needs, and if our schools fail . . . we all fail. Our citizens are struggling to define the specific changes that need to be made, but they share a sense that a mismatch exists; a mismatch between what society needs and what our schools are providing. This same sense of mismatch also exists with our national policies . . . a sense that what we are doing and where we are heading doesn't fit with a new and very different world. The frustration our nation is experiencing with government and schools stems from the same basic sense of wrong direction. The push for testing, a core curriculum, a back-to-the-basics approach is all part of this sense of unease and a reaction to it. As educators, we are in the center of a large scale realignment, and we ignore reform at our peril. The forces of change will find ways of assuring a skilled and knowledgeable workforce that can compete internationally. If the schools fail in this respect, other organizations and systems will emerge to accomplish the task. We sometimes think of our education system as here forever, no matter what. A quick look at the history of organizations would suggest this to be a very foolish view. Organizations survive when they meet social needs; they die when they do not.

There are numerous examples in other advanced nations of very different options for education. In most western and advanced eastern countries, a very close relationship exists between schools and the workplace.

Students graduating from high schools have very specific and applicable skills that are usable in the workplace. Employers provide extensive training during employment to assure a competent and knowledgeable workforce capable of assuming world class competitiveness. Nippon Denso, a worldwide Japanese manufacturer, employs high school graduates and then trains them for one full year before they begin productive work. The manufacturer does this at very expensive training centers while paying those being trained a regular salary. The "graduates" of this training are then "allowed" to begin working on the company's production lines. The production lines, of course, are fully automated, and each of the employees is a trained specialist in the repair and maintenance of highly automated and advanced machinery.

In our country, we are seeing the beginnings of this same involvement by manufacturers. They are taking responsibility for the training of their workers. The difference is that they have no sense of partnership with the schools and are not building on a commonly agreed on set of skills and knowledge. Instead, they are angry about the quality of our graduates and are focusing on training programs that provide lower level skills and basic entry requirements, tasks they believe belong to the schools.

The American school system faces a significant possibility of being replaced rather than being incorporated into the new, emerging system of education. As educators, we represent a large, cumbersome, and often very bureaucratic system designed to meet the education needs of a society that no longer exists. While we have made incremental change over the past 150 years, incremental change will no longer work. Just as we could not tinker with the jumbo jet to make it a space ship, we cannot look to small reforms in our schools to meet the worldwide changes now upon us. Our schools and our educators are not well equipped to make this change. By and large, as individuals and organizations, educators have been the protectors of the status quo. Change does not come easily to us. The following story about naval gunnery officers illustrates our resistance to change.

In the early days of the American Navy, one of the most important persons on the ship was the gunnery officer. Shooting a gun from a rolling and pitching ship and hitting the target was a true art form requiring significant experience, training, and knowledge. As the ship rose, fell, and twisted, the gunnery officer had to judge the target distance and the degree of the cannon, anticipate the roll and twist of the ship, and judge the timing in lighting the fuse. The gunnery officer was critical to the ship's welfare. In a sea battle a good gunnery officer could win the battle, a poor one could lose the battle and sink the ship.

During this time, several young naval officers used math and engineering to develop a way to keep the cannon pointed where they wanted regardless of the roll of the ship. It allowed accuracy far beyond the achievements of the very best gunnery officers. But it took over two decades to implement this innovation because it threatened the stature of the gunnery officers, and they rejected the change for all that time.

We in education are in danger of being the modern version of these naval gunnery officers. The extent of change now demanded by our society may be beyond our ability to effectively cope with it. And upon this question, we believe, hangs the future of American education.

ENTER COMMUNITY EDUCATION

There is one segment of the education community that historically has embraced change, or at least that is how it began. Community education started as a response to needed social change and has viewed its role as one of incorporating those needed changes into the system. It is unclear if being the best change agents of a culture known for its unwillingness to change is enough, but we are the best hope, now operating in our schools, for fundamental reform.

While we have been change agents in the past, we have always been agents for incremental change. We have added a program here, modified a program there. We have not dealt with the implementation of fundamental reform which, as suggested earlier, requires the rethinking of our basic understanding of what school is and what it does.

Community educators, if they are to be the change agents needed in this emerging world, must start by assuming everything is open to challenge. We must be prepared to rethink, modify, and eliminate. We must prepare for significant, sometimes radical, change. We must be prepared for this both for ourselves and for the programs we run, and we must become leaders in the inevitable process of change required for our institutions.

Community educators have a unique position. As insiders in the schools system, we can work for positive change and not be viewed as outsiders attacking our schools. As people focus on community needs, we can help prepare most communities to understand the changes that are needed and build community support for them. Our ability to unshackle our minds from the past and look at new and different options will be the critical element in whether or not we change enough to remain a viable part of our emerging future.

Community educators are exceptionally well placed to play a pivotal role in adult education, student enrichment, and parent and community involvement.

A society that is going to be built around knowledge and skills will require adult learning opportunities on a scale not yet imagined. Programs will be needed for adults who do not possess basic skills and for those who have very advanced skills that need constant updating. While programs will need fundamental reform in what is taught and how it is offered, a public school adult education structure is in place, and community educators are responsible for it.

Student enrichment, in the past, often has been focused on fun, hobby, and leisure types of activities. It could become the means of pushing fundamental reform into the core curriculum. By focusing on new needs and creating programs that successfully and creatively meet those needs, community education can become the experimental arm of fundamental curriculum reform.

Change that is as extensive as that which we face can occur only with the support of parents and other members of the community. As public institutions, our schools can change only as fast as these two groups allow. Community educators have natural ties with both parents and the community. In fact, it could be argued that we are the only public educators who have that relationship as a fundamental part of our function. Parents and the broader community need to be comfortable that the change being made is in the best interest of their children and, indeed, of the entire community. They must be active partners in the thought process and in the resulting decisions for change. Beyond planning for their children's education, our communities also need to gain a better understanding of the fundamental change that is affecting everyone's lives.

RESTRUCTURING EDUCATION

Community educators should be able to bring to any discussion on curriculum reform a broad knowledge of the community that is being served. We should be the voice of the community in these discussions. In addition, to the extent we are knowledgeable about the change process itself and the direction American education needs to go, we become essential players in that rethinking. We need to begin to view ourselves as internal change agents, and we need to develop new knowledge and skills that make us competent to carry out that responsibility.

We are reminded of an old saying from *Readers Digest*: "Even if you're on the right track, you'll get run over if you just sit there." American educators and community education first need to find the right track. And the one thing we know is that we are not yet on it. Once we find the right track, we need to aggressively pursue necessary change. If we fail to do this, we will be "run over" by other organizations, other people more in tune with the change necessary for our long-term survival. America, as a nation, will adapt, and survive. Schools, as we know them, may not.

CHAPTER VIII

IMPLEMENTATION AND DEVELOPMENT

CHANGES IN AMERICAN EDUCATION

To talk about the implementation and development of community education through a community school, it is important to recognize the nature of the change being recommended to the schools. In education, as in many fields, change often implies a superficial rearrangement of the existing programs without genuine change in the structure, a rearranging of the furniture, so to speak. Change frequently has implied some nominal tinkering with textbooks or curricula or an accretion of programs in a manner that provides little threat to the comfort zones of school persons.

One other observation should also be noted about change. There is usually an altering of the perception of change, based on age and experience. In our younger years, we tend to think of change as linear with inclines and plateaus. We feel that change becomes stagnant, then accelerates through pressures brought on the "establishment," then plateaus, and so on.

FIGURE 1—An Inexperienced View of Change

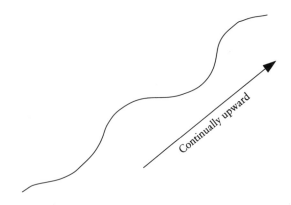

Continually upward

As we grow older and experience more changes, our perception of change is that it is more cyclical. And while there probably still is an upward direction to change, many of the ideas introduced as new are often perceived as old ideas with new names (Figure 2). Thus, one-room school houses gave way to grades and grouping, which, in turn, gave way to non-graded, open classrooms and cross-aged tutoring. Likewise, separate subjects were combined into areas such as language arts and social science, which were further combined into core curriculum and fused curriculum. These latter programs have now been broken down into separate subjects under the rubric of modular scheduling and mini-courses. Another example would be the school libraries, which were abandoned under the self-contained classroom plan and then reinstituted under the media center concept. The point is that old ideas keep coming back but with different names, and the frequent excitement about community schools, too, might be thought of as part of this cyclical pattern; indeed, many people have pointed out that most of the suggestions related to community schools are things that used to be considered well within the role of the public schools. Community schools, however, also imply something broader and more intense than a change involving the mere addition or return of some programs to the regular school, or increasing the areas of responsibility of the public schools, or changing the descriptors involved in describing what public education is all about.

FIGURE 2—An Experienced View of Change

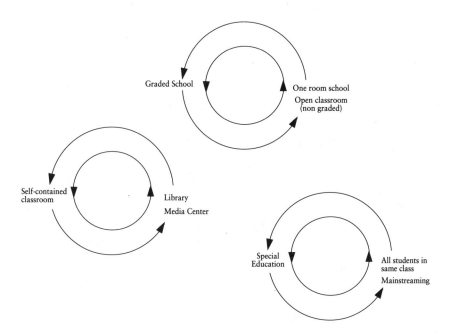

This change in role for public schools should not be bothersome to school people. This is not the first time schools have been challenged about the appropriateness of their roles. In fact, it will not be the first time they have responded to public demand by making a dramatic change in their role. This point was made in Chapter I, but it might be appropriate to review it quickly again.

The first school system we had in this country was the Latin Grammar School. It existed from 1635 to 1780. Its purpose was to train people to be good citizens, provide basic skills for a rather elitist group of citizens, and prepare students for entry into college in preparation for the professions of law, medicine, or ministry. These were the days of "old DeLuder Satan," and the best way to cope with such evil was to teach people how to read the Bible.

By the 1750s, there was great disenchantment with that school system. It was felt that American society had changed and that the school system should change accordingly. One of the leaders in such thinking was Benjamin Franklin, and through his efforts, a new era in schools called the American Academy was ushered in. These schools were co-educational, oriented to the middle-class, locally controlled, and stressed vocational training. Even though these schools dominated the American education scene for over 100 years (1750–1860), they began to lose popularity because of their preoccupation with college bound students. And so, another change took place.

This change is described as the Early Public Education Era (1821–1890). This was the first real attempt at free public education, and its popularity is reflected in the fact that the number of public schools grew from 325 to 2,500 in just a few years.

The forerunner of today's schools, however, was yet to come. The "Granddaddy" of today's schools was the outgrowth of a famous law case. In 1874, the Kalamazoo Case held that children were entitled to free public education until grade 12. The case ushered in the modern high school era which appeared on the American scene in 1890 and took us from 2,500 secondary schools to in excess of 25,000 in approximately 15,000 school districts.

The point in tracing this history is to show that suggesting a change in the role of the public schools is neither unusual nor totally unreasonable. The role of the public schools has changed at least four times in the history of America, and each change has come about because the program failed to respond to the needs of the society it was supposed to be serving. It appears likely that the circumstances that precipitated previous changes (lack of relevance) will happen again, and community schools may be the fifth major change in American education.

SUCCESSES IN EDUCATION

Dissatisfaction with the schools does not imply that everything the schools are doing is wrong. Even though they do receive a great deal of criticism, they have much to be proud of. Our schools have made us one of the most literate nations in the world, and three-quarters of our youth are graduating from high school. Thirty-two percent of our industrial growth has been credited to our education system, and about eight percent of our gross national product is the result of that system. Each year, several national studies show that despite criticism, our schools have more public support than any other segment of our society. Henry Steel Commager, speaking about our American society, has said, "No people have demanded so much of education. No other people have fared so well from their schools."

CONCERNS ABOUT THE PUBLIC SCHOOLS

While the term failure may overstate the situation, we have created a set of hypocrisies in education—things we, as educators, say we believe and yet in practice do not carry out. Following are some examples.

1. We say that the first few years of life are extremely important in terms of influencing ability to learn and developing attitudes, yet we provide few education programs for children under the age of five.

2. We say that children are products of their total environment, yet we continue to perform as though the totality of education is a result of experiences in school.

3. We have convinced our public of the relationship between education and social and economic success, and yet we deny the opportunity of education to large segments of our society.

4. We subscribe to broad education goals and then tend to stress only those programs related to cognitive learning.

5. We put large amounts of money into physical facilities but use such facilities only a small portion of their potential operational time.

6. We stress local control of schools and then deny viable input into the school operation by our communities.

7. We believe that education is a lifetime process, yet we operate as though our need for education stops at age 18.

8. We deplore duplication and waste, yet we do little to maximize the efficient coordination of our services with others or to assist in effectively bringing together problems and resources.

9. We preach participatory democracy, yet we do little to encourage the development of local advocacy or problem solving.

10. We have described education as preparation for life, yet our schools have lost a great deal of their relevancy.

THE FUTURISTS

Community school people have not been alone in their concern about changing schools or addressing these hypocrisies. A new cadre of writers and advocates called futurists have emerged to add their voices to a request for change. People like Harold Grant, Alvin Toffler, and Eric Hoffer have all suggested new and exciting roles for public schools.

Typical of this group was Mario Fantini, who suggested that education would become the dominant coordinating force for society. He felt that education would have a high priority in our post industrial society. He saw us moving from compulsory schooling to compulsory education in which we would still be interested in basic literacy, knowledge, and vocation training, but would also move more completely into personal growth, talent development, and competence in major societal roles. He predicted that the community would have more involvement in the education process in giving us direction as well as helping us to educate. He saw the school system becoming the orchestrator for many alternatives—the learner advocate.[1]

CHANGE AND IMPLEMENTATION

To this point, we have discussed major changes that have taken place in the American schools; some reasons why changes are needed in the public schools, regardless of some of their strengths; and some of the directions the futurists are suggesting for change.

There is still one more area of change that needs to be discussed because of its implication for the implementation of community schools. Change is a product of time, concept, leadership, and energy invested. The effectiveness of change will depend on whether the time is right, how sophisticated the idea is, what kind of leadership is applied, and how much time is invested in developing the idea.

If all of these characteristics are operable, then change will take place. If some are weak, then change may take place if the other components are strong enough to compensate for those that are not (i.e., extra strong leadership might make up for a mediocre concept). If components are missing, however, the change usually will not take place (i.e., hard workers with no leadership will fail as will a good concept promoted at the wrong time).

It should also be kept in mind that there is a corollary to this principle. Change will depend on how well the group promoting the change can master the components of change as compared to how well their adversaries can resist the change by using the same components. In other words, your time, concept, leadership, and energy must exceed those of your opponent.

Furthermore, the energy component is multiple, not linear. The amount of time one group invests to establish its idea must be increased by the other groups that want to throw it out. Thus, a group that has

---

[1] Fantini, Mario D. "From School System to Education System," *Phi Delta Kappan*, September, 1975, pp. 10–12.

invested two weeks of energy on a project will find that an anti-group may require four weeks to counter those efforts. This progression continues so that people who have invested eight months of time will have created a situation in which it might take as much as one year to counter their efforts. The lesson here is that if any group wants to make change, it should master the components of change and invest enough energy so that the chances of being countered by another group are minimal.

One last thought on change. Change also will depend on how well we can assure the comfort zones of the people in positions of power. When people first assume new responsibilities, they have a rather nebulous feeling about their areas of responsibility because they are uncertain of the parameters of their position. As time goes on, however, they begin to develop new perceptions from their knowledge and experience and soon develop a comfort zone which gives them the feeling of confidence and assurance. Any suggestions for change, particularly from outsiders, disturb the parameters, tear down the confidences, and recreate the uncertainties of the neophyte. The resultant behavior is resistance, alienation, and confrontation.

To guard against this phenomenon, it is important that those in power be permitted to maintain their comfort zones. This can be accomplished by allowing enough time in the change process for them to rearrange their comfort zone commensurate with the change suggested and by selling them ownership in the change. While it may be difficult for those suggesting change to be denied credit, it is important to remember that effective change often comes because members of the so-called "establishment" were able to claim the idea as theirs rather than one that was forced on them. Change will not come about for those whose egos demand ownership or who precipitate win-lose situations.

IMPLEMENTING THE CONCEPT

The development of community education is an evolutionary process that must begin and grow through the involvement of those to be affected by it. In fact, it would be a violation of the precepts of community education if it were developed in any other way. Community education surmises that common problems can be identified and resolved through involvement of community members and that programs will develop from community needs. Both programs and process imply involvement, and it would certainly seem illogical to suppose that a concept proclaiming the need for community involvement should begin without such involvement at its inception. Community education proclaims the belief that people should be done *with* and not *to*, and this belief should be incorporated from the beginning.

The initial contact should probably be made with the superintendent of schools. This is important because of the comments made earlier in this chapter about comfort zones. Superintendents are the primary leaders in the public schools, and their support for any change is absolutely essential. If the superintendent becomes interested in community education and is allowed to promote the idea as though it were his or her own, then the concept of community education has an excellent chance of being implemented. If the superintendent is not given this opportunity, the chances for success are greatly diminished. And usually, the superintendent's opposition will not take the form of confrontation but of delay, manipulation, and "killing the idea with kindness." Whether or not other administrators are involved and when they are involved should be up to the superintendent. It should be remembered, however, that the principles of involvement that apply to the superintendent apply to other administrators as well.

Interest in community education may develop in many loci within the community. Since it is the thesis of this text that it is to operate through the school system, it is imperative that the board of education, as the governing body of the school district, be the next point of contact of those desiring to implement community education. Until the board is willing to make certain basic commitments to the support of community education, there is little to be gained and much to be lost by any attempt to coerce or by-pass the decision-making body within the school system.

The initial contact with the board of education will be primarily one of information giving, and this step will have to be repeated with all groups in the community. In such presentations, there is no set pattern for selection of participants. Presentations may be made to board members exclusively or to the board members plus representative groups of teachers, administrators, and community members. In general, it has been found that community members are more readily receptive to the ideas embodied in community education, and board members consequently become more receptive when they are aware of the positive community acceptance of the concept.

At any rate, the first exposure should be a peripheral kind of presentation aimed at the overt advantages of opening schools and developing programs for community members. This presentation is intended to initiate the concept at an elementary level of understanding. The concept of community education is difficult to understand in its entirety. In addition, it is a dramatic philosophical change in educational belief. This combination of depth of conceptualization and change in traditional belief makes it almost mandatory that community education be introduced at the rate in which it can be absorbed rather than by overwhelming the listeners in an initial contact and subsequently making them apprehensive about any commitment.

The initial presentation to the board will set the tone for future activities in implementing community education. It may be that the board and others represented are not interested in implementing the concept. If this is true, then any additional efforts should be suspended until they are interested. To proceed further would be self-defeating. Experience has shown that even when no obvious interest is demonstrated, the seed has often been planted, and interest may reappear at a later date.

Under no circumstance should the board of education decide unilaterally to begin community education. This type of arbitrary decision making will only arouse suspicion and bring future problems to the program. The primary rule to follow is to move slowly and involve all those to be affected.

If the board is interested in pursuing community education, then several things should happen without any particular reference to sequence. Many additional presentations on community education should be made to the community and to the professional staff. School administrators must be made aware of the concept and its relation to their programs. Teachers must be exposed to this basic change in program and philosophy. Noncertificated staff must be made aware of what is going on, and community members must also be included in these introductory presentations. The kinds of presentations made to these groups must be similar to those first made to the board of education. Community education should be presented and explained to the degree necessary and the appropriate level of receptivity of the group. It will be the responsibility of those making the presentation to decide what this level should be. Again, let it be stated that there is no intention to defraud or to disguise community education or to claim it to be what it is not. It must be remembered that community education is a combination of programs and process comprised of student activities, use of buildings, adult activities, community service, community coordination, and community self-actualization. While the ultimate goal is to accomplish this in its entirety, it should be accomplished at the rate and to the degree to which the community is ready and able to assimilate it.

At the same time that the staff and community are receiving this exposure, it is necessary to work more intensely with the chief administrator and the board of education. If efforts are to proceed, it is important that key persons within the district be aware of the complete concept of community education and the ultimate direction in which they are moving. This is necessary so that, at a later date, the development of community education is not inhibited because of poor initial communication with the chief decision makers.

This intensive consultation should more thoroughly present the concept and its ramifications. School officials should be made aware of costs, financing, staffing, and particularly of the new role the school is assuming in its community. Again, it should be restated that if at any point there is a reluctance to proceed, all efforts should be suspended until there is a recognized need for community education within the district.

If there is, at this point, a desire to continue, then it becomes necessary to work in greater depth with the community and staff. It is recommended that a committee be appointed by the board of education to further study the concept. This committee should include representatives of the faculty, noncertificated staff, students, lay community, churches, government agencies, social agencies, service groups, and any other groups, formal or informal, who are representative of the community. This committee should now be given a more thorough exposure to the concept and its implications. Every effort should be made to familiarize this group with the theory and practice of community education. Formal presentations, work sessions, study groups, and visitations are all ways of enhancing the group's knowledge. The board of education should entrust this group with the task of completely exploring the topic and charge it with the responsibility of recommending further action to the board.

The time involved in this total activity to this point will vary. It may take a few months or stretch over a much longer period of time. While every effort should be made to keep things moving and avoid stagnation, it should be kept in mind that the most successful community education programs grow out of well-conceived plans developed by well-informed people.

THE STUDY COMMITTEE

The role of the study committee is a key one in the institution of a community school. It is the responsibility of this committee to investigate the community education concept and make appropriate recommendations to the board of education. While the involvement and presentations to this point have been relatively cursory, the in-depth analysis now becomes the responsibility of this study committee. Members of the group should be aware constantly that the future of community education in their community depends on their efforts and that they are responsible for being fully informed and recommending the direction their school district should take.

The committee must be representative of the community. Consideration should be given to the various groups within the community—organizations, government agencies, social groups, and various community subdivisions. Efforts should be made to include both the overt "power" structure and the less obvious leadership in the community. The selection of the membership of this group will greatly determine its future acceptance throughout the community. Special attention should be given to selecting people who are truly representative of the community rather than those who occupy certain "traditional positions," but do not reflect community thinking or exercise substantial community leadership.

Size is also an important factor to consider. While a small committee may prove to be more efficient and more manageable, it is doubtful if a small committee (less than 15 people) can be truly representative of the community. On the other hand, an excessively large committee (more than 50) becomes so cumbersome and unwieldy that it is difficult to get anything accomplished. The optimum size is somewhere between 15 and 50, the number depending primarily on the criteria necessary for ample community representation.

Members of the group should be those who are dependable and ambitious and who have time to devote to the study. While certain people may be desirable, it is not beneficial to the final outcome to select people who do not have time to devote to this endeavor.

After the study group is selected, members should be given certain guidelines on their function. The purpose of their efforts should be explained to them thoroughly. They should know the direction and the limitations of their function at the outset. This keeps them from wandering about in other areas and assuming responsibilities for which they were not selected. The group should also understand that its task is to complete the study and make recommendations to the board of education. Members should understand that the final decision belongs to the board, and they should be prepared to receive either an acceptance or a rejection for their efforts. This preliminary clarification will keep them from misinterpreting their role and prepare them for the possibility of a negative board reaction. In addition, the group should be given a formal appointment by the board of education, giving members a sense both of legitimacy and importance and allowing them to start on a positive note.

It is also wise, at the beginning, to set a temporary time schedule for the group. While it can be adjusted periodically, a time schedule forces the group to keep moving and places some degree of accountability for time. The committee should also be made aware of a terminal date for its activities. Generally, the committee ceases to function after it presents its final report to the board of education, thus the committee sees an end to its responsibilities, and the problems related to an indefinite appointment or an existing committee with nothing to do are eliminated.

To properly make its recommendation, the committee will have to do two things. First, it will have to understand community education as completely as is possible. This can be accomplished by reading extensively on the subject; visiting places that have community education; visiting with professors, administrators, teachers, city officials, and citizens who know of community education; bringing experts into the commnity; and attending conferences, conventions, and workshops on community education.

Second, the committee will have to become very familiar with its own community. As committee members become more familiar with the goals and purposes of community education, they will begin to perceive how the concept can be used to meet the needs and wants of their community. To properly recognize how well community education will operate in their community, they must know what things need to be done. They will need to gather pertinent information, including traditional education needs of the community, avocational interests, vocational needs, recreation needs, community attitudes, existing agencies and programs, unmet needs of the community, and overall community spirit. It is often helpful to gather information on how the community perceives the schools and what changes the community would like to see made. It is also helpful to obtain information on the use of existing schools and other community facilities.

The committee should decide whether or not community education is the direction in which their community should be moving. If members decide to support the concept, then they must pull together a plan they think would be most appropriate for the board of education to follow. One thing they should consider in their proposal to the board is the implementation of either a system-wide approach or an elementary school pilot project. The system-wide approach usually begins with the employment of one director for the entire system. This type of initial entry usually establishes a variety of program opportunities. The most that can legitimately be expected through this approach is to get lights on, buildings open, and programs in operation within the schools. While this approach does delay process for awhile, it quickly gets to overt programs that are highly visible and appealing to the board of education and the community. The developmental process from this approach would be in the direction of gradually moving toward installing building-level directors as the programs increase and eventually employing persons to operate programs as the directors move into the community with "process."

An alternative way to start would be the "pilot project" approach. With this method, one or two buildings might be selected for full-time directors. If this technique is used, it is advisable to select those buildings from both poor and affluent areas to eliminate the stereotyping of community education. This approach offers the advantage of getting to "process" much earlier. The director is now "centered" in a community of a workable size and can more quickly begin to demonstrate the advantages of community involvement and community interaction. The object of this approach is to show the growth that can occur in a particular community and thus cause other communities to request similar operations. The disadvantage is that on a system-wide basis, buildings will still continue to be closed, adult activities for the total community will be less available, and the program generally will be less visible. This approach will be better for the individual community but will tend to receive less system-wide support.

The study committee should also include in its basic plan information on staffing (full- and part-time) and financing, as well as a time schedule for implementation. The time schedule should provide for both the initial start and the full implementation of community education.

The committee must maintain a firm belief in the value of making change slowly. Once committee members become exponents of community education, they may wish to implement a total program right away. They must be aware constantly that their enthusiasm is based on information and experiences the rest of the community does not have. A small start is often sufficient and all that the school system and the community are ready for. The committee must be cautioned to curb its enthusiasm to assure the accomplishment of long-range goals and purposes.

REPORTING TO THE BOARD

Once the committee has completed its activities, it should report is findings and recommendations to the board of education. The future success of community education in that community now depends on the action of the board. If the board is supportive, it is safe to proceed with implementation, but if the board is negative or even "lukewarm" in its acceptance, more effort will have to be made to educate the board and convince it of the necessity for community education in its district. The success of community education is so dependent on board of education support that it would be a serious error to attempt to by-pass or develop community education without the board's backing.

If the board of education is supportive, it should take certain steps immediately to begin implementing community education. The accomplishment of these steps is not only necessary for the development of community education but can determine the degree to which the board is willing to make a commitment.

The first and easiest action will be for the board of education to formally resolve to support community education as a part of its basic belief in education. This resolution should declare officially the intention to make maximum use of school properties, provide for the education needs of all the community members, and promote and encourage attempts to improve community life. The most important aspect of such a resolution is that it is understood by the board members who are making it. The implications of such a resolution are far-reaching, and it is important that the decision makers be aware of both the philosophical change and practical implications that such a resolution involves.

The second action should involve financial support. While it is likely that community education, in its initial stages, will need some outside financial assistance, it is almost mandatory that some school funds be committed. This will eliminate the "something for nothing" attitude that may develop if there is no financial obligation. It is easy to tolerate almost any activity paid for by outside sources. The real test of commitment comes when one's own funds are involved. The ultimate goal is that community education will become an integral part of the total education program and consequently be paid for through the same process as are other legitimate expenses of the school system. The best way to assure the proper initial interest and continued support of community schools is to establish financial support for at least part of the program from its beginning with an understanding that eventually the program will be completely supported financially through the school system. Without basic commitment to community education, which involves adequate financial support, community schools will exist only as long as no effort is required from the school system, and operating in such a fashion it will never become more than a peripheral program in the total school operation.

The third action of the board is to hire a trained community educator. Many times a school district will attempt to assign community education as an extra assignment to someone already on the staff. The assignment of this task to someone already busy with other responsibilities often produces insignificant results because of time priorities and the level of importance assigned to the work involved. While a few successful programs have been started with part-time persons, it is generally advisable to start with a minimum of at least one full-time person. A full-time, trained person offers the best possibility for a good beginning. The right director, given time to accomplish the stated goals, is the most important factor in the success of the program.

HIRING A DIRECTOR

The director of community education will be the key person in the future development of the program, and since, like most activities, the success depends on the characteristics of the person involved, great care should be taken in the selection of the community school director.

Certain identifiable personal traits should be sought in a director. Good directors should be highly motivated persons who have a reputation for achieving established goals. They should be task-oriented so that achievement of goals takes precedence over time. They should work well with people and be able to establish good rapport quickly. They should be good administrators, able to organize, execute, delegate, and plan. They should relate well to adults, youth, and children. They should possess the leadership characteristics that will make it possible for them to play both active and passive roles, whatever is needed to bring the community into successful interaction.

A person with the above characteristics who is also experienced and trained is, of course, the ideal person for employment. It is not always possible, however, to find such a person. In such an instance, a person with the appropriate characteristics should be identified and then provided appropriate training. Minimal training should consist of extensive exposure to the community education concept and an internship with an experienced community school director.

INITIAL TASK OF THE DIRECTOR

The first responsibility of all community school directors is to become familiar with the community with which they will be working. This familiarity will include at least two things—knowledge of the resources of the community and knowledge of the people who live within the community. Included in the things they should know are:

1. *The history of the community*—this would include information about the beginning of the community and its development. Of particular importance is knowledge of the kinds of people who settled the area and the major influences that have affected growth.

2. *Government organization*—many communities are fractional parts of many different political units. It is important to know what counties, townships, cities, villages, or other units are contained in the community to be served. It also is helpful to know election procedures, inter-government relations, party organization, management types, and financial structure of those units. Of particular relevance is the knowledge of how the school relates to these governments, both financially and politically.

3. *Business and industry*—information should be obtained on the general activity of business, such as shopping centers and private enterprises, and the special organizations, such as the Chamber of Commerce, that represent them. Major business and industrial developments should be noted with special attention to their economic contribution to the community.

4. *Religion*—information of value in this category includes the kinds and numbers of denominations and sects representing the various segments of the population.

5. *Education*—not only is it necessary to know about the public school system and the area it covers but other education operations as well. This includes parochial and private schools, institutions of higher education, and any other groups engaging in some type of education.

6. *Agencies*—information in this category includes any types of social agencies, such as United Fund or government-supported agencies that deal with particular problems (i.e., unemployment, welfare, health, recreation, etc.).

7. *Communications systems*—it is necessary to know all the media sources—radio, television, newspapers, and other publications.

8. *Community members*—it is also necessary to know something about the people who live in the community. Collection of this data will help the director know more about the nature of the community and some of the needs. Information to be obtained should include such things as level of education, income, employment, family size, transiency, housing patterns, wants, and needs.

The purpose for collecting such information about the community and its people is twofold. First, the director is trying to become as familiar as possible with the community to be served. Second, a resource base is being established. The technique employed in this operation should bring resources to bear on community problems. As directors seek this initial information about the community, they should constantly be soliciting information on the services each of these contacts can provide the community. There likely will be many offers and a great willingness to aid community improvement efforts. These resources will be not only agencies and organizations, but also individuals who will have both time and talent to offer their community.

The collection of this information appears as an awesome task and is, indeed, formidable. It is, however, a necessary one and there are some techniques that will make the task easier. Much information can be obtained from other groups that have already collected such information. This would include census information, data collected by public utilities, government studies, information available at libraries, information from historical studies, and studies done by other local groups and agencies.

For the data that has to be collected, two good sources of help are students and community volunteers. Student help is unfortunately often overlooked, but many directors have successfully used students to collect data, and many have even claimed that such students are more competent and eager than some adults they have used. The technique of using community volunteers has a double value. It gets the data collected and produces participating community members with positive attitudes toward community education.

DEVELOPING AN ADVISORY COUNCIL

A basic ingredient in the success of community education is the selection and functioning of an advisory council. There is probably no one council that can best serve all functions of a community, and it is important for the director to be well aware of different levels of councils and how they interrelate.

As previously discussed, during the initial stages of establishing community schools, it will be necessary to have a working committee study the community education concept and recommend to the board of education a plan for implementing community schools. This committee should be selected to be as representative as possible so that there is maximum input into the plan. Once the plan is formed and accepted, this committee will have done its job and should be dissolved.

The selection of advisory councils can now proceed from a grass roots base. At the neighborhood level, some type of neighborhood structure should be created that provides for maximum input from the community. A block-type organization is one possibility. This allows each segment of 15 to 20 families to have a representative on a neighborhood council. These various block groups can select representatives, making it possible to have a group at the local elementary school that has direct representative contact with each member of the community.

The goal being sought here is to provide two-way communication with the community. The direction of most communication is downward.

Messages are directed to consumers and clientele with little or no opportunity for feedback, except in extreme and hostile situations. By promoting a technique that allows all community members to voice their feelings and opinions to their representatives at the local elementary level, it is possible to make decisions based on community opinion and to be more aware of individual problems that exist in the community.

Likewise, when the elementary neighborhoods are well-organized for communication, it becomes possible to improve and expand the flow of communication to a much larger number of community members. In addition, this communication system can be enlarged in a pyramiding fashion to cover a junior high area, and, in turn, a high school area, and, finally, the entire community. The premise here is that the key to good communication and community involvement is a well-organized primary unit.

The organizational pattern suggested here is aimed primarily at providing improved communication, community involvement, and identification of community problems. There will be a need also for involvement of decision makers, agency groups, government leaders, and the so-called "power structure." The difference between what usually happens and what is being suggested here is that most communities have advisory councils made up of state leaders who advise on community problems, set priorities for these problems, and frequently decide on the course of action to be taken in solving them. This procedure tends to be perceived, even if it is well-intentioned, as "doing to" certain people. The technique being offered here suggests that problems and priorities will be decided at a neighborhood level and these neighborhoods will also have input at all levels of decision making so that their perception becomes one of being "done with" rather than "done to."

STARTING WITH PERIPHERAL PROGRAMS

While the program aspect of community education is not the ultimate goal, it is often the best method by which to proceed. First of all, programs can be understood and are most appropriate in the early stages of community education. They do provide for the needs of certain segments of the community, and while they may serve only a small portion of the community, beneficial services will be provided that were not available before.

In addition, programs tend to get the buildings open and the lights on. Initially, this will meet cost expectations held by the school board, staff, and community. An in-depth understanding of community education requires an abstraction that takes time to conceptualize, but most of those exposed to community education will see the need for programs and activities. By starting classes and programs of various kinds for various age levels, there will be an immediate satisfaction and approval by school and community, and this will provide the atmosphere for future positive expansion of community education.

There has been much discussion about how these first programs should be selected and how much surveying is necessary before such activities should start. It would seem that such programs should reflect community wants. It is important to explain, however, that we are talking about initial programs that are general in nature and cursory at best. At this point, any extravagant attempt at basing these programs on community need would consume more time than would be warranted. This is not to deny that eventually all programs should reflect wants and needs, as shall be pointed out later, but during this stage of development, a satisfactory program can be developed by the director. This is also not to imply that no community suggestions should be used. Certainly if there is evidence that community members want a specific program, it should be offered. It has been found, however, that when programs are first started, there are certain ones that will be successful and others that can only be instituted at a later date when time allows for the effort needed to make them succeed. By checking with other community school directors, it is possible to find those programs that will most likely succeed in this initial stage. Spending time having community members select programs will only substantiate what is already known and result in an unnecessary expenditure of time and energy. There are many who will be affronted by this suggestion, but the affront will usually represent their lack of experience in community education or an excessive desire to demonstrate their democratic idealism.

MAKING PROGRAMS REFLECT COMMUNITY NEEDS

Once programs are operating and buildings are open, it now becomes necessary to consider making the program relevant to more of the community needs. The procedure described so far will serve to create a public image and deal with the most obvious community wants. Discovering needs and developing programs to resolve them now takes a greater investment of time. The goal becomes one of finding techniques to assure future programs based on what community members both want and need.

Part of this can be accomplished by soliciting information from those already in the programs. Either by survey or personal contact, it will be possible to get some feeling for what should be continued and what should be added. This information will be valuable since those responding are already participating and can provide some insight into executing programs. The disadvantage is that continuing to build programs by this method alone will cause future programs to reflect only the wishes of the small percentage of the community already involved.

Another technique is the community survey. This method provides an opportunity for input from each community member. The survey form may include suggestions for program offerings with an opportunity for writing in other suggestions. Other information regarding possible times, dates, and costs may also be collected. There are some problems inherent in this type of survey. It will take time and personnel to collect such information. There may also be a cost factor involved. Surveys can be sent home with students, but this leaves out the larger percentage of people who do not have children in school. Mailing is a possibility, but this requires obtaining an address list, addressing the mailings, and paying postage. This also raises the problem of return. Even with return, self-addressed envelopes, the percentage of return will be relatively low.

A very good technique is the door-to-door survey. This method assures a high rate of return and the advantages of face-to-face contact which will accommodate responses not provided through a written return form. The biggest problem with this is finding appropriate manpower to accomplish the task.

Another excellent means of collecting such information is through advisory councils. The use of this method assumes that those on the council are truly representative of the community. This method does offer the advantage of input from community leadership as well as from people who represent concerns of government units, agencies, and institutions within the community.

The best technique probably is a combination of some or all of the preceding methods. Whichever method is used, the responses will still reflect the opinions of only a portion of the population, and there will be quite a discrepancy between the number surveyed and the number who participate in the final programs. It takes a definite effort to find out what people want and need. It takes a different kind of effort to get people to do those things that will improve or change their condition, even when appropriate programs are offered.

EXPANDING COMMUNITY SCHOOLS

As indicated previously, community schools may begin either on a system-wide level (with one person serving the entire community) or on a pilot-type program starting with one or more smaller units, such as an elementary school area. In the beginning, when programs are starting to develop, the initial staffing is probably sufficient. As community education starts to mature, however, it will become important to add more staff. In fact, the most frequent hindrance to the development of community education is the plateauing of the program, generally as the result of failure to add staff at appropriate times.

The program aspect will grow rapidly. The number of classes and activities will increase, and more and more demands will be made on the director's time. Directors will soon find that surveying the community, organizing programs, advertising, staffing, registering, supervising, financing, and administering programs will take all of their time and that, regardless of their energy and commitment, they will be unable to expand their activities. It is at this point that the commitment of the decision makers in the school district is most important, for only by adding staff will any expansion be possible.

One of the immediate needs will be for additional staff to expand programs. As more and more buildings develop programs, it becomes necessary to have more administrative assistance. The program aspect is not the only concern; if community education is to reach its potential, more emphasis will have to be placed on other dimensions of community education. For example, facilitation of all government and social agencies is an important part of community education. This is a time-consuming responsibility taking a certain kind of leadership and subtlety. In addition, community education is premised on community involvement, and this can be achieved only by having at least one community school director in each segment of the community, comparable to an elementary school unit, with enough time and staff to come to know and work with the community effectively.

MOVING TO PROCESS

It may seem redundant to repeat those aspects of community education relating to involvement and process. They are so crucial, however, that they will be repeated so that the point can be emphatically underscored. The ultimate value of community education lies in its ability to bring about change and subsequently resolve community problems. This idea ia based on the belief that communities can and will tackle their own problems if they are assured of the possibility that such an effort might succeed. The belief is that true democratic process is founded on representative government which decides issues on the basis of what is good for the community, and for it to function effectively, there must be input from all segments of the community. The error in this logic is that there has been neither organization of community groups nor opportunity for them to interact and develop their community attitudes, and, as a result, they have come to feel quite powerless and disillusioned with the system.

The development of the local organization needed will take a great deal of effort by the community school directors. They will need to organize their small elementary community (about 3,000 people) in a way that allows a representative group to interact, keeping in mind that group members represent their community and must constantly strive for input from those whom they represent.

This type of development is the hub of community education and the ultimate in achievement. It takes many years to reach this level of community involvement, and boards of education must be aware that this difficult step is accomplished only by adding appropriate staff to do the job.

This, however, is what community education is all about, and it is the level to which all communities should aspire. To settle for less is to fractionate the concept of community education and to deny the community those parts of community education that can really make the difference in community life.

CHAPTER IX

ORGANIZING A COMMUNITY FOR PROCESS

In preceding pages we have attempted to establish a conceptual difference between community education programs and process. Since this has become such a controversial topic, especially among community education people, it might be worthwhile to explain our perceived differences again.

The main difference, as we see it, is in the point of focus. Some community school operations are mainly program oriented, and a review of their activities would indicate that programs of various kinds represent their primary accomplishment. In many school districts, the process aspect is becoming the main concern of those responsible for community schools, and more emphasis is being placed on this area of development.

Programs tend to be interpreted as course offerings, such as high school completion, typing, gymnastics, cake decorating, dancing, photography, and auto mechanics. Process is thought of as interaction of people for particular purposes, such as community self-actualization (the community becoming the best it is capable of becoming), community development, and community problem solving. Process generally might be thought of as involvement of community members in the activities and directions of their lives. In essence, it might be described as the development of participatory democracy.

Obviously, programs and process are not mutually exclusive. It is unlikely, and highly undesirable, to have programs in which people are not involved in some of the processes related to these programs, such as planning or implementation. It is also unlikely that process will emerge without a subsequent development in related programs. The fact that programs tend to develop faster than process does not negate the point that every community school should have both programs and process, as they are the two ingredients of the ultimate establishment of a community school.

It is also important to remember that neither of the aspects is better than the other. There is a tendency to perceive programs as being mundane and superficial and of less value than process, which is elusive, complicated, and much harder to achieve. Both are valuable and have an important place in the development and operation of a community school.

Persons willing to develop a community school should orient their thinking to an operation consisting of programs *and* process, not programs *versus* process. Our time should not be spent on arguing for one or the other but on how we develop both to their maximum potential.

BASIC PREMISES FOR PROMOTING PROCESS THROUGH COMMUNITY INVOLVEMENT

Because the United States is a democracy, people assume there is an automatic acceptance of the principle related to involvement of the community. Unfortunately, there is ample evidence to show that a significant number of the elected leaders in our communities pay little more than lip service to this concept of democracy and, indeed, are more oriented to a belief in "elitist" democracy and governmental oligarchy than in participatory democracy.

To develop true community involvement, community members and community leaders must subscribe to the following premises:

1. *Social problems have solutions.* Despite our desire to effect change, there is often a negative feeling running through the community that individual involvement makes little difference. This feeling is frequently expressed in terms that rationalize lethargy. There is a pressing need to express a constant belief in the resolution of even our most difficult problems.

2. *Ordinary people can influence solutions.* This premise implies that it is not necessary to have titles or expertise or status to arrive at good solutions to problems. It strongly suggests that while knowledge is necessary to finding good solutions, the involvement of many people, motivated to obtain the best answers to community problems, will result in better solutions than those made by a limited number of like-minded persons with status. This phenomenon has been borne out by many simulation exercises and by persons who have tried this group solution technique.

3. *People are willing to commit themselves to solving their own problems.* Many people who do not support community involvement point out that community members do not want to get involved. They argue that whenever you offer community members an opportunity for input, they frequently do not participate. This argument is probably accurate from the standpoint of initial involvement. Community members have often experienced so called community involvement that is non-viable and designed to obtain free community help, be window dressing, or get the limited involvement needed to meet the requirements of some state or federal legislation associated with a financial grant. As a result, many community people have developed negative attitudes about the value of involvement and often feel that such involvement is not worth the time they contribute. If such involvement can be made meaningful, however, especially as it touches and improves the lives of those involved, then people will make commitments of time and energy to such an endeavor.

4. *Community power is legitimate and is not being used.* The term *community power* has been associated in the past with such movements as "community control" and, as such, has come to be viewed as something suspect, something to be feared by those holding "legitimate" power. The struggle over power has become an issue, and the emphasis on deciding who should have the power has caused us to lose track of the appropriate roles of the various groups within our society and the relationship of power to these roles.

For American democracy to function correctly, three components must interact—the legally elected boards, the professional, and the community. Each of these has its own role to play, and the role of each is an absolute in the functioning of the entire system.

Despite the good intentions of all, through centralization and consolidation, and perhaps through the lack of responsibility on anyone's part to keep the system functioning, the community aspect of the trilogy has diminished greatly. As a result, the legally-elected boards and the professionals have assumed more and more control over the system. It does not appear that such a move has been either intentional or subversive on the part of the board or the professionals, although it does appear that they are aware of the shift and enjoy the extra power and authority.

There are those who have recognized this change and have become the champions of the "community." Unfortunately, a number of these advocates for community power are suggesting that to redress the grievance of lack of community input for the past several decades, we should make the community all powerful and eliminate, or at least greatly reduce, the authority of the other two. This would tend to replace one malfunctioning system with another.

The problem is that one segment of the system has ceased to function effectively, and the solution is to reconstruct the system as it was intended to operate. It does not mean that one part of the system should be elevated over the others. It does not mean that power should be taken away from someone else. It does mean insisting that the community once again accept its share of responsibility in the system and exercise the powers it once had.

And what tremendous powers these are—the power to vote and elect persons to serve on the legal boards, who in turn appoint appropriate professionals; the power to petition or initiate referendums whenever the professionals or boards do not take such action themselves; the power to recall or remove elected officials whenever they do not live up to the expectation of the community; the powers of advocacy and protest whenever the community wants to forcefully express an opinion to the rest of the system; the power of economic sanction which allows the community to express opinions in a financial way; the power of problem solving, an organized process that focuses on the thinking of the community.

These powers are not only awesome, they are probably greater than the powers of each of the other groups, since both boards and professionals derive their powers from the approval of the community. This role definition is not only desirable but mandatory if traditional authority is to be made responsible and accountable to community power, which seems to have been the intention of those who originally designed the system.

PROCESS AND THE COMMUNITY COUNCIL

As indicated earlier, process is concerned with community involvement. This involvement can be in many forms, including program planning, community assessment, community surveys, or the scores of other ways in which community members can be involved in community activities, formally or informally. In the case of community schools, involvement can and should be found in each of the six components of a community school. While such involvement is essential in each of these areas, the most sought after involvement, and perhaps the involvement that holds the greatest potential for a revival of community, is the process associated with the development of community councils.

HOW IT BEGINS—IDENTIFYING THE COMMUNITY

To develop a community council, it is first necessary to identify the limits of the community within which we are working. In this respect, we must recognize that community cannot be identified effectively by physical boundaries alone. It is true that many times community will be referred to by boundaries, such as village, or city, or other geographical designations established as legal descriptors. Definitions or descriptions of community must also take into consideration the "feeling" aspect of community. Whenever people consider their identification with community, it soon becomes evident that one of the best ways to identify what communities they belong to is to assess whether or not they *feel* a part of that community. If they do, then they are a part of that community, even though they may not live within the geographical boundaries. Conversely, if they do not *feel* a part of the community, then they are not a part of the community except as interpreted by legal descriptions. In fact, one of the aims of a community school is to attempt to revive a sense of community among those who are legally but not perceptually a part of a community.

NOT A STATIC GROUP

Community is also not a static group. The composition is constantly changing. This change may be caused by changes in *feeling*, but it is also due to the inward and outward migration of people. It has been observed that the average American will move five times in a lifetime, and in a growing or declining community where a sense of community is more likely to be missing, the percentage of people making such a move will be proportionately higher.

RELATION TO AFFLUENCE

When dealing with community, and in attempting to improve involvement, it is important to refrain from making value judgments about the community on the basis of affluence. Frequently, those attempting to work with community are inclined to imply that affluent communities are more active, have fewer problems, and are more capable of credible involvement than are less affluent communities. There is also a missionary motivation related to working with more "disadvantaged" communities accompanied by a reluctance to interfere in the more "well to do" neighborhoods. The feeling is based on false assumptions. The involvement of community members, the sense of community, and the kinds of problems found in the community are not related to the degree of wealth or education in that community and cannot be predicted on such factors. Also, the ability or willingness to be involved cannot be determined on socio-economic factors alone.

VALUE OF PRIMARY GROUP

In working with community, one also needs to keep in mind the value of the primary group. In earlier discussions, the strengths of the gemeinschaft society were identified, and these concepts are important in the development of community councils. It is true that community councils have been developed with some degree of effectiveness in larger communities, and such a procedure is certainly better than to have communities with no community council development at all.

The operation of community councils can be greatly enhanced, however, if councils are built on the basis of a primary community (small in size) that encompasses the characteristics of a gemeinschaft community. There are a number of configurations that might be used to describe the size and potential interrelatedness of such a community, but the one that most closely meets the criteria in most communities is the elementary school area. These areas are the right size, offer some basic community identity, and already exist, so there is often no need to create a new community element. It may well be that there are communities in which the elementary school area is not the appropriate unit, and in such places, other means of development should be devised. The point is that the primary unit is the key to viable community councils, and if the unit for community council development is too large, the resultant council development will have all the built in problems of most current community involvement programs: lack of community representation, poor communications, excessive status representation, superficial involvement, limited community identification, and little or no community support.

ADVISORY COMMITTEES VS. COMMUNITY COUNCILS

Probably the most frequent mistake associated with community councils is our perception that for any community there is to be one, and only one, representative community group in operation. This point has caused considerable argument about whether that group should be an existing group, such as the Parent Teacher Association; a new group consisting of representatives from the various formal groups (Boy Scouts, PTA, Recreation Council, etc.); or an entirely new group based on some democratic means of selection. As long as there is insistence that there should be only one recognized and supported group in the community, the arguments will continue.

It is our thesis that there are really two kinds of community groups and that each has a responsible and important role to play in the community. The first of these groups might be called the advisory committee type. Such groups are adhoc (for a particular purpose) and exist to do a specific thing. Included in such groups are the traditional organizations, such as the Boy Scouts, Senior Citizen Council, Parent Teachers Association, Little League Council, and numerous others. In addition, a community might seek to have several others, such as a health council, community beautification council, library council, and numerous other committees designed to focus on particular community problems. These committees might have community representation but they should also include people with the expertise necessary for each committee to function. Thus, the health committee might have a nurse or a doctor in its membership, while the recreation council might have the director of recreation or a physical education teacher as a member. The number and direction of these committees is determined by purpose, and the membership should be based on representation, interest, and expertise.

The community council, on the other hand, is quite a different organization and is based on a different set of criteria. The primary purpose of the community council is to identify community problems and seek solutions to them. While there can and should be many advisory committees, there should be only one community council in each primary community. It is essential that this council have two characteristics—be representative and capable of two-way communication.

To be representative the council should be made up of members of all of the various sub groups of that community—ethnic, religious, socioeconomic, sub-divisions, professional, business, industry, government, education, etc. While representation is important, size is also a factor. Councils with less than 15 members are often too small, while those with more than 50 members are too large to be effective.

The reference to two-way communication indicates that the channels of communication must be able to flow both inward and outward. Many times when the topic of communication is discussed, it often relates only to one-way communication—the disbursement of more information to the clients. Two-way communication implies a feedback technique, a means for clients to inject their thoughts, ideas, and reactions into the process. It is true that community groups often do communicate with their representatives, but frequently such communication is carried out at times of frustration and anger and in the form of protests. The procedure sought here is a communication system that regularly seeks and encourages two-way communication so that community input is a constant ingredient of the process.

An understanding of the difference between a community advisory committee and a community council is essential in the development of appropriate community involvement structure in a community school. Too many community school programs have developed a community advisory committee and called it a community council. The result has been a single-purpose committee, focusing on single or limited issues; antagonism from the other displaced community committees; and, most alarming of all, the lack of a community group with the broad and necessary responsibility of identifying and attempting to solve community problems of a more diverse nature.

SELECTING THE COMMUNITY COUNCIL

Several methods have been used to select membership on the council. While the proponents of different methods tend to identify their way as best, the real measure of the validity of the selection technique is whether or not it meets the criteria of representation and two-way communication.

One method of selecting the community council is by searching for an existing group that has already been selected on the basis of the recommended criteria. While this may seem overly simple, there actually have been many instances in which the community has already identified an organization, and the selection procedure is one of acknowledging the existence of such a group. In such cases, the identification of a community council is an accomplished fact, and the community school can proceed to its further responsibilities with such a group. It is important to remember that many groups will insist that they do meet the criteria and should be identified as the community council. One way of ascertaining if this is true is to sample the community to see if it supports the group's contention of community representation.

A second technique for the selection of a community council is based on the identification of community leadership. Such a procedure begins with the following assumptions.

Assumption No. 1

It is impossible to involve all people in any meaningful community organization. Some form of representation must be established. The size and complexity of our society and existing communities negate the possibility of involving all people in discussion and dialogue in a process of community problem solving.

Assumption No. 2

There is a direct relationship between community leadership and a knowledge and understanding of community problems and needs. True leaders (those who are perceived as leaders because of personal qualities rather than status position) are ascribed leadership positions because they understand, accept, and cope with the problems of life and of the community. An individual's ability to understand and assist in the solution of another's problem is an integral part of leadership.

Assumption No. 3

Most communities are a composite of many segments (both formal and informal) and by determining what segments exist in a community and finding the leadership that exists within these segments, it is possible to establish a cross section of community thinking and concern. Because real leaders do understand and reflect the attitudes and feelings of those ascribing them a leadership status, they can represent these attitudes and feelings with a fair degree of accuracy. Leadership is not authority, since true leaders are more bound by the group policy than other members.

Assumption No. 4

There are basically two forms of leadership, formal and informal, and both must be recognized and incorporated into any meaningful community organization structure. Formal leadership exists within the organized structure of the community. It includes business and industrial leaders, government officials, and other leaders emerging from the formal, organized structure of the community. This group represents the traditional community leadership.

A number of informal structures also exist within a community with their own leadership structure. The informal nature of these organizations makes them no less important. Unlike the pyramid structure of formal leadership, the informal structure appears in a parallel pattern. Important community issues, ethnic and religious concerns, and other special interests create groups with a fairly narrow scope of interest, but with a definite, although somewhat informal, leadership structure. These parallel structures, while maintaining a variety of goals and purposes, often incorporate many of the major community issues.

To ignore the formal leadership structure is to ignore the wealth, the traditional community power sources, and the vast majority of the citizenry in the community. To ignore the informal structure is to ignore the voices for change—the alienated, the concerned, and the minorities.

Assumption No. 5

Once formal and informal leaders have been found, they can be used as a communication bridge between community institutions and the general public. This is true because of the unique rapport that exists between genuine leaders and those ascribing leadership.

From the five assumptions presented, one of the best means of assessing and describing community needs and problems is by determining formal and informal community leadership, and that leadership, because of its unique relationship with the community, can provide the basis for an excellent two-way communication process between community institutions and their constituency.

With the acceptance of these five assumptions, it is now possible to initiate a discussion on determining existing community leadership. While a variety of excellent techniques exist, one that seems to allow for the determination of community leadership while assuring appropriate representation from many diverse community groups is a modified version of a plan presented by George Brower, professor at Eastern Michigan University. This plan is initiated by interviewing public figures from as many segments of the community as can be determined, including government, business, banking, industry, social services, and health.

During this interview, questions similar to the following should be considered. Questions one and two should be used and either questions three or four.

1. If you had a plan for improving some part of the community that needed total community support, to whom would you go to seek support? Name five persons and list the part of the community each represents.

2. In your estimation, who are the five most successful persons in the community? List the part of the community they represent.

3. If you wanted the thinking of the total community on an important issue, what five persons could best represent the community? List the part of the community they represent.

4. If your community was involved with other communities on a regional plan to restructure community services for the entire region, who would you select as representatives from your community? Name them and list the part of the community they represent.

The individuals identified should then be asked the same questions. The process should be repeated until the names begin to be repetitious. At this point, the data collected should be analyzed, both for frequency of mention and for cross-area representation.

In analyzing the leadership list it is important to not only find individuals who are mentioned frequently as leaders, but also those who seem to be mentioned frequently by diverse elements within the community.

There are only two modifications that are suggested to this plan.

1. Unless careful consideration is given to the initial determination of community segments, only the formal leadership structure will be included. It is necessary to identify the parallel leadership groups. Neighborhoods, special interest groups, etc., must be identified if true representation of the community is to result. This can only be accomplished at the inception of the study by recognizing the informal structure of these community segments, incorporating them into the study, and attempting to find the leaders of these groups.

2. By adding two questions to those suggested, extensive additional insight can be gained about the feelings of the community.

   a. What are the three most important problems facing the community?

   b. What are the major strengths within the community that can be used in combating the problems mentioned?

These two questions can provide insight into community concerns and potential resources for the solution of these concerns.

While the process works best on a community-wide basis, it can also work effectively on a local neighborhood basis. By identifying community segments in a local neighborhood and using the same procedures, neighborhood leaders can be identified. Because homes within an elementary school boundary often do not form a natural community, community leadership does not always fall within the boundaries of the elementary school. Provisions for the inclusion of community representatives from outside the elementary school boundaries must be made. The process described establishes leadership in a community. The inclusion of interested individuals not selected as leaders is also important. The process suggested, when used at a neighborhood level, will provide names of leaders in the community. Some leaders may not be pinpointed, and provisions should be made for their inclusion in any determination of leaders. It is at this point that community school directors must rely on their own intuition and knowledge of the service area. If they have been working with a block club, a PTA, a merchant's group, etc., and know that there are individuals in these groups who are leaders, these individuals should be included in a leadership listing, regardless of whether or not their names are specifically mentioned in a study. We are recognizing here the value of a systematic community study as well as the limitations that occur in such a study. No community study techniques are completely accurate and all inclusive in identifying community leadership.

Once data have been collected, on either a community-wide or neighborhood basis, a priority list of community leadership can be established that incorporates the various leaders of different community elements. Establishing who the leaders in a community are provides the basis for establishing the problem-solving process for the community—the community council.

A third method of selecting a community council is the block club approach. The community is broken into subunits based on geography, subdivision lines, or units containing about the same number of families. Each of these groups is asked to elect a representative to the council. This method assures representation through election, two-way communication

because of the size of the units, and diversity since each of the representatives will come from specific places rather than from the same neighborhood in the community, which is a possibility with other methods of
selection.

There are probably other effective ways of selecting the council, and
communities should be alert for other methods. The method of selection
is important only to the degree that it accomplishes the criteria necessary
for good council operation—representation and two-way communication.

One other point is worth mentioning here. The procedures described
are appropriate for the identification of the basic council related to the
primary community. Community councils for larger units can best be
achieved by pyramiding the membership of the primary councils into the
membership of the larger councils. This method of using the local councils to solicit members for the larger councils again will assure the inclusion of representation and two-way communication and will also capi-
talize on the advantages of improved decision making which accrue from
such a technique. More specifically, we have known for some time that
individual decisions are improved when acted upon by groups and that
group decisions are improved when representatives of such groups are
combined for decision making into other groups. The technique recommended here for pyramiding group representation in larger groups takes
advantage of this phenomenon.

THE COMMUNITY COUNCIL—
METHOD OF OPERATION

The method of operation of the community council and the interaction
that takes place may be more valuable than the actual solution of community problems. In many cases, the identification of community problems and the opportunity to discuss such problems provides a type of
catharsis and group process that is rewarding and satisfying in itself. The
solution of the problem is often an additional benefit but not always the
only way of measuring the positive aspects of group action.

Basically, the activities of the council can best be described as problem
solving. Primarily, the council will attempt to identify community problems and seek solutions to such problems. The method for doing this is

through the scientific problem-solving technique. While this may sound very simplistic, the fact is that most communities do not know how to identify problems or work through progressive steps to attack them. In other words, the difference between successful and unsuccessful community involvement is one of awareness of how to work effectively on community problems. Many of us have known for years that to carry out a project well, we need to know how to organize the steps for approaching such a task, and then our goal is easily and effectively accomplished. This is true whether we are trying to assemble a toy, write a term paper, or complete our income tax. Yet, in community affairs, we have not provided the guidelines for such organization or plan of operation, and as a result, we have had few good examples of community problem solving.

PRELIMINARY STEPS

Before engaging in problem solving, there are some preliminary tasks to accomplish.

1. *Select membership.* This is an important first step that has already been described in detail.

2. *Develop inter-personal relationships.* The group will be in need of group identity and "esprit de corps." Time should be taken to make the members of the group feel comfortable and needed. It is important that the group members get to know each other and to develop personal support for the group. Any time devoted to this endeavor will prove to be time well spent.

3. *Conduct group in-service.* The group will have some particular needs ranging from knowledge about the community to leadership skills. The group should have the opportunity of having these needs addressed. It might be good to consider the possibility of developing some positive attitudes about the community. Too frequently, groups are brought together to discuss problems without first firmly basing such discussions on positive factors about the community. This often results in a subtle suggestion that the community is filled with problems, causing a wave of pessimism to permeate the group.

4. *Organize.* The group will need to establish its purposes, directions, and structure. It will need to develop goals and objectives toward which to aim its actions. It will also need to develop by-laws dealing with such things as officers, elections, terms of office, membership, rules of order, personal conduct, agendas, and the myriad of other operational procedures.

These preliminary steps are very important and should not be circumvented. When the council is first identified, there will be an emotional pressure to immediately proceed to the discussion of problems. The success of problem solving, however, is directly related to time spent on building a good foundation.

One more caution. The problem-solving aspect of a community council offers a method that provides the best opportunity for identifying and working on community problems. It does not assure a method by which the problems will always be solved to the satisfaction of the community council. The council should be fully aware of the advantages of the problem solving approach; however, it should not be led to believe that such an approach will assure certain victory.

THE PROBLEM-SOLVING TECHNIQUE

As mentioned earlier, the problem-solving technique appears simplistic and yet, if followed, results in an effective means of arriving at solutions to community problems. To implement the technique, the following steps must be carried out in the order suggested:

1. *Explore concerns.* The council should identify problems it perceives as important. All problems should be listed and thorough discussion and "brainstorming" of every concern should be carried out. The group should also be encouraged to discuss each issue at length so that group members have an opportunity to express their complete feelings about the problem and that ramifications of the real issue can come forth. After all of the issues have been identified, they should be consolidated into one listing of concerns.

The next step is to list these issues in order of priority. This can be done by listing all of the issues and allowing each member of the group to identify some limited number of issues (perhaps five) he or she feels the community would perceive as being most important. By tabulating the selections, it will be possible to provide some ranking of the problems.

2. *Discuss a selected problem.* One of the problems should be identified, probably the one with the highest priority ranking. The group should identify the components and characteristics of the problem to be certain it is focusing on the real problem.

   In a manner similar to problem identification, the group should discuss possible solutions. Each solution suggested should be further discussed regarding its likelihood of success and the consequences of its implementation. The solutions should then be listed in priority order, and the group will now have identified the problem and the solutions in order of priority.

3. *Organize.* The council is now concerned with carrying out the solution. It needs to determine how it is to be carried out, who is to carry it out, and what the time schedule is for carrying it out. It is important that the council not only be responsible for the identification of the problem and the solution but that it hold some of its members responsible for the action related to the problem's solution.

4. *Act.* The activity for carrying out the solution is now accomplished with the framework identified in step 3.

5. *Evaluate.* The group now decides whether the outcome achieved was what was expected related to the problem. The evaluation will end up in one of two ways. If the problem is resolved or determined to be unsolvable, then the council can return to step 1 of the procedure and identify another problem to work on. If the group determines that the result of its efforts was unsatisfactory but that the problem is still solvable, then it can return to step 2 and proceed to implement another of the solutions to the problem.

While the previous discussion involved only one problem, it is possible for the council to be working on more than one problem at a time. One of the solutions to a problem might be to refer it to one of the community advisory committees. Thus, community advisory committees can be perceived as a part of the process rather than as competitors.

WHAT IS THE ROLE OF THE SCHOOL IN THIS PROCESS?

The school's role in this process is catalytic and facilitating. The process will not start automatically. It needs leadership and direction in the early stages until it can begin to function by itself. The school accepts the responsibility of organizing the council, training the leadership, and helping the group work through some initial problems. Once the group begins to function, the school must remove itself from the process and be available on the same basis as other resources. Its only excuse for reentering, other than as a resource, would be in the event that the council begins to flounder or disbands. The school is accountable for the existence of a viable community council as a part of the community school concept. This means that schools must assure the existence of such councils while at the same time making sure that they do not dominate the issues or actions of such groups.

SKILLS NEEDED BY THE COMMUNITY SCHOOL DIRECTOR

Initiating, implementing, and developing a community council are difficult tasks and require particular skills on the part of a community school director. Frequently, the council becomes very dependent on the director, and the director is faced with a difficult problem: the director must keep the group motivated and moving in the right direction without assuming the leadership's responsibilities. The skills needed to do this are complicated and numerous. The following skills have been gleaned from the literature and represent at least a partial list of items of which a community school director, working with community councils, should be aware. At the onset, these skills will be needed by the director, and at a later point, they will need to be passed on to the leadership or the council.

1. *The director must know his or her own motivations.* The director must keep the group moving toward its goals. It is easy for the director to assume power because of the director's leadership role with the group. It is also easy to direct the group toward the goals of the director, and the director must make every effort to assure that this does not happen.

2. *The director must be patient.* Group process is much slower than more direct and arbitrary leadership styles. It is often difficult to watch the deliberations of the group move slowly in a direction the director could have suggested in the first place.

3. *The director must not expect credit for success.* There is an old Chinese proverb which says in effect that if you provide a group with good leadership, members will say, "we did this ourselves." Most people's egos demand recognition, but if community school directors are to allow the group to grow and prosper, they must be willing to give all the credit to others.

4. *The director must remain above controversial issues.* The role of the director in this instance is much like the role of the teacher. The director should lead the council into controversial issues but represent both sides in such cases. The director's role is to help the group resolve such issues, not to be an advocate for one point of view. The group may not come to the same conclusion as the director, but it is important to learn the difference between a bad decision and one the director does not like. If the director is unable to remain neutral on controversial issues, then his or her role is with an advocacy group, not as a process person working with community councils.

5. *The director must not dominate the group.* Effective group process requires participation by the entire group. Whenever one person dominates, the process is not a group process but a unilateral one, even though the group is present. Because the director is a recognized status leader, there will be a tendency for the group to push a dominant role on that person. Effective group decisions are based on effective group participation, and the director should always keep that in mind.

6. *The director may be from inside or outside the community.* There are some process persons who feel you can achieve effective leadership with the group only if you are indigenous to the community. There is substantial evidence on both sides of this issue—enough so that a good supportive argument could be mounted for either point of view. Probably personal characteristics are far more important to group process than the locale of the director's residence.

7. *The director should be able to avoid expressions of emotion.* The role of the director is to guide and direct, not to coach and pressure. Guidance should be eclectic rather than directive. Excessive emotion will result in group deterioration and loss of confidence in the director.

8. *The director should not expect too much at the beginning.* Frequently, the director will find that the group did not select a vital issue to work on. Also, the group may not come up with what the director thinks is the best solution to a problem. There will be times when the director will have some feelings of disappointment, but he or she must be careful not to make the group aware of this or let it influence the group's activities.

9. *The director must be friendly.* Friendliness implies trust, and the director must be able to demonstrate this to the group. Friendship is often one-sided at first, and the director must be willing to share ways of life and experiences with the council. This is sometimes difficult to do if there are wide cultural differences between the director and the group. Being a good listener and always being "one's self" also help develop friendship.

10. *The director must work to assure that the group makes choices.* To do this, the director must constantly insist that solutions exist and keep the discussions going. It may even be necessary, on occasion, to serve as the scapegoat for the group.

11. *The director must be aware of the problems of original contact.* When the group first comes together, it will often convey the feeling that people really want no change, that community mem-

bers over-value material things, that there is no real sense of community, and that the group lacks motivation, feels helpless, and tends to blame others for its problems. The director must not allow these feelings to manifest themselves into inaction and dissolution. In addition, the director should seek to build tolerance within the group.

12. *The director must be sensitive.* The director must recognize the ideas of the group and be careful not to stifle participation. While the group may have many shortcomings, the director should try to see the group not for what it is, but for what it can become. It should also be kept in mind that a great deal of information can be picked up from what people do as well as what they say. The director should be very aware of body language as well as verbal communication.

13. *The director should check the motives of those in the group.* Sometimes dissidents become members of a council to promote their own grievances and political careers or to get even with some perceived enemy. The direction of the council should be for the good of the community and not to carry out personal vendettas, and the director will need to guard against take-over by self-oriented individuals with vested interests.

14. *The director should bring in outsiders only when the group is viable.* There is a need to build group cohesiveness and identity. Until this group feeling is developed, outsiders will tend to be a threat to the group.

15. *The director should see that the group starts with an easy project.* In working through the problem-solving technique, it is best to have some possibility for success in some of the initial projects. Attempts to solve major international problems or such societal issues as poverty or racial discrimination are not the best choices for first attempts at problem solving. It is very likely that the group will select a less complicated problem that will also be neighborhood oriented. If not, then the director must try to influence the choice of some of the initial issues.

The above list of skills is certainly not all inclusive, but the mastery of those listed will be of definite help to the director who plans to work with community councils. It should also be pointed out that the skills are much easier to list than to implement. Nevertheless, the component of community schools related to community involvement is highly dependent on the human skills the community school director possesses. Without these skills, the community council has little chance of success.

VALUE OF THE PROCESS

The process of community involvement through community councils has great value. For one thing, it has no end. The procedure of problem solving, as described, can become perpetual and thus need not exist only at times of crisis. In addition, it teaches the value of working together. It provides for genuine community involvement in a way that has meaning for the community. Such involvement is not only personally rewarding for those on the council but enriching for the rest of the community as members see the benefits their community realizes as a result of this process.

Finally, this process provides a basic and vital component of American democracy which has disappeared from our society. What has been described here is an itemized approach to democratic participation. The idea is not new; only the technique is. There should be no question that community involvement is what ought to be. It is a birthright and fundamental to our system of government. The process of community involvement, through community councils, is simply one way to accomplish participatory democracy.

CHAPTER X

EVALUATION

There seems to be a growing consciousness of accountability, assessment, and other terminology dealing with evaluating programs and services. And while this phenomenon has been of equal concern to almost all of the segments of our society—business, industry, government—it has taken on a special significance for education.

In many other areas, i.e., business and industry, evaluation has been a necessary part of the economic cycle. It is mandatory for such enterprises to evaluate their product, their clientele, and their management and production techniques in order to operate on a profitable basis. This has been less true, however, for government and education, and even though there often has been an awareness of the need for such assessment by these two service groups, little has been done in this direction. In fact, government and education have expended a great deal of energy explaining why evaluation is not possible in their endeavors rather than demonstrating any real interest in pursuing this end. While there certainly is a difference in evaluating products as opposed to services and while it is easier to assess inanimate objects, such as automobiles and can openers, than it is to assess multiple characteristics and dimensions of people, it is the contention here that evaluation of more subtle and complicated activities, such as education, is possible and desirable. The problem becomes one of technique. Further, this process does not have to be cumbersome and overly complex. As Wood and Santellanes say, "The truth is that successful evaluating depends far more upon clear, accurate thinking and common sense than upon advanced research techniques . . ."[1]

DEFINITIONS

To eliminate possible confusion that can result from the plethora of terms relating to measurement in education, a brief synopsis of terms, as used in this text, should prove helpful. The first is *assessment*, which generally refers to efforts to collect data and information about the community or group to be served, followed by an analysis of that information. One assesses a community, problem, or need. One evaluates a program, activity, or service.

---

[1] Wood, George S., and Santellanes, David A., *Evaluating A Community Education Program*, Pendell Publishing Co., Midland, Michigan, 1977, p. 6.

The second term, *accountability*, deals with reckoning or answerability. It implies that there is a responsibility for outcomes of education and is used primarily in charging portions of the education environment (administrators, teachers, boards of education) with the task of delivering demonstrable results. The desire to make people accountable has been a primary factor in the present emphasis on evaluation.

The third term, *audit*, deals with the importance of establishing an interim step(s) between program implementation and final evaluation to determine if the program appears to be meeting established objectives. This allows for modification of the program before final evaluation to assure a greater probability of success. An audit system is also referred to as *formative evaluation*—"evaluating that is done during a program or process, usually for the purpose of pinpointing progress and altering the process, if necessary, while it goes on."[2] *Summative evaluation*, on the other hand, is the final review and is designed to allow the evaluator to make some judgements.

The remaining two terms, *appraise* and *evaluate*, are used interchangeably. Appraise means to evaluate, and evaluation implies both examining and judging. Thus, the primary difference between evaluation and assessment is that assessment deals with the more overt acts of enumerating and collecting educational information while evaluation not only examines such data but judges it to fix a value on such information.

While the field of evaluation is diverse and is applicable to all segments of our social setting, the focus here shall be on evaluation as it pertains to education in general, and to community education in particular.

DEMAND FOR EVALUATION OF EDUCATION

Education is now under severe examination and attack and has been for several years. One need only review current and past literature to observe the number of critics who have attacked the education establishment and its methods. In fact, it might be safe to say that in recent his-

---

[2] Ibid., p. 10.

tory, no other public service activity has been so severely or continually criticized as has education.

There is probably both an explanation and a justification for these attacks. First, the education institutions of any society play an important part in that society. The literacy, technology, politics, morality, sophistication, artistry, and personal attitudes of the society can be influenced and even controlled by the education system. As a result, those who wish to achieve change in the society often attempt to use the schools as a primary force for doing so. On the other hand, the school traditionally has been the maintainer of societal values and culture—a protector of the status quo. To have two totally opposing expectations for the school by various community groups virtually assures constant dissatisfaction with the school by someone.

Second, and closely related to the first, is the scapegoat role education plays in the social setting. Since the school system plays an important part in the education of all members of the community, it becomes the object of criticism for all things that happen in that community and, for that matter, all of society. It provides a convenient institution on which to focus critical attention rather than attempting to place blame on such intangibles as the family or society in general. Unfortunately for education, the school has become not only a preferred target for social critics, but an institution whose public seems overly receptive to negative comments about its operation and function.

A third reason for such criticism comes from within education. For years educators have made diligent efforts to convince the public of the importance of education. They have attempted to show the importance of literacy, early childhood education, the need for continued education, and the relationship between education and earning power. And they have been successful. Parents are convinced of the importance of education and have become aggressive in their demands and expectations concerning schools, particularly as they relate to their own children. It is, therefore, natural to assume that if we constantly stress the importance of education, parents of children who do poorly will develop anxieties and frustrations. Such frustrations often manifest themselves in a dissatisfaction with the school—perhaps even a questioning of the whole education system.

Because we have promised so much and then failed to make good on those promises, we are open to attack. And, unfortunately, this attack is coming at a time of rapidly escalating costs in education combined with reduced enrollments. Continued requests for more and more financial support to serve fewer and fewer students is, in the public mind, ample reason for criticism.

Whether or not all of these observations are accurate, it does seem evident that schools and education systems are going to be continually subjected to more criticism and greater demands. For a number of years, the inadequacies of education were partially overlooked because of a recognition that the financial needs of education were being poorly met. There was a kind of tolerance by the public caused in part by a recognition that the support provided to the schools was minimal. This was a time when educators rationalized their shortcomings on the basis of economics. They pointed to poor salaries, poor facilities, and lack of public interest as the reasons why education was not better. In the 1960s, however, modified state laws regarding public employee negotiations coupled with a more militant profile in the teaching profession resulted in many changes in the economic factors of education. Salaries increased and became commensurate with those of other professions with equal training. Facilities were greatly improved. The public began to recognize it was paying for good education and began asking whether or not it was getting what it was paying for.

As things began to change and the overt deficiencies began to be eliminated, or at least improved upon, a demand rose for the results educators had promised. This demand first showed up in relation to federal funds. Under various legislative actions and titled programs, a large number of dollars was expended in science and math programs, libraries, counseling, poverty, and other programs for the disadvantaged. Federal legislation now began to request accountability for the funds expended based not just on accounting procedures, but on quantity and quality results. It was not long before state and local governments began to follow suit. As people began to discuss the need for improving instruction, emphasis was placed on holding schools accountable for their success or lack of it. This emphasis on accountability naturally led to a need for some measure of evaluating performance. This, in turn, has led to the broadened emphasis we discuss in this chapter—program evaluation.

This move for accountability, initiated through federal legislation, has been taken up by boards of education, parents, communities, and even students. No longer is there a willingness to accept unquestioningly the authority or the explanations of the professionals in the school setting. Schools have been asked, challenged, and now required to justify their role and substantiate that which they claim they do. Boards of education are altering their negotiation posture by coming up with expectations of their own, and one of the primary demands is for educators to account for the expenditure of funds they are receiving. If, for instance, teachers are claiming that higher salaries and tenure result in better teaching and better education, then the public is insisting on some evidence of such an outcome. Likewise, parents are no longer accepting excuses for failure from professionals whose job it is to teach, and community members are expecting justification for the increasing financial support education is receiving.

All of education is being pushed—sometimes for the wrong reason—to evaluate and reassess.

Educators will be required to clearly identify what they are attempting to accomplish, and then appraise success or failure of efforts to achieve these ends. The fact is that evaluation, right or wrong, is here to stay, and educators must either take the leadership in identifying what should be evaluated and how the evaluation should proceed or be willing to accept those instruments and techniques created for them from without.

EDUCATION EVALUATION PERSPECTIVE

The movement toward evaluation of education is not of recent vintage. Evaluation is an outgrowth of the modern testing movement which had its origin in the early 1900s. Between 1900 and 1910, the movement got underway with the work of Joseph Rice in the areas of spelling, intelligence, achievement, and basic skills. Between 1910 and 1920, the movement was pushed forward by Thorndike, who introduced such things as objective scoring, scaling of items, and established norms. This was also the period when Terman revised the Binet scale. In the 1920s, there was additional growth in measurement; group intelligence scores were developed as well as achievement test batteries. Also, the statistical techniques for analysis became more sophisticated.

The movement to this point had been concerned primarily with the measurement of achievement and intelligence. In the 1930s, this direction began to change from one of measurement to one of evaluation. The basis for this movement was the realization that while education consists of attempting to meet certain objectives, achievement was only one of the objectives to be accomplished. To look at the total system, it seemed necessary to develop more subtle measures to look at such things as map reading, use of references, and educational indices. There also had to be a concern for attitudes and personality. The idea was that we need to see the whole individual. New instruments began to appear, such as rating scales, questionnaires, judgement scales, interviews, observation techniques, sociometric devices, and anecdotal records.

These efforts continued through the 1940s and 1950s. New instrumentation was developed, and tests appeared that were designed to measure almost every facet of a person, including aptitudes, educational prediction, and even test awareness. Tests became one of the main criteria for promotion, college admission, scholarships, military placement, and employment acceptability.

Unfortunately, testing efforts still continued to focus primarily on the individual's academic achievement. Tests were and are used primarily to see if the individual is learning what he or she should. Responsibility for test scores has rarely been placed on the teacher or the school system. Testing has been thought of for the most part as a reflection of either the student's effort, intelligence, or heredity and environment.

Some educators, however, have been trying to evaluate more than the individual's outputs. They have insisted that there is a need for accountability by the school system and its staff. They hold that students are the product of that system and that achievement may reflect teaching, expenditures, facilities, and many factors other than just the personal characteristics of the student. They claim that school systems and their staffs are responsible for the products they produce, much as any other enterprise is responsible for its products.

Men like Ralph Tyler and Robert Havighurst have been encouraging us for years to do such evaluation. It is their contention that until we look at ourselves and evaluate our efforts so that we know of strengths and weaknesses, we will never be able to make those changes necessary for improving our education system. They also believe that positive change will not occur until educators accept a major responsibility for the education of the children entrusted to them.

Other educators, such as Ofelia Halasa[3], emphasized the importance of process assessment as well as product assessment. In other words, they claim we must look not only at final outcomes to determine success or failure, but also at the process established to get us to those ends. In so doing, we can then determine which activities or efforts result in a given outcome.

It should be noted here that the evaluation that has come about from federal and state requirements is not motivated by the same reasoning. The thrust from these agencies has been primarily a financial concern. As such, it lacks some of the positive values evaluation may bring about. Those requesting some evaluation have been concerned mostly with justifying expenditures, and consequently they seek information that has political significance. Nevertheless, even these requirements have had a positive spin-off since they have tended to create an awareness by the recipients of federal and state dollars that some type of accountability is expected.

The need for evaluation has been concisely expressed by Myron Lieberman when he states:

> The underlying issue is not whether to have accountability, but what kind of accountability will prevail . . . In very broad terms, one approach is through analysis of resources invested related to results achieved . . . Under this approach, efforts are made to relate input and educational output in some meaningful way . . . if school systems do not begin to do a better job of relating school costs to educational outcomes, they are likely to be faced with a growing demand for alterna-

---

[3] Halasa, Ofelia, "The Interdependency of Product and Process Assessment in Educational Evaluation," *Educational Technology*, March, 1977, pp. 55–57.

tives to public schools . . . it is difficult to see how public school education could argue this point effectively unless and until they develop more effective ways of being accountable to their patrons.[4]

APPLYING THE PRINCIPLES
TO COMMUNITY EDUCATION

Let us now try to make these comments about evaluation relevant to community education. Two comparisons need to be made. First, in the same way the public schools have not been accountable for their K-12 enterprise, they have not accepted either accountability or responsibility for their other education responsibilities to the community. Second, the charges being leveled here against the public schools and their failure to assess their traditional programs can also be made against community educators. Community education programs have made claims for change, but like their counterparts in the K-12 program, they have never made the necessary, and in some cases even minimal, effort to demonstrate effectiveness.

To be sure, there have been attempts to collect data on community education, but, in general, these efforts have been aimed at the program aspect of community education. This information has been collected primarily to satisfy the requirements for annual reports, state reports, and adult and basic education program requirements. The information collected tends to consist of numbers enrolled, numbers participating, monies collected and spent, teachers employed, rooms used, and number of credit and non-credit programs. This kind of data gathering frequently has been called the "numbers game," and while there is value in collecting such information, it supplies only a limited amount of information on which to make decisions.

Several community educators have attempted to identify the nature and scope of information that should be sought. John Warden[5], in an article, "Guidelines for Evaluating the Community Education Process,"

---

[4] Lieberman, Myron, "An Overview of Accountability," *Phi Delta Kappan*, Vol. LII, No. 4, December, 1970, p. 195.

[5] Warden, John W., "Guidelines for Evaluating the Community Education Process," *Community Education Journal*, September 1973, pp. 34–37; *Community Education Perspectives*, Pendell Publishing Co., Midland, Michigan, 1978, p. 78.

and David Santellanes[6], in the booklet, *Evaluating a Community Education Program*, achieve remarkable agreement on what data should be collected. Some of the major areas for evaluation they suggest include:

1. An Analysis of the Community-School Partnership
2. Level of Communication with the Community
3. Extent of Cooperative Planning
4. Community Involvement in Program Development
5. Interagency Collaboration
6. Use of Community Resources

Wood and Santellanes discuss the importance of collecting information of this type from a variety of people in the community to assure diverse points of view.

The collection of information of this kind is based on two premises. The first is that perceptions of people are valuable and are a legitimate means of measurement. How a person perceives something is the only true condition to him or her. No matter what factors are observed by others, you must deal with personal perceptions if you are to evaluate any condition. While this is a very subjective means of gathering information, it is the only evidence that has individual relevance. The second premise is that data other than numbers are available and can be collected, analyzed, and used in evaluation. Data that are not entirely objective are still valid as long as the limitations of the available data are recognized.

Community educators have been slow to accept the necessity of evaluation for many reasons.

THE ANTI-IVORY TOWER SYNDROME

Many of the early community educators tended to view their role as one of undoing the evils the existing programs were foisting on the community. They aptly pointed out the failures of schools to meet the need of

---

[6] Wood, George S. and Santellanes, David A., *Evaluating a Community Education Program*, Pendell Publishing Co., Midland, Michigan, 1977, p. 6.

communities and established their success at the expense of showing the inadequacies of school boards and administrators. This approach gradually resulted in an attitude toward community educators that placed all community education on the pragmatic level of operation as opposed to the school-oriented, academic countenance of their adversaries. Traditional educators were classed as being oriented to the training of college-bound students and other scholarly pursuits, of which evaluation and research were important aspects. As a result, there developed within the community education movement a kind of disdain for measurement which made evaluation incompatible with community education, at least in the minds of community education promoters.

PROGRAM VS. PROCESS

As has been pointed out earlier, while community education is really made up of program and process, many community education endeavors have stopped far short of total development and are, consequently, highly program-oriented. With only this much development, a statistical data gathering technique is often sufficient. Where the primary concern is with numbers of people and programs, the data collected generally will be adequate if they accurately determine numbers of people involved.

As the process dimension is added to community education and levels of expectations are added for all components, numerical analysis is no longer adequate. This has been a recent development in community education and thus not yet implemented in many communities.

THE DRAMATICS OF STATISTICS

A part of the success in the expansion of community education has been related to this dimension. Numbers are impressive and possess a high degree of influence. People are generally impressed by the number of persons involved and satisfied with outcomes that indicate a high level of participation.

DEGREE OF DIFFICULTY

Collecting evaluative data is an added responsibility. Frequently, the person who claims success while exclaiming that evaluation is useless or that one can "feel" the results without collecting data is rationalizing an un-willingness or inability to carry out evaluation responsibilities. If one does decide to gather information, one finds that numbers are easier to collect than more subjective data, and will therefore tend to do that which is most easily accomplished and tabulated. This often results in the estab-lishment of objectives based on whatever information is easy to collect and whatever programs are easy to evaluate rather than on what is im-portant to the community.

THE PARTIAL DEFINITION

Failure to do a complete job of evaluation sometimes is a reflection of the depth of perception of those who direct the program. A community education director who does not thoroughly understand that which is being attempted will evaluate in terms of his or her own definition of community education. Therefore, if a director perceives community edu-cation as synonymous with adult education or recreation, he or she will tend to collect numbers that show success in these programs and inter-pret them as a successful community education program. The danger evi-dent in evaluation of this type is that of ignoring many community needs while evaluating only what is being done.

CRITERIA OF DECISION MAKERS

Much of the evaluation being conducted is done to answer questions for those who are providing the monies to operate such programs—school boards, state departments of education, universities, and foundations. These groups seem to be interested primarily in numbers, and commu-nity educators respond accordingly.

INSTRUMENTATION

Instruments for measuring community education are not abundant. Be-cause of the nature and recency of the concept, test companies and professional evaluators have not developed instruments such as those available to the traditional school programs. The instruments that have been made available have been developed by local districts without much concern or attention to such test characteristics as validity, reliability, scorability, or ease of administration. The reasons why instruments for measuring other aspects of community education have not appeared are probably difficulty of construction or administration, or lack of motivation to use such devices.

MOVING FROM THE WHY TO THE HOW OF EVALUATION

We have to this point tried to establish a basis for why we should evaluate. To carry out a program of evaluation, it is assumed that this rationale has been accepted and that there is support for such action. Unless the top administration and those to be involved support starting such activities, the results may be disappointing. Successful evaluation implies that all involved want to do a good job and make use of the results. This commitment includes a feeling that through evaluation we will be able to know more about what and how we are doing; where we have been; where we are; and where we are going—a feeling that our programs can never be strong and viable unless we evaluate them accurately and sincerely. We must also acknowledge that the results of our evaluation will establish a base for the kind of direction and change that will take place in our programs of the future.

Once it is evident that there is support for legitimate evaluation, it is then possible to decide how to proceed. It may be at this point, however, that our greatest consternation appears. To say that we have been badly in need of evaluation in the past is an understatement. Evaluation more and more is being recognized as an essential part of any productive operation. It has been assumed in the past, however, that the answer lies in more data collection and various types of tests, questionnaires, and other collective devices which have been used to assimilate information in what usually ends up to be disarray of fragmented statistics. Usually, the end result is disagreement among those involved on the relevancy of the information collected and a great deal of rationalization about whether the information does or does not seem to prove some predetermined point its supporters were hoping it would prove. For example, if measurements showing achievement scores are high, then disenchanted portions of the public tend to argue that this shows that schools are only teaching subject matter, have irrelevant curriculum, and are teaching for the sake of test scores. If such scores are low, then the same public points out that this shows the inferior quality of teaching in the schools. Likewise, educators tend to claim school responsibility if test scores are high, but if such scores are low, they point to such factors as heredity, environment, or other non-school related factors as the cause. As a result, the information collected is generally not used to initiate any change, and the whole process of evaluation becomes one of frustration and futility.

The problem illustrated here is often claimed to be one of instrumentation—that the wrong things are being measured to judge the quality of the programs. And even those things that are being measured are being measured inaccurately because of the lack of validity and reliability of the instruments being used. Upon these two issues, the fate of evaluation has been hanging for a long time, and the general assumption has been that if the right instruments could be found that were mutually acceptable to all concerned, then perhaps proper appraisal could occur.

The concern over instrumentation masks the essence of the problem. Instrumentation should be the outgrowth of a process of evaluation starting with the selection of goals. As obvious as this might seem, the initial action of goal-setting is often overlooked or treated superficially so that evaluators proceed to the measurement aspect without first establishing what things are to be measured. It is true that most school districts do have objectives that often have been established by the board of education. These are, however, usually so broad, (i.e., to increase the individual potential of all the students in the school district) and so unpublicized, that there is little relationship between what is stated and what is happening.

In relating this point to community education, then, the first responsibility of the community educator in establishing accountability is to develop goals for the program.

> The underlying concept of the goal-setting approach is simple: the clearer the idea you have of what you want to accomplish, the greater your chance of accomplishing it. Goal-setting, therefore, represents an

effort on the part of the management to inhibit the natural tendency of organizational procedures to obscure organizational purposes in the utilization of resources. The central idea is to establish a set of goals for the organization, to integrate individual performance with them, and to relate the rewards system to their accomplishment.[7]

GOAL SETTING IN A COMMUNITY

To get at goal setting, it will first be necessary to decide which people should be involved in this part of the process. In general, there are two guidelines to be followed. The first is based on the premise that the greater the input, the more nearly perfect the results. It therefore becomes imperative that as many people as possible be involved. The second guideline is that there should be input from all segments to be affected by the program. This is to get away form the traditional feeling of being done "to" rather than "with." It is also to bolster a prime axiom of community education—involvement. Certainly, if a key ingredient within a program is the involvement of people, then there is no better time to accomplish this than at the inception of the program when goals are being established.

To best accomplish community involvement it is suggested that all those who should be involved be identified. This inventory should include such groups as boards of education, administrators, teachers, lay citizens, government agencies, social agencies, service clubs, churches, and business and industry, with special concern for sub-groups within these areas, such as minority groups and special interest areas. Representation from these groups should then be established so that several discussion groups can be identified and activated to develop goals and objectives. Preferably, these groups should be no larger than 20–25 persons each. The goals should be established in order of priority and should be generally agreed upon by the entire group. The general goals determined at this point are very broad and are designed to provide general direction rather than specific objectives. One very appropriate way to identify goals

---

[7] Lopez, Felix M., "Accountability in Education," *Phi Delta Kappan*, Vol. LII, No. 4, December 1970, p. 232.

is through a process such as that established by Paul DeLargy.[8] This system starts with a listing of community education goals as determined by experts in the field and then takes community residents through a series of discussions and evaluations to establish priority direction to meet their own community's needs. The opportunity for rejection of stated goals and the addition of others not listed is available throughout this process.

Once these general goals have been established, it then is necessary to become more specific. These broad, pre-established goals must be analyzed to determine specific concepts within them, to establish more concrete agreement about what the general goal specifically indicates, and to establish basic assumptions inferred in the generalization. This step is an attempt to dissect and analyze the general goals that were determined. For example, in step 1, the group may decide that one of the objectives is to provide formal education programs for adults. In step 2, the group will actually itemize the kinds of programs to be included in such a goal, such as high school completion, basic education, avocational classes, recreation programs, etc.

It is important to remember that the establishment of these goals will reflect the group's concept of community education. While it is important to share with each group the potential of community education, it is also important not to force the establishment of goals that are alien to the group. If the group develops goals that fall short of the anticipated or desired potential of community education, it is better to accept this as a need for future education of the community rather than to insist on goals that are neither identified nor comprehended by the group. By accepting group consensus, you are reaching one of the key concepts in community education—that of involving and using group process and group decisions.

Before each group disbands, it should select a representative to meet with representatives from each of the other groups. Each of the subsequent groups will be of similar size and will go through the same process

---

[8] DeLargy, Paul, "The Community Education Goals Inventory," *Community Education Journal*, May–June, 1974, pp. 38–40; *Community Education Goal Assessment*, Pendell Publishing Co., Midland, Michigan. (CEGA Kit)

as the original groups. The purpose will be to move from a certain number of groups (i.e., 15) to fewer and fewer groups until one final group contains the representation selected by all the previous groups. This final group carries with it the input from all of the other groups and will then establish, by consensus, a final set of general goals, arranged in order of priority, with each goal defined in terms of the specific concepts within it. Initially, this part of goal-setting is vital and should be repeated periodically to assure that the programs are proceeding as all those affected by the programs perceive they should be.

These first two steps provide the basis for establishing overall goals and the specifics expected by the community to be served. The general question, "What are we trying to accomplish in community education?" will have been answered. It now becomes the responsibility of the professionals to implement these goals. To do this, a third step involving the development of performance criteria, more generally called behavioral objectives, is necessary. Behavioral objectives have emerged from a concern for accountability and the need for establishing something measurable. Management by Objectives (MBO), Criterion Referenced Objectives (CRO), Program Planning Budget Systems (PPBS), and Zero-Based Budgeting are all rooted in the establishment of measurable outcomes and regular evaluation. Also all focus first on goal development, followed by the establishment of related objectives and then specific activity or programs to achieve objectives.

Behavioral objectives represent an attempt to expand universal goals (such as the Seven Cardinal Principles of Education) to a more specific, manageable objective or series of objectives. They focus on both process and product and are precise, observable, and measurable.

In establishing traditional objectives, one can say only whether a particular kind of training did or did not occur. It is possible to measure numbers attending, but it is not possible to determine the quality or effectiveness of the program. Changes in individuals will not be measured, and, as a result of improper evaluation, change in the process and output will not take place.

By comparison, behavioral objectives are based on the belief that the product of a program should result in some observable and measurable change in behavior. In preparing behavioral objectives, one should:

1. Decide on who should be affected (entire class, individual, etc.)
2. Decide on what and how much can be accomplished
3. Describe the conditions or means by which success will be measured (personal judgement, test, questionnaire, combination of these)
4. Establish a time limit—when will the things that you want to accomplish be accomplished

This is the part of the goal-setting process that is crucial to proper evaluation and yet so often is neglected or treated superficially. Both the process and its relationship to behavioral objectives are succinctly delineated in the Management by Objectives concept described by Lopez:

> The program operates within a network of consultative interviews between supervisors and subordinates in which the subordinate receives ample opportunity to participate in the establishment of his own performance objectives. Thus, the whole concept is oriented to a value system based upon the results achieved; and the results must be concrete and measurable . . .
>
> 1. It involves the whole organization in the common purpose.
> 2. It forces top management to think through its purposes, to review them constantly, to relate the responsibilities of individual units to pre-set goals, and to determine their relative importance.
> 3. It sets practical work tasks for each individual, holds him accountable for their attainment, and demonstrates clearly how the performance fits into the overall effort.
> 4. It provides a means of assuring that organization goals are eventually translated into specific tasks for the individual employee.

It is, therefore, virtually impossible to conceive of an effective accountability program that does not operate within the umbrella of the goal setting process . . . It insures that subordinate goals and role performances are in support of the goals of the higher levels of the organization and that ultimately the institutional purposes will be achieved . . . This is the essence of results compared to objectives.[9]

Once the behavioral objectives have been established, it is time to decide how best to begin implementing these objectives. It must be decided what techniques or resources will be used to accomplish the task (lecture, books, movies, group discussions, etc.). This step will provide the input necessary for achieving the tasks described.

This, in effect, is program development. It is here that the professional competence of the director is critical. It is no small task to look at an objective and to then create a means of achieving that objective with a minimum expenditure and maximum effect. The director must now develop administrative activities that deal with staffing needs, support services, awareness of those who may need service, budget control, and a host of other managerial responsibilities related to goal achievement.

After the program has been devised and made operational, an internal auditing system should be established. This is the creation of internal check points to determine if program components are operating as expected and if targeted objectives appear feasible within the structure established. The internal audit provides an opportunity for an interim review and modification prior to any final evaluation. As suggested by Moffat, "it does not assess quality or value. Its exclusive function is to look for actual or potential problems in order for administrators to make necessary adjustments while the program is in operation."[10]

Finally, it is time for the evaluation. Since behavioral objectives were decided on in terms of measurability, the techniques for appraisal will already have been decided and will be applied at the termination of the designated time period. Naturally, it is assumed that the results will be used to enhance and improve program quality. The results of any mea-

[9] Lopez, Felix M., "Accountability in Education," *Phi Delta Kappan*, Vol. LII, No. 4, December, 1970, pp. 323–324.

[10] Moffat, James G., "How to Audit a Program and Tell (before it's too late) Whether It's Working," *The American School Board Journal*, July 1976, pp. 38–39.

surement should provide information for determining how well the goals were achieved and what changes should be made in the program for the future.

One question that arises frequently is, "Who should perform the measurement?" Some prefer to have it done by an outside group. They cite advantages such as removal of local bias. An outside group is best for dealing with sensitive areas and has the advantage of bringing in a high level of expertise. On the other hand, there are certain advantages to internal evaluation. For example, it is less expensive and frequently not so complicated that it requires persons with specialized training. Also, conducting an internal evaluation engenders an awareness and involvement that is more compatible to change.

SUMMARY OF THE PROCESS

Let us summarize the whole area of evaluation by again listing the steps involved and giving examples of each step in the process.

Step I—Establish general goals

These goals will be established by involving many people in deciding what community education should do. Examples of this might be:

A. To provide for the general education needs of the adult population

B. To make people better members of their community

C. To make the community a better place in which to live

Step II—Review general goals and break them down into smaller parts or basic elements

Each of the goals listed in the first step would be analyzed to see what specific things might make up such a goal. Using (C) above as an example, some more specific objectives might be:

A. To make community members more conscious of what things are happening in their community

B. To develop a pride in community

C. To improve the appearance of the community

Step III—Establish behavioral objectives to meet the goals of the specific objectives

The responsibility for doing this now falls on the professionals responsible for the program. They must analyze how they are going to carry out their functions to meet the specific objectives of the program. In the examples cited in Step II, they might include the following behavioral objectives as sub-headings:

1. To make community members more conscious of what things are happening in the community
   a. Develop a community news organ
   b. Organize the local community for small group discussions
   c. Develop community programs on vital issues

2. To develop a pride in the community
   a. Offer social activities for the community
   b. Develop some competitive activities with other communities
   c. Provide information about outstanding people, activities, and events within the community

3. To improve the appearance of the community
   a. Start fix-up and paint projects
   b. Begin community improvement projects, such as landscaping of public buildings and improvement of parts
   c. Use community influence to get government agencies to improve streets, lighting, etc.

To complete each of the behavior objectives listed above, it will be necessary for the professional to include a statement on who should be affected, what and how much should be accomplished, the conditions by which success will be measured, and the established time limit for the accomplishment of the objective.

Thus, for the behavioral objective, "Organize the local community for small group discussion," the following information might be included:

1. Will involve at least one discussion group of not less than 20 people from each elementary school community in the school district

2. Will discuss at least four major issues of community interest

3. Will determine success by reporting on what issues were discussed, the number of participants, and the personal observation of each discussion leader

4. The time period for achieving success shall be one school year, commencing in September and ending in June

Step IV—Determine techniques for achieving objectives

The professional now must decide how to implement these established behavioral objectives by deciding what activities and programs will be used to reach the stated objectives. He or she will plan these activities and take the responsibility for their development and supervision.

Step V—Choose the evaluation instrument

Once the behavioral objectives have been established, the means of evaluation can be determined. For example, an item such as the news organ can be evaluated by describing its operation, circulation, composition, and effectiveness in communicating. Formal sessions, such as group discussions, can be described and documented as to attendance, topic, and number of sessions, and participant evaluation. Activities in the community also can be described and reported. To get a feeling for the quality of a given activity, questionnaires, random opinions of community members, and the judgement of professionals can provide information. The form the evaluation will take will depend on which technique solicits the information relevant to the particular behavioral objective.

The important thing to remember about evaluation related to behavioral objectives is this: general goals have now been reduced to behavioral terms. In other words, goals have been so specifically stated that it is now possible to tell whether or not such an occurrence actually took place. Also, as these objectives have been identified, the form of evaluation has been identified in a similar fashion. Thus, not only is the objective specific, but the evaluation has been described in terms of who is affected, what is to be accomplished, the length of time to be evaluated, and what conditions will determine success. Consequently, by collecting data on the things described, and in the fashion stated, it is possible to decide to what degree the objectives have been accomplished.

In the previous example related to community discussion groups, it would be possible to enumerate and evaluate those items listed as being necessary for success. It would now be possible to assess whether there had been a discussion group of at least 20 people from each elementary district, to check on the number of topics discussed and to have a report from the discussion leader of each group. Since these things were developed as the behavioral objectives to be achieved, and since the criteria for success was described in definite terms, the information collected at the end of the time allocated will be both valid and usable for future direction.

The topic of evaluation has seen much discussion and little activity. It would appear, however, that the day of accountability is upon us and that expectations for more assessment and evaluation will be even greater in the future. The problem seems to be one of accepting accountability as a fact of life and proceeding to implement the necessary measures. Community education will be no exception to these expectations—nor should it be. The promoters of community education believe in the power of community education and have made many claims about its capabilities. For them to say that it cannot be evaluated is to add confusion to the whole situation. Community education is a viable concept and can stand the test of evaluation. In fact, good accounting procedures will prove the claims that in the past have been supported without evidence. The question then is not should we evaluate community education, but how. The answer seems to lie in developing and following a process for evaluation by setting goals that are measurable rather than by following the haphazard, numerical techniques of the past.

CHAPTER XI

FINANCING COMMUNITY EDUCATION

THE ECONOMIC VALUE OF COMMUNITY EDUCATION

It has been said that many foreign visitors studying the United States' economic system believe that the one prominent difference between our system and others is a universally well-educated work force. Education, it is believed, has been the major force behind the expansion and development of our economic system. These same observers point out that the people who ignore this observation most, and place the least emphasis on education as a necessary part of economic growth, are the Americans themselves—especially American businessmen and industrialists.

Americans have long cherished the value of education and have demonstrated support through the development of an education system that is designed to educate every child in the nation through grade 12. No other nation has ever experimented with an education program on such a broad scale and attempted to make education the right of every child. Our belief in education is unquestioned. Until recently, however, we have never attempted to study the relationship between our massive support for education and the phenomenal economic growth of our country which has resulted in the U.S. becoming the greatest industrial nation in the world in less than 200 years.

Industrialists and economists are now beginning to recognize this relationship and are attempting to determine the extent of inter-dependency between the economic system and education, and to determine the relationship between increasing levels of education in the country and increasing national income.

Several years ago, one complete issue of the *Kaiser Aluminum News* was devoted to education. One of the sections in this issue, "The Grand Investment," dealt specifically with the relationship between educational development and economic growth. The following quotation from this article is especially interesting because it was presented in a magazine produced by a major industrial corporation.

> . . . Up until the mid 1950's it was pretty generally believed that the way to increase national income was through reinvestment of capital in material things: factories, machinery, rolling stock, power genera-

tors, etc. . . . The converse of this belief was that money invested in education was at the expense of capital investment and to that extent reduced the growth of national income. . . .

Economists at the Massachusetts Institute of Technology began, about fifteen years ago, to examine the basic assumption that capital investment in material things was the primary source of the increase in the national income. . . . They discovered that changes in the size of the work force, together with changes in the volume of physical capital, accounted for only about 15 percent of the growth of production in the United States. This left a whopping 85 percent of the growth unexplained by traditional investment theory.[1]

The article continues with an attempt to explain the difference:

Along about the same time, a parallel study was being conducted at the University of Chicago on the relationship between the level of education and household incomes, in which there appeared an invariable correspondence between higher education and higher income. When the two studies were put together, it was apparent that education and a rising national income were directly linked.[2]

To further support the link between education and economic growth, Professor Charles S. Benson of the University of California-Berkeley states:

Now, national income, that most central of all economic statistics, is the sum 'factor income,' and by far the most important of 'factor incomes' are wages and salaries (the others are rent, interest, dividends, etc.). When the work force of a country receives more education, the corresponding rise in their levels of wages and salaries is translated directly into increases in the national income . . . Current estimates indicate that between 20 and 40 percent of our growth is a result of expenditures on schooling.[3]

---

[1] "The Grand Investment," *Kaiser Aluminum News*, Vol. 25, No. 1, p. 27.
[2] Ibid., p. 27.
[3] Benson, Charles S., "The Rationale Behind Investment in Education," *Education Age*, March/April, 1967, p. 14.

In another article, "The Economic Value of the Community School Concept to Local Business," Mr. Joseph Anderson, former general manager of A.C. Spark Plug Division of General Motors provides some similar insights. He believes that as people gain better and greater amounts of education, their tastes change and are expanded and that there is then an increased desire for new, different, and better products. These increased desires will create a greater market for new homes, nicer furniture and decorations, and more appliances and conveniences. Mr. Anderson gives an excellent example of the result of ignoring the direct relationship between economic growth and education through the following story.

Some years ago, Atlanta, Georgia, had the lowest per capita spending for public schools of any major city in the United States. This low tax assessment resulted in lower costs of operation, and the Chamber of Commerce of Atlanta used this as an enticement to new business to locate in Atlanta. In an attempt to change the thinking of the business community, the superintendent of the Atlanta Public Schools did some additional research and found that Atlanta had not only the lowest educational cost per child, but also the lowest annual spending per capita for retail goods. His research gave some validity to his supposition that business was directly and adversely affected when good education was not considered a vital and necessary part of a total community's needs.[4]

Probably the most dramatic and well publicized document relating economic well being and education is *A Nation At Risk*. This presidential commission publication has become the basis for education reform in the United States. Every state department of education and the governors of almost every state have been motivated by this document to develop state plans for restructuring education. This motivation has come from the following allegations in this publication.

♦ The quality of education in a nation determines its prosperity, security and civility.

♦ Knowledge, learning, information and skilled intelligence are the new raw materials of international commerce.

---

[4] Anderson, Joseph, "The Economic Value of the Community School Concept to Local Business," *The Community School and Its Administration*, Vol. 7, No. 9, May 1969, p. 1.

◆ Individuals in our society who do not possess the levels of skill, literacy and retraining essential to this new era will be effectively disenfranchised, not simply from the material rewards that accompany competent performance, but also from the chance to participate fully in our national life.

Thus it appears that there is an interrelationship between economic growth and educational development. While research concerning this relationship is incomplete, and no accurate ratios of education to economic growth can yet be ascribed, little doubt can exist that a direct and interdependent relationship does exist.

VALUE TO THE COMMUNITY

No discussion of the economic value of eduction would be complete without including the major economic impact community education has on program participants and the community at large.

Extensive statistics are available demonstrating the relationship between the level of achievement in education and annual income. Certainly, a concept that provides programs that improve basic skills and expand levels of education has a major economic impact. As individual vocational and education skills increase, potential earning power also grows. Increased earnings mean increased spending, and people who might have been tax burdens become contributors.

The community as a whole also reaps benefit. As pride in one's community is developed and as a feeling of concern for others grows, one logical result should be a reduction in vandalism and delinquency. Communities expend enormous sums to replace and repair facilities damaged through vandalism. Much of this money could be spent more positively if communities could develop a sense of oneness, a community esprit de corps.

The community could also benefit financially by avoiding costly duplication of services. As community members begin to work together and agencies begin to cooperate with each other, former duplicated services can be eliminated and replaced by new services for about the same financial expenditure.

Despite the previous discussion, probably the most frequent excuse for failure of communities to begin community education relates to financing. School districts, already hard pressed for operating and building funds, are reluctant to take on additional financial obligations when their source of funds for traditional programs are already inadequate.

One of the greatest errors one can make in advising school districts in this matter is to attempt to convince school boards that such a program will not cost them any additional money. It should be obvious that the addition of personnel and programs is bound to add increased costs to the school district. In addition, to attempt to start community education without financial commitment from the school district itself is to instigate the old "something for nothing" game, and the results are often disappointing. The problem of financing, therefore, frequently boils down to the following situation—how can a school district secure initial funds for the implementation of community education, and how can the same district become financially supportive of such a program in the same way it supports other endeavors in education?

COMMUNITY EDUCATION COSTS

To imply that community education will not add to the financial responsibilities of the school district is to doom community education from the beginning. The very essence of community education is one of opening buildings for more hours of the day and more days of the year, expanding the responsibilities of the school district, and brokering community services, a task that has not been previously carried out by the schools. To do this will obviously require additional funds.

First, there will be an investment in personnel. While many school districts start community education with only one full-time administrator, we hope that ultimately there will be at least one director for every school building in the school district, and even this might be minimal. The needs of the community may require some buildings to employ more than one person to carry out the varied functions of a full-fledged community education program. There may be a need for specialized personnel, such as social workers, home counselors, etc., to work effectively with members of the community. In addition, there will be a need for secretarial assistance at each building level.

The program within the building will necessitate additional personnel costs too. Instructors will be needed for the various classes. This cost will vary depending on the training required, the supply and demand, and the teacher's master contract. Included in this cost will be salaries for persons who supervise activities. There also will be a cost factor for custodial help. Not only will there be additional cleaning, but many districts require a custodian to be present whenever any activity takes place in the school building. And there will be additional costs for special equipment and additional heating and lighting related to extended use of the buildings.

In addition to added personnel, there will be some other cost factors as well. When the areas of programming are expanded, extra equipment is required. For example, if a community room is established and set aside for the use of community residents, then there is a need for stoves, sinks, refrigerators, dishes, card tables, and other items necessary for equipping such a room properly. In certain communities, equipment such as washers, dryers, and sewing machines might be added. If special classes are offered to the community, then there will be an expenditure for appropriate sized tables and chairs, education equipment, recreation equipment, and vocational and avocational tools and machinery not currently available in the building. Other facilities may also have to be added or changed to carry out a community education program. For example, it may be necessary to provide expanded parking facilities, lighting for the parking area and playfields, outside drinking fountains and toilets, and a variety of facilities designed to serve adults as well as children. Added to these will be administrative costs for such things as office space, telephones, supplies, travel, and office equipment.

An enumeration of the preceding cost factors may at first seem overwhelming and could result in a reluctance to start a community school program. Closer scrutiny, however, will reveal that the problem is not as great as it might first appear. First of all, the costs listed include the maximum total of those listed in a sophisticated program. Most programs start slowly and on a much smaller basis, and the additional monies needed at the beginning of the program will be much lower than expected. Other costs will be assumed through better use of existing programs and facilities. All of these factors will result in reducing the total expenditures anticipated in starting a community school.

It is quite obvious, however, that implementing community education will require additional monies, and one of the first questions asked by boards of education will be, "Where will we get the money to start such a program?" Their concern is legitimate, particularly as they are being asked to expend funds in an area not usually judged appropriate for the spending of public school monies. There is, therefore, a need for information on sources of money available for implementing and developing community education.

SOURCES OF MONEY

FEDERAL GOVERNMENT

Many community education programs have found substantial amounts of funding available through various federal projects. No effort is made here to identify all of these sources as they are constantly changing. In the past, however, many of the programs related to the Office of Economic Opportunity, the Elementary-Secondary Education Act, the Open Spaces Act, the Higher Education Act, and others have furnished funds by which programs have been started and continually supported. The key in getting such assistance has been to analyze such legislation for its applicability to community education and then submit a proposal for funding. In general, success for such funding has come from the ingenuity of the persons writing the proposals in adapting the legislation to their particular needs. Rather than be dissuaded by the title legislation, they have attempted to work within the guidelines to get federal monies for their districts. An example of this is the Open Spaces Act. While interpreted by many as a device to help develop park areas for the city ghettos, some rural areas have successfully obtained funds to develop recreation areas within their own communities.

One caution should be noted in the use of federal funds for community education. Federal assistance is frequently aimed at programs for the disadvantaged and the urban school district. While there is no question that community educators should consider the use of such funds where appropriate, they must be careful not to get so involved with such funding that their programs become identified as poverty-related and subsequently result in the implication that community education is only for the poor and disadvantaged. The directors must also be certain that they do not become so involved in the development of programs that are federally funded that they lose sight of the total concept and therefore minimize the potential effect of community education for their community.

One of the bright spots in federal financing of community education has been the government's involvement in direct community education support. In 1974, the Congress of the United States enacted the Community Schools Act. The purpose of this act was to develop and improve community education programs at the state and local levels and to develop training programs for local and state leaders.

The first federal grants, totaling $3.5 million, were awarded in 1976. Some 660 applications were submitted, requesting a total of 37 million dollars. Ninety-four proposals were funded. Those receiving grants included local school districts (rural, suburban, and urban), universities, and state education agencies.

Despite the limited number of grants and the level of funding, the federal grants have made a significant impact. Probably the most important contribution has been that because of this legislation, the federal government has established its interest in community education and given the concept national visibility and legitimacy. The legislation has also resulted in the creation of a leadership service position in community education in almost every state Department of Education in the U.S. This investment in leadership has already begun to show its positive effect on the development of community education at the state level. Unfortunately, the Community Schools Act funds have been eliminated from the federal budget. There is some indication, however, that such funds may be restored in the future.

STATE GOVERNMENT

The advice given for seeking federal monies might also be given for state funds. Most states have allocated funds for special programs designed to meet state education priorities. With a little imagination, proposals can be written so that certain portions of the community education program can be funded from these sources.

Most applicable to the community education programs are those state funds appropriated for adult and vocational education. These funds not only support the programs for which they were intended, but often provide excess funds. In the beginning, when community education is expected to pay its own way from external funding, it is important that the school board be convinced that all funds such as these be channeled into community education and not absorbed into the general fund. It is difficult enough to find sources of funding for community education without expecting such programs to be money-makers for the traditional programs.

In addition to adult and vocational education funds, certain states have specific appropriations for community education programs (non credit offerings). Some of these states have allocated funds on the basis of a head count participation in community education classes. For example, for each person enrolled in a community education class, a flat fee is paid to the district. Other states are financially aiding community education by including specific budgeted amounts in their state aid formula for community education. Financial arrangements for this type of aid range from reimbursing a portion of each community school director's salary to providing a grant to each building that has a building director. In most cases, the dollars are to be spent on people (salaries) rather than programs.

Probably the most important part of such financial assistance is that it provides the incentive for starting community education in the school district by supplying some of the necessary initial funds. It also tends to legitimatize community education by putting an official state stamp of approval on this concept as a bona fide part of the state education plan.

One of the questions frequently raised with community educators is, "How do you justify the expenditure of state dollars for community education?" The question implies that funding of community schools and their programs is a questionable state expense.

One answer, of course, is to list the justifications related to economics and personal growth discussed at the beginning of this chapter. A second response, however, might be to point out the inconsistencies in financing that exist in most states.

All states do perceive a responsibility for financing public education for the children within their boundaries. In fact, the Constitution of the United States makes public education not only a responsibility but an obligation of the states. There will be some variance in which children are included. In some states, the target group will be described as between the ages of five and 18. Other states describe funding based on grades, such as kindergarten through twelfth grade. Some states may include "pre-school," while others may make provisions for students through age 20. Whatever the combination, there is the expectation that the state is ultimately responsible for financing education for the children and youth within its boundaries. States also provide financing for certain adults within their jurisdictions. Community colleges receive state allocations for their students, and state colleges and universities receive state funds for both their undergraduate and graduate programs. In fact, in many states, 70 to 80 percent of students' higher education costs are supplied by the state legislature. The point is that we already provide a substantial amount of money for the education of children, youth, and many adults, especially those adults who qualify to go on into post high school education. There does, therefore, appear to be some logic that states should also provide moneys for the education of those adults who have needs for education but do not fit into the current categories supported by public funds.

BUSINESS AND INDUSTRY

No group stands to profit more from community education than local business and industry. Conversely, few people realize the commitment this group has toward support of its local community. Almost every type of private enterprise expects to contribute funds to public endeavors as a part of its responsibility to that community. The fact is that few persons are really aware of the extent of the contribution business and industry might be willing to make. They tend to evaluate potential of giving on the basis of their own incomes and experiences. If there is ever a place where we must "think big," it is in regard to this type of giving. There are numerous examples across the country where school districts have obtained continued financial support from local business and industry in an amount which financially supported the bulk of the community education programs.

PHILANTHROPY

There are many more sources of financing than one might expect. Some of these sources are local persons who are looking for worthwhile projects for charitable contributions. Motivation for this, as in business and industry, is both personal satisfaction and tax considerations. Some persons wish to identify themselves with good causes by giving portions of their personal incomes to such activities. Other persons look for tax-sheltered exemptions for the purpose of donating to worthy causes.

Most foundations are required by law to expend their funds on such enterprises and eagerly pursue worthwhile causes. In considering philanthropy, one should also look outside the community. There are numerous foundations in all parts of the country looking for promising activities with which to identify. Community education has proved to be an attractive venture for many such foundations, and communities should not overlook this source of funding.

A new twist to the foundation approach is to create a local foundation. Many school districts have established non-profit foundations for the purpose of funneling dollars from the private sector into their community education programs. Gifts are solicited from individuals, other foundations, and business and industry to be used as a base for creating a foundation which, in turn, can finance community schools.

LOCAL SERVICE CLUBS AND ORGANIZATIONS

These groups, while often not as great a potential source as others, do have monies to assist community education. Although individually they are not able to provide extensive revenues, their combined efforts can be considerable. One approach in getting money from these sources is to have them finance a specific portion of the community education program. By taking on a limited project, such as providing for a singular program or purchasing some type of equipment, they can make a significant contribution. This technique for fund raising also provides a meaningful identity and involvement for the participating groups.

It should also be stressed that occasionally these groups are sources of larger amounts of money. In one small community, the Junior Chamber of Commerce took on the local community education program as its special project and in each of two successive years raised $25,000 toward the support of the program.

OTHER GOVERNMENT AGENCIES

This is often one of the most overlooked sources from which money is available. Many of the programs in community education, particularly as they relate to recreation and community service, will be concerns of other government units in the community, such as the county, township, and city. Often, these units have allocated funds for activities and are either expending them in a somewhat haphazard, uncoordinated manner or are not using the allocations because the amount is not large enough to hire the needed personnel. By consolidating these funds and channeling them through a community education program, duplication will be eliminated, resulting in better programs and increased activities.

SOCIAL AGENCIES

In most communities, many programs already are being carried on by social agencies with an extensive expenditure of funds. The problem here is again one of coordination. By drawing on the resources of these agencies and assuring a coordination of their activities with those of other community agencies, many programs and services can be offered without additional expenditures.

When activities are coordinated and duplication is eliminated, money that is saved can be used to provide new services to the community.

FUND RAISING

This source of funding offers a greater potential than might be expected. At first, one tends to think of this activity in terms of pancake suppers, bake sales, and the like. Such activities generally are limited in their fund-raising ability and can contribute only a limited number of dollars. It should be kept in mind, however, that for the purposes of community education, this type of activity offers two things: first, it does raise some money, if only a limited amount. Of more importance, however, is the fact that in such a joint effort, members of the community get involved in a worthwhile activity which brings them closer together, engendering a spirit of community. This fact alone may be ample reason for engaging in such an activity.

Fund raising also may have a greater potential for raising dollars than we realize. Many school fairs, for example, raise thousands of dollars. Some communities have raised money on such things as raffles in which the prizes are of considerable worth. Income from this type of activity is often in the thousands of dollars and the profit can be even higher if the prizes are donated or purchased at cost. One community has an annual auction in which items contributed by wealthy persons in the community are auctioned off to these same people. The charitable mood of the bidders results in a considerable income for the community education program.

In general, the techniques for raising money in this fashion are limited only by the imagination of those involved. One of the prime motivating factors is that people will often make a greater effort when the cause is known beforehand and when it is a cause in which they believe. So often, fund-raising activities in education raise the money first and decide on how it shall be spent later. By having community education or a specific community education project as the intended benefactor, it is frequently possible to achieve more input and provide greater satisfaction to members of the community.

CLASS FEES

Payment for the programs by participants in the program is often a good source of funding. Participants in most activities should be expected to pay either an established fee or a pro-rated fee for those courses they wish to take. In general, most people are able and willing to pay such tuition. Provisions should be made to provide free tuition to those who cannot financially afford to enroll in courses they need or would like to take. Some programs also provide for a variable fee structure so that those who can afford to pay more provide surplus monies that then can be used in courses where the participants are less able to afford the total cost of their class.

LOCAL TAXES

The ultimate goal for financing community education should be to obtain funds from the same sources from which we fund our existing education programs. If one truly believes in community education, then one must also believe that it is an expanded and legitimate part of the total education structure. As such, it should receive the same financial support as existing programs. To attempt to make community education pay its own way is merely a stopgap technique, acceptable only as a temporary situation. As long as school districts insist that community education directors find their own funding, they will continue to have programs that achieve less than their potential.

This means, then, that community education should be financed from the same tax structure as that provided for traditional education. In fact, many districts discover that as they make education more relevant and meet the education needs of more people in their communities, taxpayers are willing to approve the money needed for such programs. Once community education has had an opportunity to develop in a community, categorical millage for community education is often the easiest millage on which to get favorable voter reaction.

IN-KIND SERVICES

In evaluating program costs, we must look at another source of funding—one that is not given in dollars but that has the same effect on the financial needs of community education. This is probably best described as in-kind services. These services fall into several categories but have one common denominator: they all include characteristics resulting in a donation of time or materials which, if not provided, would result in extra costs and would require additional dollars to provide. These in-kind services, then, are volunteered time, materials, or techniques offered to community education that stand in lieu of money and thus serve to supplant some of the financial needs of community education.

FREE OR INEXPENSIVE PROGRAMS

Many fine programs free or very inexpensive are available to the school district if solicited. Such programs as first-aid courses by the Red Cross, gun safety by law enforcement agencies, retirement planning by social security offices, and boat safety by the sheriff's department are usually available at no cost in most communities. In addition, many clubs and organizations, such as kennel clubs and riding associations, offer free courses in their area of specialty. Social agencies, too, have various courses for the public and are anxious to find facilities in which to present them. Business and industry are also good program sources. Add to this the many other education and information programs that are one or two sessions in length, and communities will find a variety of offerings at little or no cost.

Another point to keep in mind is that many good programs have little or no expense. The cost, for example, of opening the gym to the adults in the community for recreation is minimal. Similarly, the opening of a classroom or a cafeteria for the purpose of card playing or bingo by a group of senior citizens can be done at a negligible cost. If prizes are necessary, the participants can furnish them themselves in the form of "white elephants," inexpensive gifts, or canned goods. So, too, can many other cost-free, beneficial activities be carried on.

VOLUNTARY HELP

Some of the personnel needs can be met by using volunteers from the community. In each community there are people with special skills or hobbies who are willing to donate their time. Some will want to volunteer because they want to be useful, while others will be motivated to work for little or nothing because of their tax status in relation to their retirement income. In some cases, these persons will have the background to teach special classes or offer unique programs. Others will prove useful as supervisors and aides or to help with certain custodial duties. It should be kept in mind that while these services will reduce the expenses of the program, the fact that these individuals are garnering some personal rewards from their endeavors is equally important and should suffice to justify the use of such persons.

DONATED ITEMS

The donation of many needed programming items is also of financial value. Such things as cards, horseshoes, tables, games, and any type of equipment or materials that will enhance the programs are valuable. It also may be possible to obtain items from local businesses given as a gesture of good will.

PARAPROFESSIONAL EMPLOYMENT OPPORTUNITIES

There are many occasions when local persons are capable of doing the job expected in a given area without having all the skills of a professional in that area. For example, some types of supervision or secretarial work can be done effectively by members of the community. By employing such persons at reduced salaries, the program can realize considerable savings.

COST MYTH

In reviewing costs of operating community education programs, there is a need to challenge some of the costs school officials often identify as reasons why they cannot make use of their buildings. Some of these costs, such as lighting and heat, have been amplified in more recent years as there has been increased concern about energy. On the surface, it appears as though energy arguments may be a logical reason for not opening up local buildings. There are some factors that should be considered, however, before hasty conclusions are reached.

One of these factors has to do with lighting costs. While lights will be used more, there is no agreement that the cost increase will be significant. For one thing, there is some evidence that lights burning continually may use less power than those that are turned on and off. A second point is that even when people are not using buildings, custodians frequently have the lights on, and thus, the costs are often high with or without community education. Also, too frequently the regular school program wastes electricity in many ways (turning on lights during the day when they're not needed), and some conservation by regular staff could easily accommodate the extra energy needs of the community education program.

A second factor deals with heat. It has long been thought that extra use of school facilities would use more energy for heat. Architects are now challenging this idea. Their argument is that body heat is significantly higher than room heat (about 30 degrees) and that people actually contribute heat to a room rather than take it away. All of us have experienced this phenomenon when we have attended a school function. When we enter the room it feels cold, but in time, the room, even if it's a gymnasium, becomes too warm.

Heating engineers have suggested two things: (1) vacant buildings deteriorate faster than occupied buildings, and (2) buildings could be heated by body heat. Excess heat can be drawn off and used to heat other rooms at other times or even heat the water to be used in the plumbing system. Their conclusion is that the best response to the problems related to heating costs of a building is to keep that building occupied by people.

One final point deals with a concern for total energy use. To conserve on energy, schools not only have refused to let their buildings be used for extended periods of time but have actually curtailed their regular programs for as long as several weeks. Without question, this action resulted in reduced energy costs for the school district. But while the energy use by the school district went down, it is very likely that the total energy use went up. The school, which housed groups of 30 students to a room, released those students who then turned on TV's and radios, turned up thermostats at home, drove cars around the community, and dramatically increased the number of lights in operation. The school's saving in energy was drastically offset by total energy use in the community. Putting groups of people in central facilities is probably a good way to conserve energy.

REDUCTION IN VANDALISM

As described earlier in this chapter, part of the costs in community education can be recouped through reductions in vandalism. A great deal has been written in the past several years describing the enormous costs vandals have caused local school districts to pay. Such descriptions have reported on fires, stolen materials, and ruined equipment. Glass breakage alone has accounted for millions of dollars of loss to the school districts throughout the United States.

Local boards of education have tried several techniques to deal with this problem, including placing guard dogs in the schools, fencing in the property, and employing full-time security personnel. One method, which appears to be very successful, has been the implementation of community school programs. They bring large numbers of persons into the schools for most hours of the day. School districts that have experienced a reduction in vandalism as a result of increased building use feel that there is a direct relationship between the two. They explain this interaction on the basis of two things. First, they feel that people who get greater use from their buildings are less likely to vandalize them. Second, they feel that vandalism occurs when buildings are empty and that with rooms in constant use, there is far less opportunity to destroy school property. One superintendent, who is a strong advocate for reducing vandalism through community use of facilities, claims that his community education program has cut his vandalism costs by $200,000 per year, more than enough to cover the additional expense of his community education program.

REASSIGNMENT OF PERSONNEL

Since costs for personnel frequently represent the greatest cost factor in community education, this is the area in which the greatest savings can be made. One technique for doing this is by reassigning current personnel. Some teachers, for example, can be given different schedules so that their services can be better used to cover both the regular day program and the additional activities that may occur at other times. If we can view the regular school day as not being sacred in terms of teacher assignments, then certain teachers, such as art or music teachers, might be assigned to start their day earlier or later so that their talents might be available to students or adults either before or after the regular school day.

Custodial help, too, might be more beneficially assigned. In many instances, the bulk of the custodial staff is on duty when it is least needed. The school day frequently allows for limited custodial activity, but this is often the time when most of the custodians are available. The result is that often either a limited amount of janitorial service is carried out or the school activities are limited or disturbed by window washing, sweeping, or lawn mowing. Having a minimal force in the daytime with the other staff members reassigned to late afternoon or late evening schedules makes more sense as custodians then can work without conflicting with student and teachers. By readjusting this schedule to one in which the cleaning is performed by a night crew, it is possible to maintain the building at the same level with little or no additional staff.

One additional personnel saver is recommended but with extreme caution. It is possible, in the beginning stages of the program, to have a part-time community school director. This can be accomplished by employing a building director who teaches half-days and works half-days as a director. This may be an acceptable way of getting into community education as long as it is done with the full understanding that it is a temporary arrangement. Such an assignment will result in a very limited, primarily program-oriented operation. If the intent, however, is to initiate community education gradually and show the value of such a program when no other avenue is open, then such a technique may prove beneficial.

The means of financially supporting a community education program need not be limited to those presented here. With the right person as director, funding is frequently not as big a problem as often anticipated, and the ingenuity and inventiveness of such a director will often uncover many unique ways of overcoming financial needs. It would be a serious error, however, to fail to re-emphasize a point made earlier about funding in relation to the board of education. The philosophy of community education is an expansion of the traditional school philosophy. It is based on the belief that the education needs of all communities are larger than those served by the traditional programs. It implies that schools should take on larger responsibilities in identifying and helping solve community problems. It is a legitimate function of the school, and as such, it is entitled to the same financial considerations as other school programs. Eventually, then, community education should be supported in the same fashion as the traditional school program, and once a school board commits itself to community education, it has the moral responsibility of providing the financial means necessary to support a sound community education program.

CHAPTER XII

DETERMINING AND MEETING STAFFING NEEDS

Determining staffing needs, by the very nature of community education, is unique to the community involved. Demographic differences; relationships between existing social, government, and education agencies; and expectations regarding the proposed program all come together to make each situation somewhat unique. It is also true, however, that if community education is to be more than a collection of individual perceptions of the concept, some commonalities must exist in the types of skills required to initiate, operate, and function in a good community education program.

This chapter will focus on selecting a director and his or her team, incorporating the existing school staff into a support role for community education, and using external resources to round out the program.

SELECTING A DIRECTOR

A community school program should have at least one full-time, trained community educator to coordinate and direct the effort. Further, this person should be relatively highly placed in the administrative structure to assure recognition of the person and the program as a high priority of the school system.

It is important that these two concepts be stated unequivocally at the outset. Many school districts have decided to start community education by assigning the responsibilities to existing full-time staff members, usually providing them with some form of released time. The result has been that the program never really was able to get underway. Community education implies an expanded role for the school and that expanded role implies additional staff. Until a school district is willing to accept this fact, implementation of community education should not be attempted. We believe that community education attempted without this commitment generally fails, and in failing, destroys any future opportunity for implementation with appropriate support later. The "we tried that once but it didn't work" syndrome dissuades new efforts for many years.

The results can be equally disastrous if untrained personnel are involved. "The employment of untrained community educators on a mass scale can virtually destroy community education. As people are employed who have little or no understanding of their role, have few of the necessary skills to carry out the task, and have little or no commitment to meeting the potential of community education, programs will fail."[1]

The selection of the director of community education for the district is one of the most important decisions that will be made. Whether called a director, community agent, community developer, ombudsman, or something else, the leader will, to a large extent, mold and determine the program. What, then, should a district look for in its community education leadership? Are there particular personality traits, skills, training, and employment experiences that will enhance the potential for success?

In considering this, it is important to recall the changing nature of community education. As the concept has moved from a programmatic emphasis to include the concept of process, skills required of the director of a program have changed dramatically. A good example of the extent of the change can be gained by comparing earlier writings regarding the director's role to those of more recent vintage. It is clear from this review that the earlier emphasis was on personal characteristics while more recent analysis is directed toward technical and conceptual abilities.

W. Fred Totten, in the early 1960s, described community educators this way:

> Above all else, directors must be creative and have a warm, outgoing personality. They must like people and be capable of showing compassion without pity. They must be the kind of person to be trusted by people of all ages. They must be free from prejudice with respect to people of any race and/or socio-economic circumstances. Humility and consistency are two essential qualities. Directors must be in good emotional and physical health and capable of sustained energy and vigor for long periods of time. Flexibility and adaptability are essential personal qualities. Directors should be good team members and skillful leaders.
>
> Community service directors are generalists. They must have a thorough knowledge of and be productive in the areas of curriculum, instruction, and supervision. They must be strong in organizational

---

[1] LeTarte, Clyde E., "Federal Funds for Community Education: A Mixed Blessing," *Educational Considerations*, Kansas State University, Winter, 1974.

skills and techniques. Much of their work is administrative in nature. They are also called upon to counsel and advise on many occasions. Strength in leadership, communication, and human relations skills are essential to their successful performance. Their business is composed of people and helping people solve a great variety of human problems. Hence, they must be able to assess the needs of people; then they must plan, implement, and administer programs of learning to help people fulfill their unmet needs. In doing this, they must develop expertise in approaching nonschool agencies for assistance and in bringing into contact all of the efforts of churches and other organizations and groups to serve the learning needs of people. They must also bring into use the many individuals who can serve as resources for learning. All of the building space and other space in the community that can be used for learning programs must be discovered, and arrangements must be made to use the nonschool house space needed.[2]

Ernest Melby, in discussing the creative community education administrator says, "The educational administrator who knows people in many walks of life, who is aware of the extent and depth of human suffering, who understands the ideological conflicts of our world, who has met serious difficulties and somehow surmounted then—such a person is more likely to be understanding, sympathetic, and objective than one whose outlook is narrow and whose human experiences have been restricted."[3]

This emphasis on personal characteristics was carried through in the selection of early community education leaders. They were usually "people" people, energetic and friendly, outgoing, and dedicated to helping others. The fact that few had any training in the concepts of community organization, program development, and a variety of other technical skills was often overcome by sheer force of personality. And it should be noted that in the early stages of community education development, there were no training programs nor was there certainty regarding what skills would be needed.

---

[2] Totten, W. Fred, *The Community Services Director*, No. 532, Mott Program, Flint, Michigan, p. 3.

[3] Melby, Ernest O., *Administering Community Education*, Prentice Hall, Inc., Englewood Cliffs, New Jersey, 1955, p. 235.

Community education has now come into its own. It has expanded nationwide, and with this expansion, a common set of expectations (definitions) has emerged. While, admittedly, disagreement still exists within the profession as to the role, scope, and nature of community education, there is significant agreement as well. The extent of this agreement was discovered by Dr. Donald Weaver through a national study he conducted on community education goals in 1972. The goals determined as primary by at least 50 percent of the respondents were:

Coordination
> Coordinates efforts of community agencies
> Provides effective communication
> Eliminates duplication among agencies
> Assists residents to secure educational services
> Provides forum for community problems

Surveying
> Identifies community problems
> Surveys attitudes and interests
> Identifies required resources

Demonstration
> Demonstrates humanistic approach to education
> Demonstrates methods of social change
> Provides model for community living
> Demonstrates principles of educational leadership

Programming
> Extends use of school facilities
> Increases multi-age and cross-cultural contacts
> Provides programs for senior citizens
> Provides teen-age enrichment and recreation
> Provides recreation programs
> Provides high school completion program
> Improves educational opportunity for minorities

Training
Develops leadership among lay citizens

Promotion
Increases participation in existing school program
Promotes school as primary educational agency
Improves public image of the school[4]

Dr. Weaver analyzed this listing and established skill requirements for professionals who need to respond to these goals. He suggested six: coordination, surveying, demonstration, programming, training, and promotion. In his analysis of these skills (processes), Dr. Weaver concluded that a significant change had occurred in community education requiring a much higher degree of skill and knowledge and a corresponding reduction in the emphasis on personal requisites. The job had even then clearly changed.

Human beings do not come wrapped in either all personality and no skill or all skill and no personality. We are discussing degrees of difference and where primary emphasis should be placed. Ideally, individuals selected to lead community education will possess human skills and the technical and conceptual abilities needed. Not only will the director possess the type of personality that assures comfortable and open relationships with diverse community members, but also the conceptual skills to understand problems and issues, and the technical skills to establish and carry out a plan for resolving them. No other position is so important to the operation of community education as that of director. Regardless of the other inputs, the success or failure of the program will depend largely on who fills this position. The combination of personal qualities, training, and experiences are important factors in looking for such a person. And while the suggested job description and personal characteristics may sound difficult to fulfill, the fact is that hundreds of these positions are being filled by persons with energy, ability, and dedication who meet the requirements listed.

---

[4] Seay, Maurice F., and Associates, *Community Education: A Developing Concept*, Pendell Publishing Co., Midland, Michigan, pp. 130-133.

SELECTING THE SUPPORT TEAM

In addition to a director, selecting a good support staff to carry out the various programs is also important. Usually the support staff includes secretarial assistance, building or regional coordinators, and instructors. In many instances, the community education director is required to train these individuals, as many will work part-time and are local residents who may know the community but have little background in the concept of community education.

The critical aspect here may not be past experience, but an openness to learn and an innate feeling for the need to involve the community to a greater extent in the process. All of these people are usually the initial contact between the community and the community education program. They must be sensitive to the needs of others, patient and helpful, gracious in telephone and personal contacts, and open to criticism and change. They must, in the very best sense, represent the concerns and interest of the school for its community. Within this framework, support staff include: teachers, supervisors, and community workers.

The additional programs related to students and adults will require additional teaching staff. Some of the programs, such as remedial and enrichment classes, high school completion, and basic education will require certificated teachers. Other programs relating to avocational interests, such as hobbies, recreation, and special interest areas, will have teachers who themselves have developed these specialties. Classes in the vocational area will be staffed by people degreed or licensed in that particular area. Persons staffing these positions may be paid or they may be volunteers.

There will be many activities for adults, youth, and children that will require staff in other than a teacher-student relationship. Athletic contests, roller skating, dancing, public meetings, and similar types of activities require staff to accept the responsibility for supervising the activities and providing the services necessary to carry out these aspects of the program. This staff can be solicited from local personnel, either paid or volunteer, from teachers on a part-time basis, and for some activities, from students.

Working with the community will require additional staffing. First of all, to do the massive job of organizing the community and providing for community involvement, it is necessary to have people to do the door-to-door contacting and invest the time needed to work on community problems.

Second, despite all the outstanding characteristics of the director, it is sometimes easier to use indigenous personnel for work in the community. This is particularly true if the community is significantly different from the personal background of the director.

In any event, there is a need for staff to carry out the process aspect of community education. As the responsibilities in this area increase, there will be increased need for additional staff to work in the community, either paid or volunteer.

GAINING STAFF SUPPORT FOR COMMUNITY EDUCATION

The existing staff in an education system in which community education is being implemented will be required either to work in the program in some support role or at least be supportive of the concept and lend moral and philosophical support. The difficulty that will be faced in moving the traditional educator from a limited perspective of education to a broader, more encompassing concept is not that the philosophical premises are so much different, but rather that beliefs stated do not match actual practice. By understanding these hypocrisies of education and assisting those with whom we work to better understand that they exist, greater acceptance of a broadened role for education should result.

To illustrate, let us take a look at a few of these hypocrisies of educators—those differences between what school people say they believe and how they actually perform.

Belief: The first years of the life of a child are extremely important in the development of attitudes and intelligence.

Hypocrisy: Until recently, very few programs were available for children in this age group and even now, many of the existing ones are externally funded programs, often for disadvantaged children. In most states, formal learning starts at a specific age, geared to a specific month, a condition which is contrary to most evidence on learning.

Belief: Education is a gestalt with the school being only one of the forces influencing the education of the individual.

Hypocrisy: Most schools operate as though they were the only educative force in the community. Despite the fact that a student spends less than 11 percent of his or her time each year in the classroom, there is almost no effort to recognize other education inputs. The relationship between what takes place at home, at church, or in the neighborhood and the classroom is almost totally ignored. Educators, for example, know that language patterns are almost totally influenced by the home, that success in education is a result of home attitudes toward school, and that school work will be affected by such things as diet, rest, health, and various trauma outside the school setting. Yet, educators do little or nothing to allow or compensate for such influences. It may be that some students see this more clearly than do the professional educators. "Dad says I can quit school when I'm fifteen, and I am sort of anxious to because there are a lot of things I want to learn how to do and as my uncle says, I'm not getting any younger."[5]

Belief: Education should be relevant to the society it serves.

Hypocrisy: The curriculum has moved farther and farther from the purposes it was originally established to serve. When free public education was first begun, it was designed to meet the needs of society. The three "R's" were offered to provide a more literate population for employment and citizenship. The professions offered—law, medicine, and the clergy—were aimed at providing the necessary services for the community. Like so many other institutions, the schools have continued to

---

[5] Corey, Stephen, "The Poor Scholar's Soliliquy," *Childhood Education*, 20, January, 1944, pp. 219–220.

isolate themselves from the communities they are supposed to serve until they now dispense information without knowledge as to its relevance to the community. The situation might well be described as follows:

> I can solve a quadratic equation,
> but I cannot keep my bank balance straight.

> I can read Goethe's *Faust* in the original,
> but I cannot ask for a piece of bread in German.

> I can name the kings of England since the Wars of the Roses,
> but I do not know the qualifications of the candidates in the
> next election.

> I know the economic theories of Malthus and Adam Smith,
> but I cannot live within my income.

> I can recognize the "leit-motif" of a Wagner Opera,
> but I cannot sing in tune.

> I can explain the principles of hydraulics,
> but I cannot fix a leak in the kitchen faucet.

> I can read the plays of Moliere in the original,
> but I cannot order a meal in French.

> I have studied the psychology of James and Titchener,
> but I cannot control my own temper.

> I can conjugate Latin verbs,
> but I cannot write legibly.

> I can recite hundreds of lines of Shakespeare,
> but I do not know the Declaration of Independence, Lincoln's
> Gettysburg Address, or the Twenty-Third Psalm.[6]

Belief: The quality of knowledge is increasing at such an "explosive" level that there is a need for more time to educate children.

---

[6] Freeman, Bernadine, "Is This Education?" *The Educational Forum*, Vol. 15, January, 1951, p. 139.

Hypocrisy: The length of a school year has gravitated toward the minimal figure. School districts that used to have 195 days of school at a time when 180 days were required by state law have now settled on the 180-day school year as both the maximum and the minimum figure. The hours of the school day have also decreased so that the typical school day is now about five-and-one-half hours long.

There is ample evidence to show that while knowledge has grown at a phenomenal rate, contact time between the teacher and the student has decreased significantly.

Belief: School buildings represent an expensive investment by the community and should receive maximum use.

Hypocrisy: Despite talk about year-round schools and increased use of facilities, most buildings continue to be used only by the kindergarten through twelfth-grade elements of the community. Through a combination of finances, scheduling and possessiveness, most schools are kept in idleness for almost 90 percent of the total clock hours each year.

Belief: Education should reflect the community.

Hypocrisy: The local schools have continued to usurp the right of community involvement and community control. In fact, schools have moved so far away from community that they actually have become the adversaries. Schools have become operative unto themselves so that generally the only contact with the community is an information-giving one. School administrators "tell people about the schools, bring parents into the schools, sell the schools to the people. Very few efforts of a continuing type have been mounted which allow parents [and the community] opportunities to share their feelings about the schools with school officials. Information flow has been primarily one-way. Legitimate outlets have not been provided for protest or discontent. PTAs and similar organizations have often ruled discussions of local school weaknesses out of bounds to perpetuate a peaceful, tranquil, and all-is-well atmosphere. As a consequence, school systems have not had safety valves. There are no designed schemes for absorbing or dealing with pressure; [there is] no organized way of facing dissatisfaction. The emphasis has been on how well we are doing as reported and defined only by school people . . . organizations like PTAs have been co-opted by professionals much too often. PTAs and other symbiotic organizations have paid a high price for being loved by school personnel."[7]

Belief: Education is a lifetime process.

Hypocrisy: Educators tend to limit the goals of education, such as the seven cardinal principles of education, to a specific age group. Public school education is limited to that 20 percent of our population between the ages of five and eighteen. Most other education is on a limited scope, with scheduling, facilities, and instruction allocated low on the priority list. And although there are statistics to show that there are more people who need high school diplomas outside the schools than in; that there is a substantial number of adults who are either illiterate or functionally illiterate; that there is a greater need for health programs in the adult population than in the student population; the fact remains that in all areas of education the needs of children not only get top priority but the traditional program often tends to exclude all other community education needs.

If we compare what traditional educators and community educators say they believe, one can see a great deal of similarity, at least as it applies to the traditional educative role of the school. The major difference seems to be that community education attempts to develop aspects of education for the entire community while traditionalists in education seem interested in only one segment of the population.

There is another basic difference, however, related to the "process" element of community education. In this area, community educators are suggesting that schools take the responsibility for activities formerly held to be outside the realm of the school. Community educators are saying that schools should be the catalytic institutions for bringing about coor-

---

[7] Cunningham, Luvern, *Governing Schools: New Approaches to Old Issues*, Charles Merrill Publishing Co., Columbus, Ohio, 1971, p. 176.

dination of social and government agencies, community organization, and community involvement.

Our communities are developing new expectations about the schools. The first expectation is that schools carry out their traditional job better in relating curriculum to the community, involving the community in making decisions about education, and opening opportunities for education to all members of the community rather than just a selected few. But schools also have the responsibility of establishing a new role. They must be the catalysts in helping the community develop esprit de corps, identify its problems, and use its resources to influence the decisions related to these problems. This role implies not only opening its doors, but reaching out to those community members who do not respond to the program aspect of community education.

How does all of this relate to modifying traditional behavior and moving toward expanded support for community education by colleagues in the system? Assuming that people want to perform in a manner consistent with their philosophical beliefs, then a change in beliefs—or a recognition of inconsistency—should result in a corresponding modification of behavior, or at least an expanded openness to change.

If the community education director can help others understand that community education is a new and broadened role for education consistent with most philosophies of education, opportunities for support from other educators are greatly enhanced.

USING EXTERNAL RESOURCES

Earlier, the importance of involving other agencies and groups in community education programming was emphasized. Community education is not intended to become either the provider of all services or the system that replaces and assumes many activities that are already in place. It does, however, have an important coordinating role, one that assumes that many services will be provided by others and that staffing for these services will be done through other agencies. In the broadest sense of community education, then, all staffing will not be controlled by the community education director.

Generally, the community school staff will have little input into the selection of the staff of other agencies. The important thing is to be aware of all of these resources and to incorporate them into the total program of community education. In addition, it is also important that these people from other agencies recognize the community education concept and their part in it. This will be a difficult and time-consuming task. The immediate reaction by agencies to community education is often one of mistrust and threat. It will be the responsibility of those building the community education program to work with these other groups to define the concept, illustrate its value, and involve outside groups in its implementation. At first, it will be necessary to reassure such groups of the need for their services in the total plan. As they become more involved, they will begin to realize that their programs and services actually increase in size and scope and that such coordination is the most appropriate way to attack community problems and improve conditions. Once the initial concept is understood and accepted by such groups, the primary concern becomes one of establishing techniques for cooperation, coordination, and effective communication.

TRAINING

While the preparation of people for work in community education is not directly related to staffing problems and interests, it is important to understand what can be expected if someone is a well-trained community educator. Obviously, based on preceding statements in this section, this training is of great importance.

First, a person should be an experienced educator with a broad and encompassing understanding of the education process and the education system. This means that an undergraduate degree in education is necessary. In that many of the director's efforts are administrative, training in school administration will necessitate advanced study. Many universities that prepare people for community education leadership have established this tie between education and administration and offer advanced degrees in community education leadership through their departments of educational administration.

The placement of such programs in educational administration has not been accidental. There is a logic behind why most institutions have moved in this direction in their training.

1. Community education seems to be most productive when worked through the public schools. While this may not be the only way such a program can be successful, to date, it has proved to be the method most likely to succeed. Thus, if the programs are to be run through the school, it seems logical to conclude that preparation programs might also be handled by the colleges of education at the higher education level.

2. If one accepts the idea that the school should be the vehicle for implementing community education, then there is some advantage to making the director's role administrative. Such a position will give the director certain relationships with the school staff, and will allow the director to operate on a task-oriented basis without the restrictions of time imposed by a master contract.

3. The career direction of most people in community education seems to be toward administration. During the past 40 years, it has been possible to determine, from a review of their aspirations, what professional direction community educators will take. While many have stayed in their positions as directors of elementary-size districts, most have gone on to other administrative positions. Some of these positions have been as coordinators of community education for the school district, but a large number have moved into more traditional administrative roles, such as principalships, central office staff, or superintendencies.

4. There is great value in attaching a new role to a traditional discipline. When a new position and new responsibilities are identified, it takes some time for them to be accepted or perceived appropriately by other members of the staff. Most new programs and positions have had a difficult and prolonged battle in trying to receive acceptance both by other educators and the commu-

nity. By identifying with a traditional discipline (such as school administration), identification, role definition, and acceptance are more immediately accomplished.

5. If the point about identifying with a traditional discipline is accepted, then the only task left is to discover which identification is most appropriate. A close look at the responsibilities of directors of community education reveals that they hire and discharge people, build schedules, arrange for rooms, handle registration, deal primarily in education, work at public relations, relate to people of all ages, and do many other administrative tasks. Thus, this position seems to be more akin to school administration than to any other position in education.

The graduate training program of community school directors generally consists of core courses, cognate courses in the field of education, and electives from areas other than education. The training program will usually be made up of courses in such areas as leadership, education organization, community organization, the conceptual base of community education, community education administration, adult education, research techniques, and school and community relations. Elective areas, both in and out of education, should be aimed at the development of individuals in areas that will improve their understanding and ability to deal with the individual and the community.

Specific goals of a good program for community education leadership should emphasize and assure competence in the following areas.

A. *Understanding the Community Education Philosophy*
Each graduate should:

1. have established a philosophy of community education and should be able to defend it among his or her peers

2. be able to define community education and illustrate specific programs and processes by which it is to be implemented

3. be able to analyze a community education program, and determine the strengths and weaknesses of the program and the extent of community involvement within the program

4. have achieved a level of competence sophisticated enough to allow him or her to initiate and operate successfully a community education program

B. *Technical Skills for Implementing Community Education*
Each graduate should:

1. be able to analyze a community power structure and understand how this power structure can best be used for community growth

2. be able to establish an effective community council

3. know how to conduct and analyze a community study

4. understand the relationship that should exist between schools and other community agencies and how to organize these agencies to accomplish the purposes of the community education program

5. be able to initiate and operate specific programs found within the general framework of community education—of adult education, recreation, student enrichment, special programs designed to meet special needs, etc.

C. *Humanitarian Concerns*
Each graduate should:

1. be able to describe the complex nature of the society and the resulting effect on individuals

2. recognize internally an increased tolerance for human differences and an increased feeling of concern for those within the society

3. understand the shortcoming of our existing education system and possess a desire to create change within the system

D. *General Administrative Skills*
Each graduate should:

1. be able to describe different types of administrative organizations and specify where community education fits into these structures

2. understand the roles and responsibilities of the superintendent of schools, elementary and secondary principals, curriculum directors, school business officials, and other selected administrative personnel

3. understand the basic principles involved in budgeting, decision making, team management, and current administrative theory

4. understand group processes and know how to lead a group toward goal attainment

5. understand how to create an organizational climate in which all members may make significant contributions

6. be able to communicate orally and in writing clearly and precisely

TEACHER TRAINING

Training of teachers of classes in the community education program will deal primarily with techniques. Teachers employed in these classes are usually well-equipped with regard to the subject matter they are teaching. The shortcomings are generally in the area of methodology. For those who have never been teachers, there is a need for training in teaching techniques. For those who have been teachers, the problem usually centers around their lack of experience in teaching adults. There are few programs established for dealing with these problems. Some colleges and universities have recognized this need and are attempting to establish such programs. In general, however, the efforts being made are being carried out on a local, school district basis.

TRAINING SUPERVISORS AND ASSISTANTS

The training of supervisors and assistants is an easier matter and usually can be handled locally through in-service education. The responsibilities of these jobs include opening buildings, providing operational services, and interpreting rules and regulations. As such, there is little training needed, and usually individuals are able to function effectively in these positions after limited experience. These individuals should be encouraged to seek further training to expand their competence and to establish a cadre of individuals trained to advance in the system and assume additional responsibilities.

It appears that the need for trained community educators will continue to increase. While personal characteristics certainly are of prime importance, our contention is that additional and appropriate training will enhance the individual responsible for community education and subsequently enhance community education itself. The programs for training are not all alike and will most certainly change as community education becomes more sophisticated.

Chapter XIII

Establishing
an
In-Service Program
to
Meet Staff Needs

In-service education is probably one of the most maligned, misused, and misunderstood processes in education today. At the same time, it is potentially one of the most important tools for change within the educator's "bag of tricks." Many educators feel that education goals and objectives can never truly be reached without a vibrant in-service education process in operation within the education system.

If change is to take place within a system, it must be done through the people already employed within the system. It is recognized that this usually is difficult, since these same people are usually the ones who created a need for change in the first place. It must also be recognized, however, that in a time of decline or stabilizing enrollments, little staff change will occur. Former means of creating change through a continuous infusion of new blood will no longer be viable. Staff employed now will be, for the most part, the same staff employed five and ten years from now. A process for encouraging change and growth must therefore be established to assist these individuals in improving and maintaining their skills and competence.

To state that in-service education is of major importance is an understatement. To state that community education can never reach its true potential without in-service training is redundant. And to state that in-service education is normally at best poorly done, and at worst ignored, is stating something most people know and accept.

These statements are all true . . . most community educators accept them as fact . . . but what is being done to expand insights and to improve the general quality of education? How else can community educators gain commitment to an education philosophy as demanding and time-consuming as the one they espouse without a sophisticated, comprehensive, and dynamic in-service program? The basic point is this: while educators recognize all of the negative attributes of existing in-service education, it is simply impossible to develop good community education without good in-service programs.

Educators must recognize that knowledge does become obsolete, that new ideas must be not only learned but accepted and integrated into our education philosophies, that people do have to recharge old batteries and be stimulated and excited, and that educators, like all people, lose perspective in their day-to-day routine and must be provided with opportunities to continually reassess and re-evaluate their performance. In-service education can and should provide this.

ESTABLISHING A BASE FOR IN-SERVICE EDUCATION

Three basic ingredients seem to make up the poor programs that education leaders have historically forced upon other educators as in-service training: tradition, noncommitment, and poor financing. By analyzing each, and avoiding all three, we move toward a significantly improved effort and result.

TRADITION

Educators usually have viewed any in-service program as that period of time when they call together a given staff for one or two hours at the beginning of the year to somehow, in some way, improve their performance. This is usually done through a speaker of stature making a presentation to a rather large group—people who have mixed emotions about their presence, the content, and the value of the whole activity.

The rationale for this approach is simple: it is safe and has been done this way for years. There seems to have developed a tacit understanding between the educators planning the in-service and the educators receiving it. If you sit through a rather dull presentation without too many complaints, you won't be expected to change and improve performance. While this may overstate the case, it is basically true. Information is presented rather traditionally and is seldom internalized by the recipient. When knowledge is not internalized into a basic education philosophy, it is not used. As a result, little, and usually nothing, results from these attempts.

This same sentiment is expressed in a publication of the National School Public Relations Association: "Staff development has always been a stepchild of the American educational process. A necessary stepchild, perhaps, to meet the technical requirements of states toward permanent teacher certification, but basically a stepchild nevertheless."[1]

---

[1] *In Service Education: Current Trends in School Policies and Programs,* National School Public Relations Association, Arlington, Virginia, 1975, p. 5.

NONCOMMITMENT

The second most common reason for failure in in-service programming is noncommitment. In very simple terms, the in-service programs presented suffer from lack of thinking and lack of planning. While most educators stress the importance of in-service education, few are willing to spend the time necessary to make it successful. They ascribe to it great importance in words, but not in the amount of time they are willing to spend to assure success. To be meaningful, in-service education must be given a priority of time to assure adequate planning and program development.

POOR FINANCING

The third reason in-service often fails is financial. It is continually underfunded. Educators must not only be willing to spend substantial amounts of time in developing a good in-service program, but must be willing to spend the money necessary to see it through as well. In a world of financial priorities, educators seldom give proper priority to the development and growth of the staff that turns ideas into action and determines the success of the entire program.

As community educators establish a base for a good in-service program, these three negative characteristics must be accounted for; however, they should be stated positively. In-service education should be designed to insure positive desired change. To do this, adequate time and money must be expended and creative approaches to change should be encouraged and used. While this statement attempts to avoid reasons for failure, it does not provide any ideas for assuring success. It cannot be assumed that success will be achieved by merely eliminating negative aspects. Positive insurers of success must also be established. Some of these include: involving participants in planning for group and individual differences, establishing objectives, and assuring adequate evaluation.

PLANNING FOR PARTICIPATION

If there is one thing educators have learned from sociologists, psychologists, and group process people that can assist them in planning in-service education, it is that participants must be involved in the total program if they are to gain the most from it. It is important that conclusions reached and plans established in an in-service program emerge from within the group. This insures that the product will be a group product, and the group then shares in the responsibility of success or failure in the decision. By establishing a program that insures maximum participation of the people that will be involved, greater chances of success are assured. Programs should be geared around the group's unique problems and needs and around the concerns common to the group. Programming must start where the group is and move toward the desired goal. It would be wise, for example, to consider whether or not the members of the group know each other. If they do not, it is necessary to get them to know each other well enough to participate effectively in the program that has been planned. If they do know each other, what is the relationship among members of the group? Are they friendly? Do they have negative feelings about each other? Are they indifferent?

Another concern that might be considered in terms of the group is gearing the in-service program to the level of sophistication of the group members. Determining this general level of sophistication and how much difference there is between members of the group are but two considerations of many that must be accounted for in recognizing the unique differences within groups.

CONSIDERING THE PARTICIPANTS

In planning an in-service session, it is also important to consider what participants appreciate and expect. An example of this type of consideration for teachers is provided by Hilmar Wagner in his review of what teachers prefer in in-service programming:

Ten Suggestions on What Teachers Like at In-Service Meetings

◆ Teachers like meetings in which they can be actively involved. Just as students do not want to be passive, most teachers prefer Dewey's 'learning by doing.'

◆ Teachers like to watch other teachers demonstrate various techniques in their teaching field. Demonstration teaching can serve as a model that teachers can take back to their classrooms.

◆ Teachers like practical information—almost step-by-step recipes—on how others approach certain learning tasks. Too often, in-service programs are theoretical and highly abstract.

◆ Teachers like meetings that are short and to the point. The introduction of guests at a meeting is often ego-filling for those introduced, but cuts into valuable in-service time.

◆ Teachers like an in-depth treatment of one concept that can be completed in one meeting rather than a generalized treatment that attempts to solve every teacher's problems in one session.

◆ Teachers like well-organized meetings.

◆ Teachers like variety in in-services programs. If the same topics are covered every time, attendance may drop off.

◆ Teachers like some incentive for attending in-service meetings; released time, salary increments, advancement points on rating scales.

◆ Teachers like inspirational speakers occasionally. Such speakers can often give a staff the necessary drive to start or complete a school year.

◆ Teachers like to visit other schools to observe other teachers in situations similar to their own. These visits, even when observing poor teachers, are highly educational.[2]

While many of these suggestions focus on teacher in-service efforts, many of the issues raised should be considered when planning any type of in-service activity.

DEVELOPING THE IN-SERVICE PROGRAM

Developing an in-service program is quite different from planning an in-service training session. The in-service program entails the total plan developed for the entire year. It will include a variety of activities and training sessions within it. Planning this total program requires much thought and discussion. To begin, it is important to get rid of the old notion that

---

[2] Wagner, Hilmar, "What Teachers Like," *In Service Education: Current Trends in School Policies and Programs*," National School Public Relations Association, Arlington, Virginia, 1975.

in-service education always centers around meetings and group get-togethers. Much effective in-service education can be handled through subscriptions to appropriate journals; establishing a regular means of communication, such as a newsletter; suggesting specific reading; or developing a professional library that is easily accessible to the staff. Mini sabbaticals, planned visits to other programs, and encouraging professional involvement in associations are other less common but often effective techniques. Even within the standard concept of in-service education (meetings), there is much room for innovation. Instead of the traditional lecture or lecture-discussion, meetings can be developed around simulation games, the case study technique, two- or three-day retreats, or a free-wheeling, totally unstructured session inviting people to brainstorm on a given problem or issue.

These suggestions are not intended to be all inclusive, but rather to initiate some thinking and present some creative possibilities for in-service education. The community educator, in planning an in-service program, must consider as many techniques and innovations as possible and determine which ones, or which combination, best fit the training needs of the staff that will be involved.

The establishment of a good in-service education program seems to fall naturally into six basic areas:

1. Defining the problem to be attacked
2. Determining what can be accomplished through in-service training
3. Establishing general goals and objectives for the in-service effort
4. Determining how the goals and objectives can best be reached (program planning)
5. Carrying the program out as planned
6. Evaluating

It has been stated previously that inclusion of participants from the beginning is essential. It is restated here to underscore its importance. Participation by those who will be involved is essential for a truly effective in-service effort. This involvement should start at the very beginning with the determination of what is to be achieved through the program.

While it is impossible to include all participants in the planning, it is possible to select as diverse a group as possible to assure that many are incorporated into the planning. This is often avoided in the interest of expediency, and individuals are selected who tend to agree with one another and who can complete the task quickly. Selections of this kind are little better than having no group participation at all, because diverse opinions are never heard.

DEFINING THE PROBLEM TO BE ATTACKED

Once the task force that will assist in planning has been determined, members should be asked to define the general problem with which they should be concerned. At this point, the community educator should express specific purposes and provide committee members with any supplemental materials that might assist them. A new director of community education, for example, might explain that the purpose for providing in-service education the first year is to establish community education in the system as a bona fide part of education and to make sure that there is general understanding of what community education is. This process allows the committee to think through the general purposes of the in-service effort and to redefine these purposes into more meaningful terms for them.

DETERMINING WHAT CAN BE ACCOMPLISHED THROUGH IN-SERVICE

As the committee begins to study the problem, it will become evident that some of the purposes discussed will not be met through in-service alone. Such purposes should be identified so that the committee eliminates discussion of general education issues and considers only those issues relevant to the proposed in-service training effort. It is necessary to remember, at this point, that the committee is not rejecting some of the existing education concerns because they are unimportant, but rather because they cannot be best achieved through the planned in-service. This redefining and narrowing of scope helps the director determine which general purposes must be accomplished through other means.

ESTABLISHING GENERAL GOALS AND OBJECTIVES FOR THE IN-SERVICE EDUCATION EFFORT

Once general consensus has been reached on the general purposes of the in-service efforts, specific objectives should be established. The objectives should be stated in specific terms so that an evaluation can be made upon the completion of the program.

At this point, for example, the committee might determine that since a general goal of the program is the establishment of community education as a bona fide part of the system, the specific behavioral objective might be: a minimum of 80 percent of all teachers and administrative personnel participating in the in-service program shall feel strongly enough about the value of community education that they will sign a prepared statement to this effect at the conclusion of the program, and the statement will be submitted to the superintendent of schools.

The objective is measurable and can be evaluated at the end of the program. Other factors that might be in an in-service program designed to initiate community education could include the upgrading of teachers in specific program areas (such as adult education, recreation, or student enrichment), the reconsideration of existing school system priorities, or the rethinking of custodial job descriptions. Whatever the committee decides, members should attempt to put their thinking into definitive and measurable objectives. If time is a problem, the director can assist the committee by taking the general goals and writing the initial drafts for the behavioral objectives. Committee members can then take these and rewrite and rework them until they are satisfied.

DETERMINING HOW GOALS AND OBJECTIVES CAN BEST BE REACHED (PROGRAM PLANNING)

Once goals and objectives have been established, the committee must turn to the problem of planning the in-service program that will best meet these objectives. At this point, the community educator can be of great assistance by providing the group with information concerning a variety of possible techniques. He or she should also discuss what makes a success in an in-service program to assure that proven concepts will be incorporated.

CARRYING THE PROGRAM OUT AS PLANNED

While this step seems quite evident, it is important to stress the need to carry out the program *as it was planned*. Too often directors have become involved with a variety of other activities and forget the responsibilities they had assumed, or some of the specific plans of the committee. Whenever group process is used in planning, it is essential that the intent of the group be carried out. Failure to do this is often interpreted as the administrator's attempt to subvert the advice of the committee. At this point, group process begins to disintegrate.

EVALUATING

Assuming that the previous steps have been carried out, the evaluation process is a rather simple one. The behavioral objectives must be evaluated at the completion of the program to determine whether or not they were met. If they were not met, some assessment must be made as to why they were not, and a decision then made about what must be done to see that they are met. This phase also provides some information to assist in making future decisions about the value of in-service efforts and the extent of funding that such activities should receive.

EXISTING NATIONAL TRENDS IN IN-SERVICE

The preceding suggestions seem consistent with several national trends in in-service education presented in a National Education Association Research Bulletin:

> Teachers or their representatives are usually involved in planning the in-service program. Administrators, supervisors, and teachers work as a team.

> Greater use is being made of the professional staff within a school system. Non-college credit programs are conducted by school personnel.

> School systems are offering a wider variety of opportunities and activities for professional growth in in-service.

> School systems are providing more released time during the regular school session for in-service activities.

Compensation is being given for time contributed to in-service education by the teacher outside regular school hours.

School systems are extending the period of teacher employment; the additional time is used for in-service education.

Salary practices recognize experience and preparation.

In-service programs are receiving financial support from sources other than the school system.

Nearly all in-service programs have subjective evaluation; systematic statistical evaluations are not widespread.[3]

PLANNING FOR COMMUNITY EDUCATION IN-SERVICE

The preceding pages have been directed to a general discussion of in-service education. The information presented provides some broad guidelines for the community educator or any other person planning an in-service effort.

While the general guidelines presented establish some concerns that all educators must face in planning in-service education, there are specific issues that also must be considered in planning an in-service effort in community education.

1. Promoting a new philosophy—The community educator must understand from the outset that in-service success in community education will be more difficult to achieve than in most other areas of education. Most in-service efforts are geared to solving a specific school problem, to the development and use of a new technique, or to the stimulation of teachers to encourage a greater teaching effort. While these efforts are often challenging, they usually do not require significant change.

   Community Education presents a concept substantially different from that held by most educators and community members. To succeed in an in-service effort in community education,

---

[3] "Professional Growth of Teachers in Service," *NEA Research Bulletin*, XLV, March, 1967, pp. 25–26.

old belief systems and patterns of operation must be broken down before new ones can be developed. It is always difficult to change existing patterns of behavior. Community education requires this change before success can be achieved.

2. Most education in-service efforts attempt to change people whose lives are dedicated toward a specified responsibility. The second-grade teacher should become the best possible second-grade teacher. The high school English teacher should teach English in the most effective way possible. In most instances, the people involved have accepted a full-time professional responsibility in their given area of concern.

   The community educator, especially in the early stages of community education development, is forced to work with part-time people. This group often perceives its part-time assistance as a means of making a few extra dollars—nothing more. While it is difficult to change individuals involved on a full-time basis, it is even more difficult to establish change if the involvement is perceived as something of secondary importance.

3. Earlier in the chapter, the general problem of underfunding was discussed. While this is a problem faced by all who attempt to provide in-service programs, it is even more acutely faced by the community educator. In the early stages of development, when in-service is most needed, finances are the most difficult to obtain. It is a simple fact of life that most community education programs are not adequately funded initially. The conflicting demands for existing dollars, then, are much greater in community education than they would be in programs that have had time to develop and establish. Community educators often face the difficult dilemma of adequately supporting important in-service efforts at the expense of establishing two or three essential community services.

4. Because community education does not limit education to the schools, or its in-service efforts to teachers or administrators, any in-service planned must deal with extremely diverse groups who

have specified and unique functions within the general program effort. It is impossible to establish one or two major in-service efforts to adequately serve all groups. How, for example, could you combine the in-service needs of all teachers in the program with those of the building directors; the needs of school administrators with those of paraprofessionals; or the needs of the school board with those of a staff employed to provide high school completion opportunities to adults.

Unique diverse needs require many different in-service efforts in community education. Directors must consider the scope of the program, the diversity of the groups involved, and the in-service requirements of each.

WHO NEEDS IN-SERVICE AND WHY?

The preceding pages have described general in-service needs and the diverse groups with whom community educators must concern themselves. Each of the groups has unique needs that must be met through different techniques. The administration, for example, must have a fairly sophisticated understanding of the concept before true support can be gained. An in-service program for this group must be designed to clearly portray the concept and define the role the administrator will play within it. It must be done on an intellectually sophisticated level, incorporating a rationale for the concept based on existing knowledge in the field.

Teachers also need to understand the concept and to identify their role within it. The specific concerns of this group, however, focus on the classroom and the effect community education will have on the relationship between students and themselves, parent involvement, and increased community expectations. In-service efforts for teachers must include methods of relieving teacher anxiety, demonstrating the positive impact of community involvement, and stressing the importance of educational relevance to the needs of the community.

In addition to teachers and administrators, it is also important to include the school's noncertified staff in an in-service effort. If this group can develop an acceptance of the concept, it can then accept work schedule changes, new responsibilities, and new problems with less difficulty.

In-service efforts for this group must stress the important role that non-certified personnel play in community education, attempting to make them feel they are an important part of the team.

Because of the broad nature of community education, in-service efforts cannot be limited to the staff of the public school. In-service efforts must also be developed for social and government agencies, lay citizens, and the business and industrial community. Each of these groups, while unique, shares the need to understand its role in community education, the advantages that may be obtained through its involvement, and the new sense of purpose that may be established in the entire community.

As previously indicated, extensive planning for in-service is crucial. Before involving others in the in-service planning process, it is important to clarify what is to be accomplished in your own mind. This often can best be established by using outside professional assistance. A consultant with special expertise in in-service planning may be employed to help. There are also many professional community educators throughout the country who can provide extensive leadership experience and expertise. State and national community education associations exist that provide consulting services to community educators, and many state departments of education are now staffed to assist districts in the development of community education. In addition to this, extensive reading may also provide appropriate assistance, and numerous books, articles, videos, and other types of media are now available with excellent supportive information.

The every static nature of the present situation in education will require creative in-service efforts—and these efforts, if done well, can greatly assist in moving community education from a conceptual base to a practical reality.

CHAPTER XIV

FACILITIES
PLANNING

The proper design of any facility depends on the use for which that facility is intended. Any other premise will result in an edifice disappointing to those who are to benefit from it and dysfunctional to those who are to use it.

The design of a school building thus depends on identifying the objectives to be accomplished and the means by which these objectives are to be promoted. This has always been a truism in the design of education facilities. When schools were to serve as town hall meeting sites, facilities were planned for such use. When free transportation was not viewed as a public school function, schools were located on main highways for easy access.

ARCHITECTURAL SPECIFICATIONS

In the early years of school construction, school buildings began with the employment of architects whose function was to design the school and oversee its construction. Unfortunately, there were many communities that acknowledged a perceived expertise among architects and consequently often entrusted them with total responsibility for the entire building project. There was an assumption that if architects knew the amount of money available and the type of buildings needed (elementary, junior high, or senior high), they could then proceed to develop appropriate buildings on the basis of professional know-how and experience.

SCHOOL SPECIFICATIONS

Unfortunately, and to the chagrin of many districts, it was often discovered that the completed facility was not as they had expected and that many of the buildings lacked some of the basic ingredients of a good education program. It soon became evident that the expertise of the architect should be supplemented by input from the profession—the teachers and administrators. As a result, more and more school plant planners began to recommend that in addition to the architectural specifications relating to heat, light, acoustics, and physical space, there was a need to have educational specifications. These specifications were intended to provide the architect with vital information only a teacher or experienced educator might possess.

Through teacher involvement in planning, buildings were improved. The observations and suggestions related to such things as recessed drinking fountains, blackboard glare, lighting problems, closet space, boot and mitten storage, and placement of electrical outlets proved essential. By itemizing those things in a given building that had led to less effective learning, the architect was able to eliminate some of the previous problems in school buildings. Furthermore, by knowing the goals and objectives the teachers had established for their courses, as well as the type of curricula to be offered and the techniques to be used, the architects were more realistically able to perform their functions.

In most cases, other specifications were also added. By including the custodians, the secretaries, the bus drivers, the cafeteria workers, and others who were expected to function in this facility, it was possible to do a better all-around job, and the final product more nearly met the expectations of the staff members of that school.

COMMUNITY EDUCATION SPECIFICATIONS

To develop a community school requires a similar approach; the main difference is one of goals and involvement. While it is true that community members have been included in drawing school specifications, their task has generally been one of expressing their points of view on the traditional school program as perceived by parents.

To more clearly state the difference, we must first look at the goals and objectives of such a facility. In the book-centered era, the specifications were designed to match the goals of such an endeavor. If book-learning was a major theme, then it would logically follow that specifications would describe a building concentrated on the role of a school that disseminated information, stressed academic discipline, and provided for the teacher-learner process of education.

In the child-centered era (the prevailing ideology today), the specifications required a different approach. It became necessary to provide for individual instruction, with small group activity, and facilities such as blackboards and bulletin boards scaled down to student size. With the focus on the learner, furniture became moveable, rather than stationary. Flexibility became the byword, with chairs that adjusted, walls that moved, variance in space, and floors that could be walked or sat upon. Schools became the center of child or youth activity in which the very design suggested the exclusion of all others.

If one were then to attempt to identify the main difference in building design as suggested by community education, it would be necessary to identify the differences in goals and objectives. At the risk of committing educational heresy, community education believes that education facilities should be available to all persons on an equal basis. It then becomes necessary to develop specifications that take into account the differences in age, size, and availability of those to be served. Thus, if instead of serving a group of children ages five to 13, the school is to provide for the education needs of all persons, then a different design is needed for that facility.

The job is not as formidable as it might seem. First of all, it is a matter of making an already flexible program more flexible. Second, it is a matter of involving the community in planning the specifications. And third, it is simply keeping in mind that students function quite well in the adult world at home and in the communities and can, in a similar fashion, function effectively in a learning climate designed for both adult and child use.

The first task, then, in developing community education specifications is to identify the goals and objectives for such a concept. While the overriding philosophy of community education will be the same for every community, it will be necessary to interpret this philosophy into behavioral objectives according to the specific needs of that community. To do this will require an assessment of the community to understand the nature of the community and the areas of need. It will also be necessary to have information about the physical factors of the community, the economic and business activity, social and government aspects, social agency operation, and other facilities available for community education. With this knowledge, and with community involvement, it now becomes possible to develop objectives and begin to draw up specifications. Such specifications can then be used by the architect to design a school facility that will meet the needs of all it is to serve.

The culmination of these efforts will result in the construction of the building. The ensuing operation of the building will provide for programs and operation of activities within the building which, when properly evaluated, will reflect on how well the original philosophy has been interpreted and implemented. Evaluation, then, becomes the technique which allows the community to again look at its philosophy and regenerate the cycle so that such planning becomes an ongoing and self-perpetuating process.

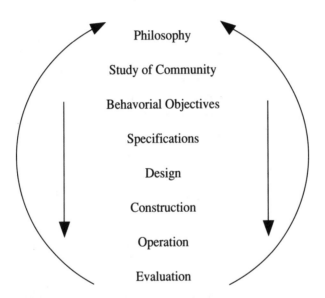

Philosophy

Study of Community

Behavorial Objectives

Specifications

Design

Construction

Operation

Evaluation

The difference between this approach to school construction and previous methods is that frequently our past efforts have started at the specification level, and the inputs have been primarily from a limited representation of those to be affected by the outcome. It has already been strongly pointed out that since the design of the building will reflect community needs and objectives, each building program will be somewhat unique. Nevertheless, there has been a degree of commonality in districts that have designed buildings for community education. Following are some specific suggestions to assist districts in their planning.

EXISTING FACILITIES

In evaluating building needs for providing community education, one should consider existing facilities and avoid duplication when possible. Many public and private facilities frequently can provide adequate space for community activities. For example, many existing school buildings, both public and private, have special facilities, such as shops, home economics facilities, and auditoriums, that are both accessible and available. Such facilities should not be duplicated unless there is a definite need to do so. In a similar manner, lodge halls, churches, government buildings, YMCA and YWCA facilities, theaters, public parks, recreation areas, facilities of business and industry, and even private homes provide suitable space where community education activities can take place. A part of facility planning is to make effective use of existing facilities through identification and coordination. Expensive duplication is an unacceptable and potentially dangerous approach to facility planning.

Too frequently, the many services and agencies in a community plan and construct their facilities without deference to what others are doing in the same community. The end result is of schools, libraries, senior citizen's buildings, and recreation facilities built with little or no relationship to each other. The administrators of these separate units seem to support this system of duplication, but the tax payer and consumer often view the non-coordinated operation as costly and unnecessary.

While the focal point of this discussion is the building of school facilities for multiple community use or the use of school buildings for community services in addition to schooling, it is also desirable to follow similar thinking related to other combinations of buildings and services. In one community in the eastern United States, for example, the fire hall was combined with a public library and a recreation area. The end product was a facility that served three functions. In addition, the staff of the fire station was available to help operate the library and direct recreation programs during the times when they were on duty but not responding to fires or other emergencies.

THE SCHOOL SITE

There are some generally accepted guidelines for a traditional school site. School plant planners often use such figures as ten acres of land plus one acre for each 100 students in an elementary school and 30 to 40 acres plus one acre for each 100 secondary students. In designing a school for community use, these may not be adequate sizes. Added school use and additional activities may necessitate more space. As the needs are identified, adjustments may be necessary to do an adequate job. The main caution here is that it is first necessary to identify the activities to be carried out before arriving at a site size. Accepting a suggested size based on a traditional program will result in inadequate space for carrying out the program.

SCHOOL-PARK SITE

In many large cities, sites of the recommended size are simply not available. If they are available, the land expense is too great. In most large cities, the cost of an acre of land would exceed one million dollars, and building on a adequate site would be prohibitive. In those areas, the need for community education and a community center, however, may be greater than in any other type of community. To accomplish the objectives of community education, therefore, it becomes necessary to be more inventive and innovative. A high-rise building with additional facilities below ground may provide part of the answer, and development of roof space and other available space may be the only means of increasing the facilities in the school.

One promising practice has been the school-park site. In most communities, planners have provided for city parks which are generally located throughout the city. Such parks are usually the only open space areas in the community and generally include such things a ball fields, picnic areas, play areas, and playground apparatus. They may even have a stream, lake, or pond. These parks make ideal playgrounds and are frequently least used at the time when school is in session.

With cooperative effort, it is possible to build a school building adjacent to such a site to get the best possible use from both facilities. The schools, with buildings built to community specifications, can use the park area for their student activities. In fact, the park area is frequently better developed than a traditional school site and subsequently, can provide for more and better student activities.

Similarly, the school building can also serve the members of the community by adding to the facilities that already exist in the park. Community members now have meeting rooms, classrooms, a gym and other facilities. Furthermore, cooperative planning can result in joint financing of such facilities as a year-round attached swimming pool and a social service wing of the school that can provide an employment office, medical center, dental chair, counseling offices, and other necessary community services. The end result is a combined venture which enhances the program for both the children and the community and, because of mutual planning, eliminates unnecessary duplication. This saves funds for the community which can then be used in better ways.

OUTSIDE FACILITIES

Consideration of the areas surrounding the school can frequently proceed from the assumption that such areas will include all the traditional facilities plus those needed to serve the additional activities of persons not currently provided for in such planning. Ball fields, play areas, hard surfaced sites, play apparatus, basketball facilities, underground wiring, proper drainage and nature trails are all things to be considered in such site development. In addition, however, the extended use of the site and the additional groups to be served will necessitate other considerations. Lighting of the activity area will allow for evening activities. Increased parking will become necessary to accommodate adults who use the facilities. Other types of games for more sedentary persons, such as horseshoe pits and shuffleboard, should be available. Pools for expanding summer programs should be considered, either as permanent facilities or by using some of the temporary or portable units available. Outside functions will demand toilets constructed for winter as well as summer use. Hard surfaced areas for such things as roller skating should be provided, and such areas can be constructed so that ice skating is available during the winter months. Picnic sites for family and group outings should also be included.

While such suggestions are certainly optimal and may not be possible in all communities, the limitation on such planning should be in terms of space and finances and not the planning. Again, it is important to remember that the criteria for such planning are community needs and interest.

THE BUILDING

The primary consideration in planning the building is, again, based on who is to use it and for what purposes it is to be used. Naturally, one of the prime considerations will be planning for the traditional student population that will be using the building. Everything should be done to develop a building that allows for maximum learning opportunity for the children who will attend that school. The only restriction is that no design should be permitted that will eliminate other groups to be served by that facility.

The inputs for the traditional student program will not be discussed here. Suffice it to say that in addition to the needs of the students, a community-planned building should include the following things.

First, rooms should be planned so that in addition to those needed in the regular day program, there is enough space for room use by other groups in the daytime. The usual procedure is to plan a building, such as an elementary school, for enough space to handle those students generated by the kindergarten sessions. Thus, for every kindergarten room (which can accommodate two classes a day) there would be two classes for each grade. It is simply recommended here that additional classrooms be provided for community use in the daytime.

Community rooms should also be provided. These rooms should provide comfortable spaces where citizens can meet, study, work, or just relax. They should provide the kind of pleasant atmosphere necessary for attracting citizens to the school. They should have a private access so that classes are not disturbed, and citizens can feel a bit of privacy in using the space. The rooms should have comfortable furniture with chairs and tables available when needed. They might also have a stove, refrigerator, sink and running water, cupboard space, dishes, curtains or drapes, carpeting, rest rooms, television, radio and may even have a washer, dryer, and sewing machine. The rooms should be reserved for community use, and requests by teachers and other school groups should not usurp the community's use of them.

There should be a multi-purpose room or a gymnasium and an auditorium. Where cost permits separate facilities, it is best to have both. In many cases, however, and particularly in reference to elementary schools, the two facilities will likely be joined as one unit.

In the gymnasium and auditorium, the ceiling, apparatus, dressing rooms, lighting and other parts of the facility should be designed to accommodate the adults as well as the children. There should be lockers, showers, and seating space for activities. The floor should be designed for the multiple activities. A portable stage can also increase the potential use of the gym.

There are still some other factors to be suggested in the design of a community education building. Zoning of the building for heat and lighting will make it easier to use parts of the building without having to heat and light the entire facility. In a similar way, zoning of the building by moveable gates will also help control the use of the building and limit occupancy to one area without opening the entire building when not necessary. Portable coat racks make it possible to handle the coats for large crowds. Flexible furniture, for use by both adults and children, should be provided. This is not as difficult as some might claim, since most homes accommodate adults and children in the same facility and do it rather easily. Serious thought should be given to air conditioning for the building. Unfortunately, this is still thought of as a luxury and frequently is omitted from the planning. With added use at night, on weekends, and particularly during summers, however, such an installation is as feasible as heat in the winter. One might also look at extra facilities such as shops, art rooms, home economics rooms, etc. While these will be found at most secondary schools, they are not always available at elementary schools. It should be kept in mind while planning such facilities that each building does not have to have everything. Duplications in facilities should only be encouraged when there is an absolute need for such duplication.

There are certainly many other things that might be included in planning a building for community specifications. Only some of the most obvious have been mentioned here. Different communities will dictate different things. For example, some communities have taken their pool, cafeteria, gym, and auditoriums, which traditionally are a part of the high school, and designated them as community facilities. They are on the school site but are viewed as community centers which the school uses at certain hours. Many districts are finding new materials to help in their planning. New gym materials, for example, make the high school gymnasium a usable place rather than a restrictive shrine. Other communities have discovered that to get maximum use of their buildings, they are having to build more traditional types of facilities that will accommodate all ages and then are achieving flexibility through greater use of audio and video technology.

Attention should also be given to existing buildings. While the description to this point has dealt with planning new buildings, the points made and suggestions given apply to existing buildings as well. If existing buildings are to serve community needs, then changes will have to be made in these facilities. Generally, this is not as satisfactory as building new facilities, but many communities have made adequate changes in their existing facilities.

Usually this means adding to or changing present structures to meet the demands of service to the community. Most of the suggestions can be added to current facilities, and the fact that the buildings are already completed should not be an excuse for failing to provide facilities that represent the goals and objectives of the community.

There is also the issue of existing school buildings that are not being used but that still require costly maintenance and continued mortgage payments. In specific instances, these school buildings have been converted into apartments, shopping centers, corporate headquarters, office buildings, art centers, and community college satellite centers.

One very promising practice is to convert surplus schools into community centers. The rationale for doing this is based on the assumption that community need for services should be of a higher priority in considering the use of public buildings than the selling of such buildings for private use. Such use has not only proved to be popular but highly logical when one considers that public schools are within walking distance of about 90 percent of our population and that about 80 percent of the population do not have children in the public schools.

In the actual renovation of one of these recycled schools, the classroom and administrative space was altered to become a day care center, senior citizen club, art gallery and museum, community theater, branch public library, garden club center, community club room, and reading garden. In another example, a 2,500-student high school with declining enrollment was converted into a 1,250-student high school and a community center, which housed a health club, handball courts, public pool, branch library, community club rooms, health clinic, agency office space, a day care center, and a center for the elderly.

CURRENT STATUS OF SCHOOL FACILITIES PLANNING

There is a great deal of speculation and projection as to what the possibilities of school renovation and new construction might look like in the years ahead. In general, the direction seems to be one of perceiving schools as community centers to be used by many different groups in the community rather than as classrooms for use by a specific population for limited purposes. It should also be pointed out that the issue is not one of conjecture and speculation. There are already several hundred buildings that either have been built or renovated on these new premises. There is also a great awareness on the part of architects and facility planners of this topic, and the literature on such an approach is growing rapidly.

At any rate, the design of facilities with community specifications, while relatively new, is increasing. It has great potential and will certainly mature as it develops. And while there is still much that can happen as communities and architects view this concept, it is important to keep the basic tenets in mind. Namely, that if schools are to be a moving force in the development of communities and community education, they must reflect that concept in their facilities. And that will be possible only by designing buildings whose specifications reflect the goals and beliefs of the community education philosophy.

Chapter XV

The Future of Community Education

Developing predictions about the future is an obviously risky venture. Kenneth Boulding stated the problem well when he said, "One thing we can say about man's future with a great deal of confidence is that it will be more or less surprising."[1]

Recognizing these limitations, a new breed of educator has emerged in recent years—the educational futurist. This individual attempts to look into the possibilities and probabilities of future development by looking now at the directions being pursued by various disciplines, and then projecting these directions into the future. While it is clear that no one can predict the future with any real accuracy, generalizations can be drawn regarding probable future events, and these generalizations can be used as guides for future education planning.

It is important for educators to attempt to assess the future if we are to maintain educational relevance—to begin planning for the necessary changes. In an attempt to do this, this chapter will be divided into three parts:

1. The World of the Future
2. Dehumanizing Forces in Tomorrow's World
3. Education Programming of the Future

THE WORLD OF THE FUTURE

". . . two major trends are likely to continue for a least another thirty years: The population will continue to grow, and technology will continue to be a major source of change in the affairs of men."[2] Within these general areas, Robert L. Shinn and others suggest that most of the difficulties we will experience in the future will be related to "human problems" rather than technological ones.

---

[1] Boulding, K., "Expecting the Unexpected," *Designed Education for the Future*, No. 1, Edited by Edgar Morphet and Charles Ryan; Citation Press, New York, 1967, p. 199.
[2] Miller, George, "Some Psychological Perspectives in the Year 2000," *Daedalus Journal of the American Academy of Arts and Sciences*, Vol. 96, No. 3, Summer 1967, p. 88.

1. *Increasing Population*

While the population in this country appears to be stabilizing, this is not true for the rest of the world; most futurists do not dwell on the technological problems, such as food supply and housing, that this will create. Rather, the emphasis is on the individual's abilities to cope with the changes that will be forced upon us. Alvin Toffler,[3] for example, discusses the problems of transience facing people in an increasingly urban society. He suggests that a new form of limited involvement is developing in our relationships with others—a type of nonpermanent plug in-plug out structure that allows each of us to use others as we do any other type of service. A throw-away friendship, in effect. The impact this type of life style could have on our ethics, values, and perception of self is truly dramatic.

In that population growth is now occurring most rapidly in countries that can least sustain it, people in the "have" nations will be increasingly faced with the ethical question of how much to support the "have not" nations and the effect on them if they do or do not provide that support.

It is clear that population growth and the resulting increase in urban-suburban density will force us to rethink concepts of privacy, individual rights, responsibilities toward others, and the establishment of a more appropriate relationship between man and environment.

2. *Technology*

With an expanded population will come an expanded technology. It is inevitable, if only to sustain the increasing numbers of people. Cybernetics, for example, will expand the powers of humans and the length of life in ways we cannot yet imagine, and with these changes will come new and demanding ethical questions regarding the very nature of people. Toffler suggests, for example, that within the relatively near future scientists will be able to redesign both individual bodies and entire societies through genetic intervention with the DNA molecule. The ability to trans-

---

[3] Toffler, Alvin, *Future Shock*, Bantam Books, 1971, pp. 96–99.

plant organs from one body to another will continue to expand, and our ability to replace existing organs with synthetic ones will also improve rapidly.

It does not require significant amounts of imagination to recognize that we may well face decisions that get to the very soul of mankind.

3. *The Shrinking World*

Competition for natural resources will grow increasingly more intense. Countries possessing scarce resources will become inordinately wealthy; those possessing few resources will become increasingly poor. International trade and interaction will flourish as never before, requiring an expanded awareness of cultural difference and a new ability to function effectively within these societies.

The military situation will become increasingly complex. The number of new nuclear powers will continue to increase. This increases the chances of military disaster, but also increases the impulse of people for international control. Bertram Russell has written, "The human race has survived hitherto owing to ignorance and incompetence, but given knowledge and confidence combined with folly, there can be no certainty of survival. Knowledge is power; but, it is powerful for evil as much as for good."

4. *Human Rights*

Human rights will continue to be a major issue. The United States has a tradition of freedom and justice. It now faces the ethical problem of making good on that tradition in a world dominated by pragmatic and security issues that tend to overwhelm ethical considerations.[4]

It seems evident that the world of the future will certainly be different from the one we know today. The forecasting of technological advance is relatively easy. The forecasting of our capacity to effectively accept and use this technology and control it for our own purposes remains open to question. As previously suggested, it is probable that the greatest

---

[4] Shinn, Robert L., "Human Responsibility in the Emerging Society," *Designing Education for the Future*, No. 1, Edited by Edgar Morphet and Charles Ryan; Citation Press, New York, 1967, pp. 243–246.

problem the world will face will not be in creating technological devices but in being able to function as human beings within the technical maze that will be created.

DEHUMANIZING FORCES IN TOMORROW'S WORLD

There is little question that the problems the future will bring are immense. These problems are multiplied by our existing society. At a time when the society needs all of the resources and human potential possible, it is becoming decreasingly capable of handling these problems. Many sociologists fear that America is becoming a mass society—a society that reduces an individual's capacity to truly gain a unique identity. The society this group perceives is one that dehumanizes and depersonalizes individuals. It is an interesting dichotomy that during a time of emphasis on personal development and "doing your own thing," sociologists are becoming increasingly concerned about a society that forces conformity and mass identity. There are several characteristics of the mass society that many sociologists point to as existing in America today.

1. The loss of a feeling of community and a loss of community conscience

2. The establishment of a mass culture created by the mass media

3. The alienation of individuals from the society, resulting from their individual loss of identity

4. The dissolution of mediating groups and individuals who work between the extremes within the society

5. The growth and development of an institutional bureaucracy that in its immensity often forgets the individual and loses its initial purpose for existence to become self-serving and self-perpetuating

The basic problem within the mass society is the dehumanization that takes place within people. As people become dehumanized, they lose a sense of personal responsibility, feeling for the larger community, and acceptance of authority.

At a time when the society most needs uniquely creative and concerned people, it is establishing a system that destroys individuality and diversity. Educators, in preparing for the future, cannot ignore the general direction society is taking when they establish education programs relevant to both the individual and to the society.

Ralph Keyes,[5] in an article, "In Search of Community," expands on the dilemma we face in reestablishing a sense of community. While, in general, we appreciate the advantages of anonymity and freedom provided through the lack of close relationships, we lose an ability to establish a common sense of purpose or direction. We cannot establish trust, true friendship, or the ability to count on people when we need them. This loss is difficult to accept in any society. It is devastating, however, in a democracy. The loss of a sense of community as described by Keyes in 1975 is very similar to the problems perceived by Ferdinand Tonnes almost one hundred years earlier; the very complexity of a society which is necessary for the economic advantages upon which we are so dependent is also the destructive force in human relationships.

The issue we must now face, is how to maintain existing and potential future economic advantages while restructuring our human interactions to again establish a sense of community. We must recognize that it is quite possible that some economic gain, some technological advantages may have to be forfeited to regain that lost community interaction. This modification in life style may come as a result of a conscious decision, or it may result from limited, finite resource availability.

EDUCATION PROGRAMMING FOR THE FUTURE

Before we decide where we are going, we should assess where we are and what we are doing. John Goodlad points out that there is an unwillingness on the part of educators to state the purposes to be served by education, schools, or specific programs of instruction, that the structure

---

[5] Keyes, Ralph, "In Search of Community," *National Elementary Principals*, Vol. 54, No. 3, Jan./Feb., 1975, pp. 9–16.

of schools with certain learning coming at specified times is not in concert with our knowledge concerning individual difference and how children learn. Much of our curriculum is justified on no criteria other than habit and tradition. Large portions of the education reform being discussed scarcely have touched the teacher in the classroom. Many innovations designed to unshackle the school program are, instead, tacked on to the existing school structure. Educators and school systems have a great hesitancy to experiment.

Goodlad feels that by attacking these problems now, education institutions will be able to meet the needs they will face in the future. To do this, we must develop a sense of purpose within the school; we must bring curriculum change about by careful planning and design.[6] Because we have established no specific goals, generations of students are denied whatever education program is out of fashion at a particular time. The pendulum swings every 20 years or so in curriculum development, and students receive whatever type of education program that happens to be in vogue. We must incorporate into the curriculum the problems likely to be facing young adults in the future. Some of these will include population, poverty, pollution, technology, and use of free time. Goodlad also suggests that there will be an increased emphasis on nonremunerative pursuits and that we should attempt to gain a greater balance for cultural and nonutilitarian aspects of the curriculum.

Perhaps the greatest concern that will be faced by the educator of the future will be in the area of ethics. Ethics are now in an extensive process of change. There is no longer a continuity of belief patterns or a commonly accepted moral base. The major social changes that are coming will provide both an opportunity and a threat beyond the present rapidly changing structure. The several major ethical questions that face us now can result in either an opportunity for or a threat to humanity.

---

[6] Goodlad, John, "The Educational Program to 1980 and Beyond," *Designing Education for the Future*, No. 2, Edited by Edgar Morphet and Charles Ryan; Citation Press, New York, 1967, pp. 47–60.

Some of the issues related to ethics that the schools must face include:

1. *The undermining of authority.* Established authority is losing relevance, and there is more demand for experimentation and change. In the future, authority will not be able to exist based only on tradition.

2. *The question of affluence and poverty.* This will greatly affect the ethics of the future. Affluence will continue to expand; poverty, if allowed to continue, will create great ethical and political difficulties. We are experiencing vast shifts of power related to affluence and poverty. What will happen, both within systems and within world politics, when these shifts of power occur?

3. *Individual identity.* Will individuality give way to a mass culture with a confusion of value and a confusion of identity? Will personal identity and role identity become fused?

4. *Separation from institutions* that we have created to assist us, separating ourselves from those aspects of the society that have traditionally strengthened us and bound us together.

These and many other issues will be raised, and the schools will have to address them. The crucial point is that major modifications within the society will demand major modifications in the schools, and as people lose faith in their institutions, the schools may face an increasingly heavy responsibility.

It is important that we approach planning for future education programs cautiously. There is a danger that we can become so engrossed in our technological advances that we lose sight of the most important things in education. These are things that aren't new or exciting, but things that we have been working toward for several decades.

Paul Miller states that five basic goals remain constant:

1. To learn about self and seek self-realization

2. To learn about others and the art of human relations

3. To learn about economic life, to provide food, clothing, and shelter

4. To learn about organized man and his civic responsibility because organized resources—government if you please—make it more certain that self-preservation becomes possible

5. To learn to battle the elements with attendant successes and failures, and thus to become a philosopher to contemplate the purpose of things[7]

It seems evident that the demands on the education institution of the future will be extensive. Radical change will be forced on educators. The vast changes that will occur and be required will require new expenditures of funds. Unfortunately, it appears that we are approaching, in the immediate future, a period of increasingly inadequate financial assistance for education. This will remain true unless a significant break occurs in attitudes concerning the importance of education. Schools cannot rely on the complex political process required for the passage of millage. This greatly hinders the education system and its ability to get funds. Present attitudes and funding procedures indicate that our supply of education services will greatly lag behind the growing demand for them. Modernization of state tax and financial structures needs to begin immediately. Local school district financial structures are in need of sharp and prompt revision. Only through initial adequate funding will we be able to begin to plan to meet the needs of the future.

FROM PROGRAM TO PROCESS

Both the education system and society are facing a crisis—both, it seems, for the same reason. As our education institutions have grown and developed and our society has become increasingly organized, structured, and complex, we have left out a very basic element in the structure—the humanity of man. Our institutions do not work well for us unless we are involved personally in seeing that they work.

---

[7] Miller, Paul, "Major Implication for Education of Prospective Changes in Society," *Designing Education for the Future*, No. 1, Edited by Edgar Morphet and Charles Ryan; Citation Press, New York, 1967, p. 4.

In earlier times, when life was less complicated, people were involved in their government, in their schools, and in their communities. They cared about what happened and what did not happen. They were concerned. This is a far cry from the transient, cold, self-seeking society that exists today.

Recognizing this, the schools must initiate a transition back to some very basic elements in a democratic society. Democracy requires involvement—it cannot survive without it. We must turn our attention back to local human involvement in very basic issues and problems if we are to survive. Leadership for this move logically should come from the schools. Educators must begin now to involve community members in planning their own destiny.

Community education in the future must be established on the premise that people need to be involved in community decisions that affect them, on process rather than program. For if community education remains committed only to providing program opportunities and not providing problem-solving and involvement opportunities, it will fail. Education must become what former President Lyndon Johnson foresaw when he stated:

> Tomorrow's school will be a school without walls—a school built of doors which open to the entire community. Tomorrow's school will reach out to places that enrich the human spirit; to the museums, to the theaters, to the art galleries, to the parks and rivers, and mountains . . . Tomorrow's school will be the center of community life for grownups as well as children, as shopping centers for human services. It might have a community health clinic or public library, a theater and recreation facilities for all citizens—and it will not close its doors anymore at 3 o'clock. It will employ its buildings around the clock, its teachers around the year. We just cannot afford to have an $85 billion plant in this country open less than 30 percent of the time.[8]

---

[8] President Lyndon Johnson at A.A.S.A. Convention, Atlantic City, New Jersey, 1966.

President Jimmy Carter also understood the potential of community education when he said:

> The community school concept offers our people the chance to participate in the learning process when they can—which is often outside regular school hours. In so doing, it offers us the chance to extend the learning process to the whole community . . . We have a tremendous need to develop more sense of community throughout the nation, and I feel that the community education concept, if fully implemented, could make an impact in meeting this need.[9]

The schools now have the opportunity to move beyond the confines of the kindergarten through twelfth-grade curriculum; beyond the limited perspective that education occurs only between the ages of 5 and 18 and only within the confines of the school building. We are talking about a new philosophy of education—one that builds on centuries of thought and growth. While the changes suggested are dramatic, the concepts proposed have been philosophically accepted for decades by educators. The time is long overdue to move toward the integration of philosophical ideals and education practice. We are attempting to recognize that education throughout life and the interrelationship between education and the community are essential components of a good education system and suggesting a new and broadened role for the schools that goes far beyond our current system.

We believe that what we are proposing is nothing short of revolution—but we are recommending revolution within the existing structure.

The decision of which direction education takes—which road we follow—will be made by that small group of dedicated people who believe in community education. These people will make the decision to work like they never have worked before, and they will accomplish the lofty goals community education can reach. Or, they will let the opportunity slide past because of inaction, timidity, or lack of human compassion, and our very democracy will be threatened as a result. The decision must be made—it must be made now.

---

[9] Community Education Advisory Council Report No. 5, "Statements on Community Education, A Report Prepared as Part of a U.S. Office of Education Grant," 1974.

INDEX

INDEX BY TITLE AND SUBJECT

INDEX OF AUTHORS, INSTITUTIONS AND ORGANIZATIONS